Metawritings

EDITED BY JILL TALBOT

Metawritings
Toward a Theory of Nonfiction

UNIVERSITY OF IOWA PRESS
Iowa City

University of Iowa Press, Iowa City 52242

Copyright © 2012 by the
  University of Iowa Press

www.uiowapress.org

Printed in the United States of America

Design by Teresa Wingfield

The University of Iowa Press is a member
of Green Press Initiative and is committed to preserving natural resources.

Printed on acid-free paper

Library of Congress
Cataloging-in-Publication Data

Metawritings: toward a theory of
nonfiction / edited by Jill Talbot.

  p.   cm.

Includes index.

ISBN-13: 978-1-60938-089-2 (pbk)

ISBN-10: 1-60938-089-4 (pbk)

ISBN-13: 978-1-60938-105-9 (ebook)

ISBN-10: 1-60938-105-X (ebook)

1. Creative nonfiction—Authorship.

2. Authorship—Literary collections.

I. Talbot, Jill Lynn.

PN145.M485 2012

808.02—dc23   2011042198

Contents

ACKNOWLEDGMENTS vii

PAM HOUSTON
Prologue: Corn Maze ix

JILL TALBOT
Meta-Introduction xxi

RYAN VAN METER
I Was There 1
Interview with Ryan Van Meter 9

CATHY DAY
Genesis; or the Day Adam Killed the Snakes 13
Interview with Cathy Day 18

ANONYMOUS
The Facts of the Matter 21
Interview with Anonymous 29

SARAH BLACKMAN
The Girl Is a Fiction 37
Interview with Sarah Blackman 41

DAVID LAZAR
On Dating 47
Interview with David Lazar 55

BRENDA MILLER

The Dog at the Edge of the World   61

Interview with Brenda Miller   65

ANDER MONSON

Facing the Monolith   68

Interview with Ander Monson   112

ROBIN HEMLEY

The Pickpocket Project   115

Interview with Robin Hemley   133

LENA DUNHAM

Excerpts from *Creative Nonfiction*   139

Interview with Lena Dunham   163

BERNARD COOPER

Winner Take Nothing   167

Interview with Bernard Cooper   184

BRIAN OLIU

Adventure Island   187

Interview with Brian Oliu   188

KRISTEN IVERSEN

How to Be Tough in Creative Nonfiction   195

Interview with Kristen Iversen   202

CONTRIBUTORS   209

PERMISSIONS   213

INDEX   215

Acknowledgments

I would like to thank Joseph Parsons, who indefatigably supported this project. I would also like to thank the contributors for their thoughtful submissions to this anthology and especially for their time and patience in the interview process. Thanks to Charles Blackstone for the interview angle and for always hitting "Reply." Special thanks to the Spring 2010 Readings in Nonfiction class, who revealed a fascination for and appreciation of metawriting that inspired me and this anthology. Finally, as always, thanks to my daughter Indie, who displays unyielding understanding during the writing hours.

Prologue
Corn Maze

WHEN I WAS FOUR YEARS OLD my father lost his job. We were living in Trenton, New Jersey, at the time, where he had lived most of his life. With no college education, he had worked his way up to the position of controller at a Transamerica-owned manufacturing company called Delavalve. The company restructured itself and dismissed him. My parents decided to use his sudden unemployment as an opportunity to take a vacation, to drive whatever Buick convertible we had at the time from New Jersey to California. My parents loved the sun and the beach more than they loved anything except vodka martinis. They promised to take me to Disneyland. We stopped at Las Vegas on the way.

We stayed at the Sands, where my mother had opened, decades before, as a singing, dancing comedian for Frank Sinatra. I got to swim in the kidney-shaped pool and then we ate a giant slab of prime rib each for a dollar. My mother and I went up to the room to bed, and my father stayed downstairs to gamble. I woke up to my mother standing over my bed and sun streaming into the hotel room window. I was four-and-a-half years old. "Pam," she said, "Go downstairs and get your father out of the casino."

I found him sitting at an empty blackjack table, looking 110. I took his hand and led him through the hazy cigarette air, up the elevator and down the long hall with the zigzag carpet to our room. He had, of course, lost everything. The money we were meant to live on until he found another job, the money for the trip to California, the money for the hotel bill. Even the car.

My mother's old boss at the Desert Inn loaned us enough to get the car back, to pay the hotel bill, to take me to Disneyland. A few weeks later my father started a new job in Pennsylvania, and we moved there, though when my mother had run away to Manhattan from Spiceland, Indiana, at age 13, because she had won the bet with her Aunt Ermie, who raised her, that she *could* get straight Cs, and as a result had, for the first time in her life, fifty whole dollars, she'd vowed she would never live west of the New Jersey border again.

ABOUT FIVE YEARS AGO, I was asked to be one of four writers to participate in an evening called "Unveiled" at the Wisconsin Book Festival in Madison. Our assignment was to write something new that had never been tried or tested, and to read it aloud to an audience of roughly a thousand. I not only accepted, I took the assignment so literally that I didn't start writing until I was on the plane to Wisconsin. I wrote for the entire plane ride, and all evening in my hotel room. I stayed up all night and wrote, and I wrote all day the day of the reading. When I started to panic that I would not have something ready in time for the reading, I told myself what I tell my students when they get stuck: *write down all of the things out in the world that have arrested your attention lately, that have glimmered at you in some resonant way. Set them next to each other. See what happens.*

By late afternoon I had twelve tiny scenes. I have always, for some reason, thought in twelves. I don't believe this has anything to do with the apostles. One scene was called Georgetown, Great Exuma. Another was called Ozona, Texas. Another was called Juneau, Alaska. Two hours before I was to read, I looked back at my instructions to make sure I had done everything the assignment asked of me. The only caveat, it said, was that the piece had to mention Wisconsin. I knew nothing about Wisconsin, so I left my hotel room and sat on a street corner downtown and waited for something to happen. In less than thirty minutes, something did, and I went back to my room and wrote it down. When I added Madison, Wisconsin, to the original twelve, I had to take out Mexican Hat, Utah, but that was okay with me.

"Jesus, Pam," Richard Bausch said, after the reading, "Write a hundred of them, and that's your next book." I thought, "No, not a hundred, but possibly 144."

WHEN I WENT ON TOUR with my first book, a collection of short stories called *Cowboys Are My Weakness*, I was asked, more than any other question, *how much of this really happened to you?* "A lot of it," was my honest answer, night after night, but the audience grew dissatisfied with that answer and seemed, more than anything, to want something quantifiable, so I began saying, also honestly, about 82 percent.

Eight years later, when I published my first "nonfiction" book and went on tour with it, I would often be introduced in some version of the following manner: "In the past we have gotten 82 percent Pam, and now we are going to get 100 percent," and I would approach the microphone and feel the need to say, "Well, no, still coming in right about 82."

BETWEEN DAVIS AND DIXON, California, in the heart of the Central Valley, just off I-80, right under the historic sign where the cow jumps over the moon, is the *Guinness Book of World Records'* largest corn maze. If you get off the highway and drive to it, you find out that technically speaking it was the *Guinness Book of World Records'* largest corn maze in 2007, and not in 2010. But, you figure they figure, once a winner, always a winner.

In the corn maze, as in life, there are rules. No running. No smoking. No strollers. No drugs. No inappropriate language. (The corn has ears too!) No tampering with the signs and the maze markers. If you misbehave you will be asked to leave, though in a corn maze, you understand, that is not always so straightforward. Surprisingly, dogs are allowed in the corn maze, and there is nothing in the rules prohibiting handguns. Sex in the corn maze is also apparently okay, as long as you use appropriate language.

The computer-generated grid that the corn maze sits upon runs from A through QQ and 1 through 52. It contains 2,193 squares. When you enter they hand you a map. To complete the maze successfully, you will make approximately 189 right turns and 156 left turns, though there are a few places when more than one option will get you out, so your individual numbers may vary.

An ear of corn averages 800 kernels in 16 rows. A pound of corn consists of approximately 1,300 kernels. One hundred bushels of corn produce approximately 7,280,000 kernels. In the U.S., corn leads all other crops in value and volume of production. The corn in this maze *is* as high as an elephant's eye, if we are talking the world's largest elephant, in heels.

I have a painting in my kitchen by my friend Marc Penner-Howell of a giant ear of corn with the word *hallelujah* written in red letters running vertically up the ear and lots of little ghostly gas pumps in the background. When my boyfriend Greg eats corn on the cob his lips swell up so much we call him Angelina Jolie.

THE REASON I HAVE BEEN AFRAID, until very recently, to make any kind of general, theoretical, or philosophical statements about women, writers, westerners, environmentalists, academics, western women, western women writers, outdoorswomen who grew up in New Jersey and eventually became academics, women who dreamed of running white water rivers and falling in love with poets and cowboys (though not cowboy poets), women who got on I-80 West on the other side of the George Washington Bridge one day and just kept driving . . . is that I have never felt comfortable speaking for anyone except myself. Maybe I had been socialized not to make declarative statements. Maybe I thought you had to be fifty before you knew anything about the world. Maybe I was afraid of misrepresenting someone I thought I understood but didn't. Maybe I was afraid of acting hypocritically. Maybe I have always believed it is more honest, more direct, and ultimately more powerful, to tell a story, one concrete and particular detail at a time.

So I did. I put my boat into the river, some things happened, and I took it back out on the other side. In time, though, I began to suspect that linear narrative was not doing a very good job representing life as I experienced it, but I still tried to stretch the things I originally conceived of as Slinkies into straight lines. I don't mean to suggest that I was unique in this. There are so many of us out there, trying to turn Spyrograph flowers into rocket ships. In time I began to gain confidence in my Spyrograph flowers and Slinkies. Eventually, I began to speculate about where they came from. Just for starters, I never met any of my grandparents. Also, every single one of my relatives (except a second cousin in Alaska who is oddly afraid of me and his illegitimate son who likes me but lives in Prague) is dead. Also, when both of your parents are alcoholics, one thing never leads to another. There is no such thing as how it really happened. When both of your parents are alcoholics, the only way to get to a narrative that is *un*-shattered would be to run the tape backward, like a car accident in reverse, where the windshield that is in a million pieces magically mends itself. This is not necessarily the bad news. A mind that moves associatively (as my mind does and probably your mind too) like a firefly in a grassy yard on a late June evening, has more fun (and other things too, of course, like static, like trouble) than a mind that moves logically or even chronologically. Just the other day, for instance, someone said the word *tennis*, and I saw in my mind's eye a lady in a pig suit with wings.

NOT TOO LONG after grad school, I was hired by a magazine to write an article about why women over forty take adventure vacations. I was barely thirty and had no idea why, but I needed the money, so I called some power women I knew who had climbed Kilimanjaro or whatever and asked them. They gave flat and predictable answers like, "for the challenge," so I made up some smart, funny women who said surprising and subversive things about why they took adventure vacations, and wrote the article up.

When the fact checker called me, I said, "You're a what?" like an asshole fresh out of graduate school. "You actually believe in things called facts?"

The fact checker, whose name was Bethany, asked for the phone numbers of the six women I wrote about. I gave her the three that actually existed.

"What about Katherine and Louise and Samantha?" she said.

"Well, Bethany," I said, "I made them up."

There were five seconds of silence; then she said, "Well, I guess we don't have to call them then, do we?"

IN 2010 IN LAS VEGAS, in a gondola, in the canal that runs from Barney's New York to Kenneth Cole, *up*stairs in the mall they call the Palazzo, a very young man is proposing to a very young woman. He is on one knee, and the acne-faced gondolier in his straw hat and red kerchief steadies the wobbling boat. The shoppers pause a minute to look over the railing and watch. The girl is either genuinely surprised or good at pretending. She whispers yes, and then shouts it for the small crowd. The twenty-five of us gathered clap and cheer, and the boy stands up and pumps both fists, the same exact gesture he uses, one imagines, when he hears that his fantasy football quarterback has gone 18 for 24 with 4 TDs and no interceptions. The gondolier turns the boat around with his single long paddle, and pushes them back toward Bed, Bath and Beyond.

Every day in Vegas is upside-down day. Walking along the canal, young men in wife-beaters say sentences into their cell phones that, if they were not in Las Vegas, they would never say. "I'll meet you in an hour in St. Mark's square," or, "I applied for a job with the KGB," or, "Let's meet up in time to see the volcano erupt." People pay money—a lot of it—to see Donny and Marie Osmond. On the poster for the Garth Brooks show in the Wynn Encore theater, there is a picture of Garth in his big black hat and a one-word review from the *Los Angeles Times*: *Genius*.

We are staying at the Golden Nugget, downtown, a hotel where, if you want to, you can go down a waterslide, which is really more like a water straw, through a two-hundred-thousand-gallon shark tank. At the guest relations desk there is a very pretty girl with quarter-inch-thick makeup and long blonde hair that has been dyed so many times it is leaning burnt sienna, and the kind of ultra-thick, ultra-blunt, square false eyelashes that only transvestites wear, and the whole ensemble makes her look like somebody cross-dressed as herself.

Every time we leave the hotel, the junkies are sitting on the steps of the church across the street shooting up under their toenails. The lady in front of the sign that says Hotel–Wedding–Cuban Buffet looks right through the driver's-side window into my eyes and says, "Put a muffler on it you fucking bitch," right before she sits down in the middle of the street and tries to scratch her own scalp off.

WHEN IT WAS DECIDED (*When* was that again, and by whom?) that we were all supposed to choose between fiction and nonfiction, what was not taken into account was that for some of us truth can never be an absolute, that there can (at best) be only less true and more true and sometimes those two collapse inside each other like a Turducken. Given the failure of memory. Given the failure of language to mean. Given metaphor. Given metonymy. Given the ever-shifting junction of code and context. Given the twenty-five people who saw the same car accident. Given our denial. Given our longings.

Who cares really, if she hanged herself or slit her wrists, when what really matters is that James Frey is secretly afraid that he's the one who killed her? Dear Random House Refund Department: if they were moved, then they got their twenty-four dollars' worth.

BACK IN THE NINETIES, a magazine sent me to the Ardèche region of France. They wanted me, among other things, to kayak the Ardèche river canyon, one of the five river canyons the French call the Grand Canyon of France. But they sent me in late October, the days were short and getting shorter, all the kayak rental places were boarded up tight for the year and it was thirty-six degrees with freezing rain. So I hiked the canyon of the Ardèche, thinking it would be an acceptable substitute.

When I turned in the article, the editor said, "We really wanted you to kayak the Ardèche."

"I know," I said, "but it was too cold, all the rental places . . ."

"No," she said, "we really wanted you to kayak the Ardèche . . ."

"Ah . . ." I said.

"And while you're at it," she said, "could you make it rain a little less?"

I found her request neither difficult nor surprising. The river had, at that time of year, hardly a riffle on it, and would have been a pretty, if chilly, float. To spice things up, I added a water fight with three Italian kayakers. There was some good-natured flirting across the language barrier. It didn't rain that day at all.

Some years later, the editor of an anthology asked my permission to reprint that essay. He said, "I really liked your story, especially the part about the three Italian kayakers."

"Funny," I said, "I made that part up."

Maybe I should have anticipated the depth of his outrage, but I did not.

This was pre–James Frey, of course, and who would have ever anticipated that? The editor called back a few days later and said he had removed the kayak trip from the essay. He had added a scene in which I carry my kayak down to the river's edge, and a fog bank rolls in, and I decide not to go.

"I don't want to be an asshole," I said, which of course, wasn't true either, "but if I can't make up three Italian kayakers, I don't think you can make up fog in my essay."

It is hard, all these decades after *The Things They Carried*, to stand here and say the scene with the three Italian kayakers is the truest thing in the entire essay (though of course it is), even though it never really happened. Nor would I turn an entirely deaf ear to the complaints of those who actually use travel magazines to plan trips. Not to mention war crimes, genocide, sex offenders, presidents who lie about weapons of mass destruction . . . certainly I do believe that sometimes it is necessary for us all to pretend together that language can really mean.

But if you think about it, the fact that I did not *really* have a flirty exchange with three Italian kayakers doesn't make it any less likely that you might. I might even go so far as to argue that you would be more likely to have such an exchange because of my (nonexistent) kayakers, first, because they charmed you into going to the Ardèche to begin with, and second, because if you happened to be floating along on a rainless day in your kayak and a sexy, curly-haired guy glided by and splashed water on you, you would now be much more likely to splash him back.

DUE NORTH OF NEWFOUNDLAND, there is a small, rocky island in the Labrador Straits called Quirpon (pronounced kar-poon). The island is roughly ten miles long and three miles across, and on the seaward tip there are a lighthouse and a lighthouse keeper's house—both painted bright red and white—and no other buildings to speak of. Inside the house, two tough and sweet women named Madonna and Doris fry cod, dry clothes, fix mugs of hot chocolate, and hand out maps to soggy hikers who've come to stay the night.

Marked on the map along with the fox den and the osprey nest is an old townsite called L'Anse au Pigeon, and underneath the name in parentheses it says, "site of mass murder." When I ask Doris about it, she tells me she isn't much of a storyteller, but when I press she takes a deep breath to get into what I recognize as the Newfoundlanders' storytelling mode, a half-performance, half-trance state that suggests stories are serious matters, whether they are about mass murders or not.

"And now," she says, "I will tell you the story of the mass murders on Quirpon Island." She brings her hands into her lap and folds them as if she's getting ready to pray. "A long, long time ago," she says, "not in this time, but in the time before this time, there was a settlement—several fishing families, living together on Quirpon Island. And one day the government saw fit to send them a schoolteacher. Now this schoolteacher, mind you, he was a handsome fellow, young and smart, and one of the fisherman's wives fell head over heels in love with him. And the husband was terrible jealous, terrible, terrible, so he decided to trick the schoolteacher into drinking a little bit of the stuff—what is it? I don't know what the stuff is called . . ."

"Arsenic?"

"No, it's the stuff they use in the lanterns."

"Kerosene?"

"Like kerosene, but different from kerosene."

"White gas?"

"Like white gas, but different from white gas . . . anyway, he gave it to him a little, a little, a little at a time, and finally the poor handsome schoolteacher died."

Doris nods her head as a kind of punctuation, unfolds her hands, and stands.

"And that is the story of the mass murder on Quirpon Island."

"But Doris," I say, "Why call the death of one schoolteacher a mass murder?"

Doris sighs heavily. She sits back down and brings her hands back into her lap. "A long, long time ago," she begins, "not in this time, but in the time before this time, the fisherman who had given the schoolteacher the poison to drink became more and more afraid that the men in the town were getting ready to confront him. There wasn't law back then like we have in these times, so he probably would have gotten away with it, but his guilt made him believe his friends were not his friends. So deep deep into one dark night he soaked one of the fishing boats with the liquid that goes into the lanterns . . ."

"The same liquid," I say, "that he gave the schoolteacher to drink?"

"The very same!"

"The white gas?"

"Like white gas . . ." Doris says, "but different from white gas."

"Didn't they smell it?"

"This is the liquid that has no smell. Anyway, all the men in the town went fishing the next morning and one of 'em struck a match to light his cigarette and the whole lot of them burned up or drowned or died of hypothermia. You can't last long in that iceberg water," she says, nodding her head toward the window. "And that is the story of the mass murder on Quirpon Island."

PAM HOUSTON

I WAS DRIVING OVER Slumgullion Pass listening to *Ashes of American Flags* with the volume at fifty. There were three feet of new snow on the ground and I watched a herd of two hundred elk gallop through it. I had spent hours the night before on baby-naming Web sites trying to find something I could search and replace for Pam in my forthcoming novel of 144 chapters. The book is more or less autobiographical. I have, of course, taken massive liberties with the truth.

In past books I have used Millie, Lucy, and Rae. For the sake of sentence rhythm, I was leaning toward something with one syllable, but it would also be convenient to the book if the replacement name meant something as embarrassing as what the name *Pamela* means, which is *all honey*. I had considered Melinda, which on some sites means honey and could be shortened to Mel. I had considered Samantha, which means listener and could be shortened to Sam. But in the car with the elk in the pasture and the snow on the road and Jeff Tweedy in my ears I was all of a sudden very angry at whoever it was who put all that pressure on Oprah Winfrey. This book was in danger of missing the whole point of itself if my name were not Pam in it. If my name were not Pam in it, who was the organizing consciousness behind these 144 tiny, miraculous, coincident, unrelated things?

ABOUT TEN YEARS AGO, I was looking for an epigraph for a book of my travel essays. I arranged a lot of my Asian travel in those days with an excellent San Francisco outfit called Geographic Expeditions, a company famous for their catalogs, which are full of heart-stopping photos and quotes from writers such as Goethe, Shakespeare, Chatwin, and Plato. That year's catalog contained a quote from Seamus O'Banion: *Eventually I realized that wanting to go where I hadn't been might be as fruitful as going there, but for the repose of my soul I had to do both.* I found it wise and pleasingly self-effacing, and I shamelessly stole it for my epigraph, without taking the time to find the original source.

A season later, I was invited to a cocktail party at the offices of Geographic Expeditions, and since my new book contained essays about trips they had arranged for me, I brought them a copy. "And look," I said, "I thieved my epigraph straight from your catalog," and showed them the O'Banion quote.

When they could contain their laughter long enough to explain it, they said, "There's no such person as Seamus O'Banion. We made him up, one late night several catalogs ago, and now we bring him back whenever we need him to say something profound."

WHEN I TOLD MY FRIEND Shannon how rattled I got in Vegas, she twisted up her mouth and said, "Well, it seems to me that Vegas is the distillation of American-style capitalism, where what is desired is a facsimile of old-world decadence (Venice) exchangeable only by complete ignorance of its actual cost (the wasteland at its margins). And that the lower-middle-class who go there with their obese children are the real fools, because it's their money that keeps everyone else either rich or poor."

For the first time in my life I truly understood the difference between a writer and a cultural critic. A cultural critic goes to Vegas and lets it serve as proof of everything she's been trying to say about the world. A writer goes to Vegas, and it makes her want to kill herself.

IT IS POSSIBLE that I will be advised to change the character Pam's name to Melinda. It is also possible, though less so, that I will be advised to change the names that I have changed back to the actual names, or that I will be advised, the first time I introduce a character called Rick, to say "the man I'll call Rick." It is possible I will be advised to do that with all the characters' names I have changed, which is somewhere in the neighborhood of thirty. In the instances where I have combined two or more real-life people into one character and thrown a little something in there to make them blend—a little storyteller's Petit Verdot—or even made a character up altogether, this method becomes even more problematic.

The Rick I've put on the page bears only a modest resemblance to the man I love and live with—less and less with every draft. But the point I am trying to make here is that the two wouldn't resemble each other much more than they currently do if I called him by his real name and tried with all my might to make the two characters match. Nor would the Pam on the page resemble me any more or less than she currently does (which is only so much) if I am made to call her Melinda. Except inasmuch as her name would be Melinda, and my name would still be Pam.

I UNDERSTAND THAT IT is in bad taste to love Venice, the real version. The city exists, now, more or less for the tourists who number an astounding 7 million a year. None of the employees can afford to live there, and the whole city shuts down by ten thirty each night because the waiters have to run for the last boat, train, or bus for the city of Mestre, where there are apartments they can actually afford. Eighty percent of the palazzo windows are dark at night because they are all owned by counts or bankers or corporations, and now, because of the wave action of speedboats, the wood pilings that have stood strong under the town for more than a thousand years are finally rotting, and the whole city is sinking, slowly but surely into the Adriatic Sea.

And still, leaving the rent-a-car at the San Marco car park, and slipping onto a Vaporetto at 8:00 PM on a foggy January night, leaving the dock and watching the first palazzos come into view, some of them still adorned with Christmas lights, puttering past a gondola, its gondolier ramrod-straight in his slim black coat, passing under the Bridge of Sighs, with the dark water lapping softly against the bow, it is hard not to feel like you have entered the world's single remaining magical kingdom.

And when you tell the Sicilian owner at Beccafico, "we have only one night here, so just make us whatever you think is best," and he brings a whole fish cooked in wine and capers and olives and it is so fresh it is like the definition of the words *fresh fish* in your mouth, and afterward, your sweetheart buys you for your birthday a small piece of Venetian glass, various shades of umber, in the shape of a life preserver to wear around your neck, and you drift off to sleep in a room that has had fancy people sleeping in it since at least the 1400s, you think, if the worst thing they ever say about you is that you have an underdeveloped sense of irony, that might be quite all right.

DID I MENTION THAT when James Frey was an undergraduate, I was his creative writing teacher?

IN SAN FRANCISCO, at Alonzo King's Scheherazade there was one dancer who was head and shoulders above the others. I mean that literally, he was a giant, and figuratively . . . every time he leapt onto the stage, all of our hearts leapt up too.

It was a difficult problem, I imagined, for the choreographer to solve, to have one dancer, in a troupe, who was so outstanding, so lithe and fluid, so perfectly free inside his own body, that he made all the other dancers, who I am sure were very fine dancers, look clunky, boorish, and incontrovertibly white (even the black ones). And yet, having seen that dancer perform, wasn't it Alonzo King's duty to let us see him, even if he couldn't be on stage the entire time, even if every time he left the stage, we all died a little bit inside?

I DID NOT ACTUALLY BELIEVE, for example, until I saw the signs with my own eyes, that several places in Vegas offer drive-through windows for weddings.

IT HAS BEEN FIVE YEARS since my trip to Madison, Wisconsin, and I have 144 chapters. Of those, 132 are titled with a place-name, divided into groups of 12 by 12 single stories that take place no place, on an airplane, 39,000 feet above the ground. I had to make a decision as to whether the airplane stories would count as 12 of the 144, or over and above the 144, but that turned out to be easy. If I stuck to 132 non-airplane stories, I needed just 12 airplane stories to serve as both dividers and bookends. If I wrote 144 non-airplane stories, I would have needed 13, which would have ruined everything.

In the final stages of editing, I sent an e-mail to my editor saying, "Is it wrong of me to want to call myself Pam in this book? Should I just change my name to Melinda and be done with it?"

She wrote back saying, "No, I like Pam. I think we want people to think it is both you and not you," and I sat in front of the computer and nearly wept with gratitude.

Six months before my father lost his job and we drove to Las Vegas, he threw me across the room and broke my femur. I think it's possible he meant to kill me, and I spent the rest of my childhood, the rest of his life, really, thinking he probably would. Speaking only for myself, now, I cannot see any way that my subsequent well-being depends on whether or not or how much you believe what I am telling you—that is to say—on the difference (if there is any) between 82 and 100 percent true. My well-being (when and if it exists) resides in the gaps language leaves between myself and the corn maze, myself and the Las Vegas junkies, myself and the elk chest deep in snow. It is there, in that white space of language's limitation, that I am allowed to touch everything, and it is in those moments of touching everything, that I am some version of free.

When my agent read the first draft of my forthcoming book she said in dismay, *you haven't taken us anywhere and yet you have taken us everywhere!* I know what she was asking for was more resolution, which she was right to ask for and which I subsequently provided, but I still don't know how to inflect her sentence in a way in which it doesn't sound like praise.

One thing I am sure of, having spent the last five years inside a shattered narrative, is that time is a worthy opponent. It does not give up quietly. It does not give up kicking and screaming. It does not, in fact, give up at all. Time is like when you break a thermometer and all the mercury runs around the table trying like crazy to reconstitute itself. Or like the way PCB can start out in a glass transformer in Alabama and wind up on the island of Svalbard, inside a polar bear cub's brain.

A shattered narrative is still a narrative. We can't escape it, it is what we are.

PAM HOUSTON

JILL TALBOT

Meta-Introduction

IN HIS INTRODUCTION TO *Ernest Hemingway on Writing*, Larry W. Phillips begins with this sentence: "Throughout Ernest Hemingway's career as a writer, he maintained that it was bad luck to talk about writing." The introduction is followed by thirteen chapters with titles such as "What Writing Is and Does," "The Pain and Pleasure of Writing," "What To Write About," and "Titles." The collection, a collage of excerpts from Hemingway's works, letters, and interviews, would probably baffle Hem as much as the collection of pennies covering his grave; nevertheless, it establishes a paradox, a contradiction, something Kris Kristofferson would describe as "partly truth, partly fiction."

Yet Hemingway, like countless other writers (insert your favorite one here), did in fact write about writing: the struggles, the strategies, the publishers, the editors, the advice. Hemingway advised Fitzgerald, "I think you should learn about writing from everybody who has ever written that has anything to teach you." During the arduous writing of *In Cold Blood*, Truman Capote wrote a letter insisting, "One can only learn to write by writing—and reading." And a year after the publication of *On the Road*, Jack Kerouac wrote in a letter to Joyce Johnson, "the details are the life of any story." Departing Africa, Isak Dinesen wrote: "At the moment I really cannot foresee what I will, or can, do, so I will not begin to write about it." These insights into writers are but one of my fascinations with metawriting, the writings about the writing. It is true, I enjoy thinking about texts. Thus, one of my most significant friendships for over ten years now has been one with a fellow writer. We often joke about the volumes of e-mails that will survive us, the ones, often tens, we exchange daily about our current endeavors: the drafts, the re-re-re-revised sentences, the forwarded rejections from editors, the authors we are currently reading. (I just e-mailed him that sentence.) Writers record the thoughts, misgivings, frustrations, especially those triumphs that seem to arrive just when we need them, but now in various ways, rather forums. Fast-forward from centuries of handwritten implorations, diary notations, and ALL-CAP telegrams to the digital age of Facebook status updates, Tweets, blogs, and the latest text from your friends: we're all in metamode, writers or not. Everyone now has a blank screen, "Compose Post," status block, 140 characters, to record. As I first learned in graduate school, art reflects or influences society. So as I began to notice that more and more writers were collapsing the distance between artist and artifice, I wanted to see what writers would do if I asked them to deliberately write a piece of metawriting.

IN THE INTRODUCTION TO *Narcissistic Narrative: The Metafictional Paradox* (1980), postmodern theorist Linda Hutcheon writes:

> Reading and writing belong to the processes of "life" as much as they do to those of "art." . . . On the one hand, [the reader] is forced to acknowledge the artifice, the "art," of what he is reading; on the other, explicit demands are made upon him, as a co-creator, for intellectual and affective responses comparable in scope and intensity to those of his life experience. (5)

The life-versus-art issue is a recurring conversation in this anthology, as is the idea that writers themselves, on the page, are works of art. Particularly in metawriting, writers admit, via self-consciousness, self-reference, and self-reflection, the artifice, the representation of the I, the author, the narrator, the essayist, and how that artifice shapes the artist's reality. And vice versa.

PART OF ME WOULD LIKE the introduction to this anthology to consist of only the following:

Metawriting is _____.

Turn the page.

WHEN I INITIALLY QUERIED AUTHORS, I pointed not only to the metaquality of current fiction and nonfiction but also to the ways in which writers were addressing genre boundaries as they examined, within their writing, what it was they were writing. I specifically referenced Nicole Krauss's "The Painters," which had appeared as part of the *New Yorker*'s 2010 Summer *20 under 40* series. In Krauss's story, an excerpt from her novel *Great House*, a writer is told a story at the end of the evening by her host and retells it through her own writing. Within the story, the writer grapples with the fiction-versus-nonfiction aspect of the story. When I teach the story, students always hover around these lines a little longer than the others, "In her work, the writer is free of laws. But in her life, Your Honor, she is not free." Krauss provides an example, one that is emulated again and again in this anthology and beyond, of metawriting as a means to discuss genre, its limitations and its suppositions. As Brian Oliu, a contributor, notes in his interview here, metawriting can be viewed as "the act of doing something outside of the game in order to impact what is actually occurring in the game."

"I DO CARE, SOMETIMES, whether it's fiction or non-fiction." A line from Nicholson Baker's *The Anthologist*, which is about a man struggling to write the introduction to an anthology. (Uncomfortable cough.)

THE GENRE OF EACH PIECE is not identified (at least not by me) so that discussions and contemplations may arise regarding genre. True story: in my contemporary literature courses, I teach the tenets of contemporary fiction. I also teach the ones of the personal essay. During a recent final exam, I gave students two essays and two stories that we had not read so that they might showcase their literary analysis skills on new readings, rather than regurgitate what we had discussed about a piece in class. I did, however, identify the genre. And still, some students wrote on their exam that a story had more essayistic qualities or the essay's elements were more reflective of contemporary fiction. We had not, in that class, ever conflated the two genres or discussed overlap or the blurring of genre. In his preface to *A Moveable Feast*, Hemingway closed with this: "If the reader prefers, this book may be regarded as fiction. But there is always the chance that such a book of fiction may throw some light on what has been written as fact." Indeed.

WE CAN NO LONGER DISCUSS fiction versus fact in literature without invoking the name of James Frey. Five years after his post-Smokinggun .com appearance on *Oprah*, the one in which the talk show host and media mogul excoriated him for a "lie," Frey returned during her final season as one of her "Most Memorable Guests" over a period of two shows that aired on May 16–17, 2011, explaining, "When I sat down to write the book, I didn't think of it as a memoir. I didn't think of it as a novel even. I thought of it as, as some, in a way, statement of defiance." He also described the moment he got off the phone with Oprah in 2005, when she told him she was choosing *A Million Little Pieces* for her book club. Frey turned to his wife and said, "Our lives just changed." We of the literati concur, James.

IN *THE ART OF FICTION*, John Gardner refers to the law of the "vivid and continuous dream." Yet this law is no longer operative in metafiction, he tells us, as "the breaks in the dream are as important as the dream."

CHRISTOPHER ISHERWOOD, another example of a writer writing about his writing (that sentence is very Gertrude Steinesque, I feel), muses in his diary, "Why invent when life is so prodigious?" These contributors speak to this very question, and with aplomb, I might add.

IN HER 1998 NOVEL *The Antelope Wife*, Louise Erdrich gives one of her characters, Cally, this line: "You make a person from a German and an Indian, for instance, and you're creating a two-souled warrior always fighting with themself." I underlined the line in blue ink, marking my recognition of Erdrich, of German and Chippewa descent, peeking behind the pages, but it would take her at least a decade to become more stripped, more exposed in *Shadow Tag*, which closes with a metafictive chapter, in which the daughter in the novel reveals, "So you see, I am the third person in the writing. I am the one with the gift of omniscience." Louise Erdrich: she's making her metamove.

METAWRITING DOES NOT MARK a recent shift or trend in writing. In *The Poetics of Postmodernism* (1988), Linda Hutcheon notes its earliest incarnations: "Self conscious metafiction has been with us for a long time, probably since Homer and certainly since *Don Quixote* and *Tristram Shandy*." In her work, she has also noted her unwillingness to attach, and thus limit, the concept of metafiction as postmodern. Some writers in this anthology are as well.

IN "LEAVING THE MOVIE THEATER," Roland Barthes admits, "I must be in the story . . . but I must also be elsewhere." In some of the works in this anthology, writers wave loudly from the balcony, insisting that their persona as a writer be an integral part of the work. In others, metawriting is the experience. In still a couple others, the metawriting zooms in for a close-up in the final scenes or rolls through like final credits. Yet these distinctions may be interchangeable: the film is different for every person in the theater. Such is art. Lena Dunham, a filmmaker and contributor to this anthology, describes metawriting as "the interplay between reality and fantasy in the stories I (we) tell."

WE LIVE IN A WORLD of deleted scenes and DVD commentary. We live in an NBC hallway in which people look into cameras and talk to us outside of *The Office.* We get our news from a comedian named Jon Stewart who consistently interrupts his own news stories to discuss the audience reaction to the name of the story ("You like that? We just threw that one together in like two seconds.") We watch Tina Fey impersonate Sarah Palin and wonder which one is more real. And for that matter, we watch Tina Fey's creation *30 Rock,* a sitcom loosely based upon her experiences as the head writer on *Saturday Night Live.* Live from New York?

> Chapter One. He adored New York City. He idolized it all out of proportion. Eh uh, no, make that he, he romanticized it all out of proportion. Better. To him, no matter what the season was, this was still a town that existed in black and white and pulsated to the great tunes of George Gershwin. Uh, no, let me start this over. —Woody Allen, *Manhattan* (1979)

I am teaching a seminar in nonfiction, and the students repeatedly tell me, in responses, essays, and office visits, that they are inextricably drawn to meta-nonfiction, an aspect of the course that gains more momentum as we progress through the texts. Early in the semester, it's the slight nod of Edwidge Danticat's *Brother, I'm Dying,* in which she tells the reader in the introductory chapter, "I am writing this because they cannot." When we are in the middle of discussing the pieces in *In Brief: Short Takes on the Personal,* the students comment on the inclusion of metaessays in the mix. A few weeks later, metawriting commands center stage in Michael Chabon's *Maps and Legends: Reading and Writing Across the Borderlands,* with lines like, "I wanted to tell stories, the kind with set pieces and long descriptive passages, and 'round' characters, and beginnings and middles and ends."

Yet it's through the final text in the course, *The Best American Essays 2009,* edited by Mary Oliver, that students are starting to suspect a conspiracy on my part. Is this a course in nonfiction or meta-nonfiction? (Is there a difference?) The selections "(En)Trance," by Chris Arthur, and "The Dark Art of Description," by Patricia Hampl, are particularly pertinent, as each speaks to the essayist's attention to metawriting, as well as the predilection for wandering rumination, versus a fiction writer's consideration of linear arc. Either way, both claim a difference between the How and the Why of what is emphasized and how that emphasis works to its genre's end. Moreover, fifteen essays of the twenty-one in the 2009 edition are in some way writing about writing. What is going on here? I ask. The students are not nonplussed. After all, as they slump in their seats waiting for class to begin, their lives are on constant "meta." They are Tweeting and updating their Facebook status.

MILLIONS OF 140-CHARACTER Tweets, RTs, and FB thumbs-ups are being generated at this very moment. Lady Gaga, Rachel Maddow, Charlie Sheen, *CNF* Online, Richard Brautigan's ghost, you, even that guy at the next table is currently updating his own version of reality. What are you doing now? Jill Talbot is writing an introduction.

IN THE INTERTEXTUAL, critically acclaimed, meta–teen comedy *Easy A* (2010), the protagonist Olive Pederghast broadcasts her own experiences onto YouTube in order to salvage her scarlet reputation. (Olive is studying *The Scarlet Letter* in school and creates a twenty-first-century twist on Hester Prynne.) Olive's English teacher complains, "I don't know what your generation's fascination is with documenting your every thought, but I can assure you, they're not all diamonds. 'Roman is having an OK day, and bought a Coke Zero at the gas station. Raise the roof.' Who gives a rat's ass?" Answer: Mark Zuckerberg, and *Time Magazine* named him 2010's Person of the Year. Like the social network created by Zuckerberg, art does indeed reflect or influence culture, or does both. And the current fascination with documenting and sharing, with self-awareness, may perhaps be linked with the influx of metawriting and the dissolving barriers between experience and the representation of that experience. Some of the interviews in this anthology address what I see as the "selfolution" of our times. @pamhouston: what percentage are we on FB or Twitter? Everyone now, not just writers, creates a written, published persona on a daily (hourly) basis. Artifice abounds.

SOME WRITERS IN THIS ANTHOLOGY warn against the self-congratulatory tinge that metawriting is capable of producing (though they phrase it more delicately and constructively than "Who gives a rat's ass?"). For example, Ryan Van Meter warns, "At its worst, meta- can feel self-congratulatory or pretentious or condescending." Ander Monson, in his interview, notes, "[It] can pretty quickly devolve into a recursive spiral of self-consciousness and neurosis, which is usually a frustrating and uninteresting reading experience." However, Kristen Iversen points to the potential for another type of distraction: "The danger of meta-narrative is that it can become too intellectual or too busy with its own pyrotechnics or—worst-case scenario—trivial or dull."

WHEN MY READINGS IN NONFICTION course ended in 2010, I had already contacted most of the writers who appear here. I began with writers who had already published a work of metawriting, as well as writers I admire and writers whom I knew, from interviews or their social media comments, to be engaged in the fiction-versus-nonfiction issue. Note: I have only met one of the contributors in person, and even then, only once, briefly. How's that for writing in the digital age? Or maybe it is my predilection for technological exchanges in lieu of human contact, but I digress. I initiated conversations (interviews) with the assumption that we all had a dictionary-based, working definition of metawriting (writing about writing, writing that refers to itself), which allowed me to focus upon their perception of its presence, impact, and purpose in literature, and, as you will read, their favorite metawritings. One characteristic of metawriting stands out after compiling and looking back over all the interviews, and that is the directness inherent in it.

Sarah Blackman, for example, sees metawriting as "more immediate," while Cathy Day recognizes that "Metagestures ... remind us that we're reading or watching something that is not real, that has been created. There's something even more 'real' than the carefully rendered reality we're being presented with." Brenda Miller describes its "naked, physical quality." Still, David Lazar zings us with this one: "[It is] a yearning for the perfectly flawed sentence that is the comet's tail of an idea."

IN ALL OF MY ADVANCED COURSES, the final project for students is not an exam or a completed manuscript but a representation of what they are taking from the course. This is for you, I tell them, not for me. Think of something that you will keep as a reminder of the works, the concepts, the class. For most students, the freedom of this "final" affords them the opportunity to reveal beyond what can be measured in traditional ways: I've had students create works of art, photographs, paintings, (anything on a poster board is forbidden), buy a suitcase and a bus ticket (from a course on the road narrative). In one class, two students took off to Minneapolis over spring break, to Louise Erdrich's bookstore, bringing back store bookmarks for each student in the class. Read on, keep writing, is at the core of each final. But this nonfiction final was different; during that final on an early May morning, I, too, took a number.

When my turn came, I projected the image of a mock book cover with the pending title *(Meta) Writing in (Non) Fiction* (titles, they change— Tennessee Williams initially had *The Poker Night*) onto the screen, then clicked to the beginnings of the list you now see in the table of contents. Like my students, I wanted to read on, keep writing. And a fellow writer, the one I e-mail about my writing, suggested I interview each contributor. The interviews, conducted over a period of a year, allowed me to engage with each writer, sending one question and waiting for the answer, on and on, in order to develop conversations that never turned in on themselves, but went in their own direction, as had been my goal in including them—interviews, by nature, are "meta," and I asked some of the writers here to respond to interviews of other contributors, thus acknowledging the artifice of what you're holding—this is an anthology.

PHILLIP LOPATE, in his introduction to *The Art of the Personal Essay*, begins, "This book attempts to put forward and interpret a tradition: the personal essay." I insist: this book sets out to turn a spotlight on metawriting in order to showcase the various ways in which it is currently being performed in writing. I believe it's more of a collection of How. And Why.

ACCORDING TO SOME of the essayists here, all writing is metawriting. I like the way Robin Hemley puts it: "We read the essay to see a mind at work on the page." As a preface to each piece, I have chosen one of the most salient quotes from each writer: about metawriting, about genre, about truth. I hope they illuminate the anthology's focus as well as the writer's piece within the collection's framework.

THE OTHER DAY, a student came into my office and told me she was struggling with her essay. She mentioned not feeling connected to her work, not feeling like it was something that she truly wanted to write. I told her, "Write what you would want to read." This is the anthology I wanted to read.

THE BEST CREATIVE NONFICTION 3, edited by Lee Gutkind, features essays that are prefaced by a metawriting, in which writers address the writing of the genre or the specific essay. Gregory Orr's "Return to Hayneville," begins, "When I write prose, I find myself acknowledging truths that elude me in poetry." Truth, you will find, is a recurring issue in this anthology. And it's as elusive as ever.

ON HIS PENULTIMATE APPEARANCE on the Oprah show, James Frey claimed he was told that the now-infamous show he originally appeared on in 2006 was going to be called "Truth in America." "It was going to be a discussion about, sort of, the flexible definition of truth," he recalled, "or if there is a flexible definition of truth." Oprah nodded, responded with one word, "Truthiness." We have Stephen Colbert, or his writers, to thank for that one. *Truthiness*: Merriam-Webster's choice for #1 Word of the Year in 2006.

A PROLOGUE, an introduction, and a foreword walk into a bar, er, a book.

YEARS AGO, MY MOTHER gave me a birthday card featuring stamps of famous authors: John Steinbeck, Robert Frost, Shakespeare, William Faulkner, Edgar Allan Poe. The front of the card reads: "None of these famous writers could say it better." I framed it and keep it on the wall near my writing desk. To be sure, the writers in this anthology explain metawriting better than I ever could in an introduction or elsewhere, so let's indeed, turn the page.

RYAN VAN METER

"I like reading work that tips me into a world already in motion, and enjoy creating that effect in my own work. . . . [T]his kind of storytelling technique also underscores the 'truth' of literary nonfiction by creating the sense that there's been a life going on before the opening moment of the essay."

I Was There

MY BOYFRIEND STEPPED ON the parking brake of the U-Haul, switched off the engine, and the weight of our stuff pushed from behind as we sat on the severe slope of Lyon Street, pointing down. All of us—boyfriend, dog, me—felt the relief of journey's end, but just as quickly, as I unlatched my seatbelt, the gravity of our new place tugged hard. I realized I didn't want to move from my cushion. Too much movement, it seemed, and the parking brake would uncatch under the strain of that terrible street angle and the mass of all we'd carried across two time zones, sending all of it and us into the buzzing intersection below, a line of cars and the stout trees of Golden Gate Park.

But once my feet hit the pavement, and I stood and marveled at the pitch of the view with the fog arriving as easily as a cliché, our steep hill felt reassuring. Yes, we were in San Francisco, where turquoise houses perched on improbably sloping hills and where fog rolled across vast parks like the hippies used to, and I'd find out soon, sometimes still did. I'd never stood there before but it was somehow familiar.

Because of the slope, unloading the truck meant trudging up its ramp to the bed deck and then walking down and pulling our stuff up out of it—something like rescuing a fallen sofa from a cave. I hated standing inside the truck at that angle, always thinking of that parking brake— had it been tested at this slope, with this amount of stuff? Shouldn't we have told the woman at the U-Haul counter we planned to park the truck on a steep hill right after driving over a mountain range? As much planning as we'd done, there was still so much I hadn't thought of, and there was the sudden sense that I needed to move very carefully inside the facts. After my boyfriend wrangled a chair from the heap, the whole truck shimmying in the struggle, he paused to scratch his beard and discuss our unloading strategy again. I wanted to shake him for making us stand in there and talk, and would have, if such movement wouldn't also have killed us.

Later, as I heaved crates of records and kitchen junk into our new place on that first San Franciscan afternoon, over the crest at the top of the block came a tour bus. Double-decker and softly blue, it was vaguely designed like the streetcars from Rice-a-Roni commercials, but with an open top and all-road tires. The bus floated down and parked behind our gaping truck. The voice of the guide mumbled out of the speakers and into the faces of the tourists sitting under the sun. Everyone looked to their right, to a house on the other side of the street. Even so, I felt part of their scrutiny—the moment of us heaving my giant desk across the street for- ever connected in their memory with whatever important thing had hap- pened there. On our block of our street. The bus hissed, rolled, and floated on, turning at Oak Street and disappearing around the corner.

We emptied and returned the truck, unpacked boxes, filled dresser drawers with folded squares of t-shirts and tight balls of socks. Arranged furniture, plugged dozens of cords into power strips and shoved the jum- bles behind cabinets. And each day as we worked, setting everything in order, standing in the middles of rooms with hands on hips wondering where some bookshelf might be placed or look better, the tour bus tinkled down the street and stopped halfway down. Then a couple of other times a day, groups on foot marched down the hill, clumps of out-of-towners with cameras wound around necks. They stopped in front of our house and nodded when their guide pointed across the street—to a house that was not the house where the tour bus aimed its attention.

Then I started noticing people tramping down the hill, without tour group or bus, just people with companions and camera. Younger or older, usually in pairs, often gripping a guidebook. All day they came from Haight Street to climb the stairs of one of those two porches. Some sat on a top step's lip, others stood proud and leaned over a railing. Many stood next to a door, next to house numbers tacked on in gold. Sometimes they held up a two-fingered peace sign. The friend on the sidewalk fussed with the camera, an eye in the viewfinder, framing a smiling face. Half of them stopped at 112 Lyon Street, a dusky lavender house with a bright belt of white panels cinching its middle and a pristine round balcony off the sec- ond floor. That was the tour bus house. Further down the hill, closer to the park and directly across the street from my apartment was 122 Lyon, where the tour groups on foot and the other half of the trampers stopped to climb the cement stairs of a stone-colored house with a wrought-iron railing, white trim, and a big black door.

"God, what happened on Lyon?" I asked my boyfriend as we ate take-out from containers balanced in our laps. "Who was murdered here?"

Later our landlord stopped in, a former tenant of our apartment herself, and she told us about our house and neighborhood, about how Jimi Hendrix stayed somewhere nearby back in those days, and how on our block, right up there (and she pointed to 112, where the tour bus had idled), Janis Joplin had once lived.

Though it had been at least fifteen years and possibly more since I had put on a Janis song, there was a time when her Greatest Hits CD was among my most cherished music. In high school, I liked her music's old-fashionedness, and liked too that listening to her old songs made me look a little weird, nostalgic. Among the kids at my school, it wasn't popular and neither was I. Her music beckoned from the past and had meant rebellion, wildness, and ease to me—which was the opposite of what I felt on my own, in the present tense of high school. My parents' record collection had many other high school favorites—the Carpenters, the Mamas and the Papas, the Doors, the Supremes—but Janis was mine, discovered somehow on my own and purchased on compact disc with birthday money so I could listen to her in my bedroom, behind my shut door, as opposed to vinyl, which had to be played on the turntable in the basement.

"Me and Bobby McGee," track number five, was my favorite, a celebration song in which the volume knob was turned to the hilt of what was allowed in our house, six on a dial of ten. On tiptoes, in front of the mirror screwed to the back of my door, I sang, danced, swung my head like a censer, my tone-deaf notes drowning Janis's while I secretly wished for a restless man of my own named Bobby to take me off somewhere, anywhere, away. As I saw him, Bobby had a dark beard and a darker voice, a white t-shirt and almost-gone blue jeans. That I had imagined Luke Duke from earlier childhood Friday nights spent watching *The Dukes of Hazzard* wouldn't occur to me until later.

Another, bigger revelation about Bobby came from my high school best friend Angie, who like me had been cheated in life by being born a couple of decades late. On my bedroom floor, she pointed to the songwriter's name on the liner notes. Kris Kristofferson, a name I recognized from country music, the music I considered at the time to be the most awful of all music, possibly because while growing up in Missouri the last thing I needed more of was "country."

"Bobby," Angie said, hand over her heart, eyes pointed out the window, "is really a woman." This truth was crushing, but because displaying any of my heartache about that bait-and-switch would be yet another revelation, one about me that wouldn't break open for another ten years, I shrugged and said, "That's so weird."

As terrible as the news about Bobby was, there was something heartening to it, because more than just connecting with her music in the deeply serious way that no one else in history had ever done, I was also kindred to Janis: we both needed secret saving by a handsome hero, Bobby McGee, as in Robert and not Roberta or anything else dreamed up by Mr. Kristofferson. Much later, it would make perfect sense that my closeted high school self would fall in love with an imagined male version of an actually female character—I was always having to translate my fantasies: squinting my girlfriends into boyfriends or veiling tortured crushes on a rare straight friend as brotherly affinity or swapping the cheerleader on the running back's arm with me. I was trying to seem plausible as myself, for my pretend desires to be believable, for my true ones to be invisible. No wonder I desired rescue.

"Piece of My Heart," the first track on the disc, was my mournful song, played during grief or frustration. The morning, for example, that Angie and her family left for a ten-day summer vacation, or the afternoon the cast list was posted for the school production of *Winnie-the-Pooh*, and I was not to star as Christopher Robin (or anyone else) even though I looked and talked exactly like him. This song was set between four and five on the dial while a burning stick of incense unwound a rope of smoke toward the ceiling. I then lay across my neutral carpet, miniblinds squeezed shut, overhead light off. With the song on repeat, Janis rose up and faded down every three minutes as piece after piece of our hearts was taken, slowly in the dark, and I felt myself disappear, until my mother stood at the end of the hall and called, "Supper!" In one song I was taken away to another life somewhere else and in the other, I was just taken away.

So I should probably have been more embarrassed by how thrilled I was that Janis had at one time lived on my block. But this fact became part of my standard "How is San Francisco?" answer, part of the way I made sense of my new city, familiar as it felt when I arrived, until a local friend trumped me by revealing that the Symbionese Liberation Army once holed up in his apartment. "So Patty Hearst was held hostage in my closet," he shrugged. "Someone famous once lived everywhere in San Francisco."

And even if it felt adolescent to fawn over Janis again, I still stomped up the hill to take a picture of the lavender house, 112. That the tour bus continued to swing by, day in, day out, seemed proof that she'd lived in that one, so I sent it to Angie. But as more and more young people continued to smile for photos at 122 Lyon, I was bothered that I didn't know where she *really* lived.

"Half of those people are wrong," I said. I started imagining myself in San Francisco during my Janis days—drunk on nostalgia and sentiment instead of anything else, goody-two-shoes that I was, in my oversized Beatles t-shirt, a five-dollar pair of Lennon lenses, and the Birkenstock sandals given to me for my birthday in June that I had requested right after Christmas. What if I had a photo taken of me standing on Janis's porch, surely flashing that peace sign to the camera, and had found out later, possibly decades later when I returned to that block of Lyon Street to live, that she hadn't ever lived there? That of all the apartments in all the houses in San Francisco, and in California, and even in the United States, I had come so very close to hers, closer than most people, but was in fact four houses off?

My boyfriend sat in our still-curtainless window and typed into his laptop. "Both addresses come up," he said. "She lived at 112 or she lived at 122."

But only one could be true. I stood beside his chair and hunched to look under the tree shading our side of Lyon. If curtains weren't hanging over there, at 122, I could have looked right in, and if it had been forty-three years earlier, the Summer of Love, and Janis was home and sitting in her window, and she had just moved in so she didn't have curtains either, we might have been looking at each other. Suddenly, even if the lavender house was lovelier, I wanted Janis's house to have really been 122. Instead of saying she lived on our block, I could boast she lived *across the street*.

But 112 Lyon Street was her address according to the blue tour bus. She also lived there according to onlyinsanfrancisco.com, the official visitors' site for San Francisco, which is maintained by the San Francisco California Visitors Bureau. And she lived there according to virtualtourist.com, goldengatebi.com ("bi" in this case being an abbreviation for "best inn"), shoestring-traveler.com, as well as *San Francisco* by Tom Downs, published by Lonely Planet in 2006, and *Walking San Francisco*, also by Tom Downs, out the following year from Wilderness Press, where he states that Janis's place "was on the second floor with the curved balcony off the front." Before we moved to the city, my boyfriend bought me a copy of *San Francisco Secrets: Fascinating Facts about the City by the Bay*. During our first trip to the city together, about a month before arriving in the truck, I cleared my throat and pointed to various sites to share essential scraps of trivia. "Did you know that the Golden Gate Bridge wasn't supposed to be *that* color?" I asked, out of breath, as we crossed it. "That's really the primer. It's called International Orange." This book of secrets was actually shaped like the bridge and also put Janis in number 112 in the year 1967, saying it was a one-room apartment shared with boyfriend Country Joe

McDonald (instead of our Bobby McGee). Frommer's, a giant of travel book publishing, in its *Irreverent Guide to San Francisco* by Matthew Richard Poole, lists 112 as Janis's address, but in its *San Francisco Day by Day: 24 Smart Ways to See the City*, by Noelle Salmi, Janis lives down the hill, in the house right across from mine, at 122. I wondered then which I considered to be more accurate—a "smart" book or an "irreverent" one?

In either case, Janis also lived at 122 in *Roadtripping USA: The Complete Coast-to-Coast Guide to America*, *Let's Go San Francisco*, and *Little Black Book of San Francisco*, as well as on strollsanfrancisco.com, sanfrancisco cityhotel.com, haightshop.com, singlemindedwomen.com, in an article titled "The Hills—and Heels—of San Francisco," and on roundamerica .com, a Web site devoted to the 148-day trip by car that Bill and Barbara Windsor of Marietta, Georgia, took to more than 2500 towns in all fifty states. Though one of them was sick for most of their California stay, they both were still able to visit the "center of hippydom in the 60s," which included Janis's former apartment at 122 Lyon Street.

Scribbling down the various sources, I was suddenly the tourist out there tramping around, my finger pressing a spot on a map, trying to find my way to a landmark. In a notebook, I tallied the number of listings under a column for 112 and another for 122. In the absence of something definitive, I decided the truth, or mine anyway, would be determined by which address gathered more hash marks. But if one travel company as famous as Frommer's couldn't even get its own books published within a couple of years of each other to agree, what kind of truth would ever be definitive? So I kept looking.

Back in those incense and carpet-sulk days, I would have been among the writers posting to the fan forum of the official Janis Web site at janis joplin.com, if our family's Apple II GS could have connected to anything but an electrical socket. Like many of the writers of those posts, I used actually to mourn having missed the 60s, romanticized and clichéd as my idea of them was. The fan forum divides its thousands of discussion topics into three categories: "Official Site Talk" (for questions asked frequently, as well as issues with usernames and links that lead nowhere), "I Was There," and "I Wasn't There." The former for firsthand memories of Janis performances, of backstage glimpses, hugs, shaken hands; the latter for fans who came around after Janis's passing, like me, for celebrating her music and celebrity posthumously. While the forum is open to any reader, more than six thousand members are registered.

"There," as it applied to either "I Was There" or "I Wasn't There," meant not just a place but also a time, or many possible times, as many possible times as Janis was anywhere. And not even just a single place, but many possible places, and not just her two possible apartments on Lyon Street, but her apartment on Noe Street or Cole Street or anywhere else she might have been in the city—the "Grateful Dead" house or the "Jefferson Airplane" house, which are both nearby—and not just San Francisco or California, but any concert anywhere, any roadside stop on the way to those concerts, any jam session or shopping trip or picnic or party. "There" was any place or time (or both) where the 60s were, and though I had literally never been there, back when I had been my foolish, nostalgic self in a brand-new suburban house built in 1987, stretched across new carpet with my CD manufactured long after Janis died in 1970 (five years before my own birth), I would have claimed that I had been "there." In fact, I had been "there" many times. And knowing what I knew about "there," I wondered how it could ever be possible to find it on a map, walk up its steps, turn and face a camera, and smile.

Organizing them under the topic "Janis Lived Here," fans posted photos and comments about visiting Janis's various dwellings, especially her San Francisco addresses. On this thread, the debate about where she really lived on Lyon Street bounced back and forth. Azhippiechick asked, "Can anyone shine some light on the 'correct' house. They are very close to each other and I went to see both in Feb. when I was there. The 112 house is prettier, but I am just curious??????????"

Then another member posted blurry scans of Janis's California driver's license. The hazy address was 122 Lyon, and another fan wrote that the 1967 San Francisco phone book also put Janis at that house—two definitive sources of truth, it seemed. The end.

I felt relief then that I could claim she was "there," right across the street. But bigger than relief, I felt regret at having sought the truth so doggedly that I had found the answer. Without realizing it, I had enjoyed Janis eluding us, being something like that cliché fog impossible to fix on a map. As a writer of true stories, I was used to looking for the truth. What was strange this time was being disappointed at finding it.

Under "Janis Lived Here," fans also speculated about the source of the discrepancy. Darkstar, a fellow Haight-Ashbury resident, attributed the decades-long mix-up to the tiniest of mistakes. "The 112 address came about when in the book BURIED ALIVE the address was miss printed as 112. It was a total typo error and it has caused 30 years of confusion over the address. Janis had nothing to do with 112 Lyon." The biography by Myra Friedman was first published in 1973, three years after Joplin's death, and had been updated and reissued ever after, as recently as 1992. But thumbing through *Buried Alive*, the only reference I found to Lyon Street didn't list a house number, 112 or 122. Instead: "Janis's Lyon Street apartment had a quaintly curved balcony that soaked up the rays of the afternoon sun." Pulling aside my miniblinds and leaning to look under the tree branches again, I confirmed there was no balcony on the façade of 122 and that four houses up, at 112, spread across the front and facing west to catch the sun as it set, was a perfect half-circle in white trim.

One of those travel books by Tom Downs also described the same balcony, so perhaps Darkstar was right. If the *Buried Alive* curved balcony confused visitors and travel writers after its publication in 1973, then it could have been the source of the confusion. But glancing up Lyon Street again, I counted a couple of curved balconies on that side alone. Even 122 had a balcony, if you considered fire escapes. On paper, 112 and 122 were only a typo apart, a simple mistaken keystroke of the next-door key, 2 for 1. But how do you accidentally describe a curved balcony on a house that doesn't have one?

I couldn't stop looking, but instead of the truth, I was searching now for its confusion. In 1999, the *San Francisco Chronicle* published a story about Golden Gate Community, which was opening its new rehab center for single mothers with addictions at 124 Lyon Street, the house on the corner of Oak, next door to 122. In the organization's press release about its grand opening, they boasted that Janis had once owned their huge four-story yellow Victorian back in that Summer of Love, as they had believed for decades. After the paper published its story about the center, local readers wrote in to set straight the claim. The *Chronicle* then issued a correction, and the second story's third paragraph stirred up my murkiness even more: "To believe the dizzying variety of versions from tour guides, history books and local lore, 'Pearl' Joplin lived in any of four different houses on the block, right near two separate houses where Jimi Hendrix supposedly crashed—not to mention two more houses where newspaper heiress Patty Hearst was reputedly kept prisoner in the basement." Suddenly my San Francisco friend's closet across town was emptied of its story—though still crammed with his stuff—because that blonde hostage could have been on Lyon, could as easily have been tied up and blindfolded in my basement, or could have been in one of Janis's two or three or even four different Lyon Street basements, or could have been in any other basement on my block, or any other block in this neighborhood, this city.

And that friend of mine had been right. Someone famous once lived everywhere in San Francisco because we kept putting them there. Why were we trying so hard to tie ourselves to such nostalgia?

Clichés, like the fog in San Francisco, worn down as they are by frequent handling, are almost always true. Nostalgia almost never is. It's a story about the past, a desire about it, how we wish it or we had been. The slope of Lyon Street was a fact. That the streets of San Francisco sloped sharply was a cliché. That Janis once lived there, somewhere: a story. That the truth about where eluded us: a better one. So it didn't matter which house Janis lived in. Just like it didn't matter to her fans, including my high school self, that she'd left the world at age twenty-seven on the floor of a hotel room because there was too much heroin in her blood, or that her voice was beautiful precisely because it sounded ruined much too early.

She had been an actual person, despite the way she and Bobby appeared through my Lennon lenses, and she had lived there instead of "there," with bills in her mailbox, curtains to hang, a bookshelf that didn't look right no matter how many times she and Country Joe heaved it from wall to wall. Later, at the top of the hill on Lyon, I'd look down and see scrawled in permanent marker along the curve of the gutter: JANIS JOPLIN PUKED HERE. Another point on a blurry map, and not any more or less true. Knowing the difference about her addresses, I wished I didn't. But everywhere, all over the planet, were the photographs. People who came by streetcar, bus, or feet. Standing on her porch or just looking at it, and her porch was that porch and also that porch, and maybe many other porches. Those people had wanted to find her too. And hadn't they? Couldn't they still point and say, "That's me, I was there"?

INTERVIEW

Ryan Van Meter, author of "I Was There"

Q: This essay, like others of yours I have read, begins *in medias res*. Is that a stylistic tendency or a coincidence?

A: Yes, in medias res is a stylistic choice, if not a tic. I like reading work that tips me into a world already in motion, and enjoy creating that effect in my own work. But in essays, I think that, as important as it is for the action to start in the middle of something already unfolding, it's just as important for the thinking of the essay also to be in medias res. Even if you're only making your reader sensitive to certain important ideas that will be explored more explicitly later in the essay, I think all those clues and hints need to be there from the very beginning. And it's not only for the sake of the essay's pacing; this kind of storytelling technique also underscores the "truth" of literary nonfiction by creating the sense that there's been a life going on before the opening moment of the essay.

Q: In "I Was There," you ultimately arrive at the idea that "where truth eludes" is the story. Would you say that your work seeks to examine these elusive truths, and beyond the accurate address of Janis Joplin's house on Lyon Street, what other evasive truths have you sought to explore in your work?

A: Sometimes the truth is so elusive that it's just not available, so I usually think of essays as looking to gain clarity on an experience instead of looking for some single tidy answer. And sometimes the fact that you can't know something leads you to another more important discovery. In my book *If You Knew Then What I Know Now*, I have an essay called "Specimen," about a time in seventh grade when I developed a sudden, paralyzing fear of being abducted by aliens—seventh grade being the year in school when we all kind of feel like aliens ourselves. I watched one episode of *Unsolved Mysteries*, and then that was it, I was utterly convinced that I was going to be abducted, it was just a matter of when. In writing the essay about that experience, I was convinced for a long time that it wasn't working because I couldn't figure out why I was afraid of aliens. I sat and imagined it all again, I thought and thought, wrote pages and pages over several years in several versions. Then one day, I just let it go, and started thinking about the essay as not trying to solve a riddle of why, but as a way of understanding what was changed by my fear, and what that change revealed about my experience of seventh grade. It was ultimately more complicated to change the focus in that way, but if I'd had some simple cause-and-effect truth available from the beginning, I'm not sure the essay could have gotten there.

Q: A few weeks after you submitted "I Was There," you Tweeted this: "Someone wrote 'Janis Puked Here' in black marker on the curb on my street corner." And I couldn't resist but to reply: "And would that be 'here' or 'there'? Thinking of your essay." I mention in my introduction to this anthology that due to Facebook, Twitter, YouTube, and other venues such as blogs, we're ALL living meta-lives. Yet how do you see such sites impacting writers and their writing? Yours?

A: It's probably safe to say that regardless of what those sites have done for us as writers, they haven't made us more productive. But that's another story. I was aware of course when I Tweeted about Janis that I had been writing about her, and that anyone who had read the essay (namely you) would read that Tweet differently than anyone else. And I guess that's what is engaging to me about our living these metawriting lives—that we've found a way to invite others into our writing process. On Twitter and Facebook, I'm friends with writers who post how many words they've written on a particular day. But is it a way to keep track? Or to be held responsible? Other writers ask questions of their friends and followers, needing an answer for their project. Or share links to articles and reviews that presumably other writers would find interesting. And so on. It's a curious symbiosis. Then the complication is that all these Tweets and statuses are themselves being written. I actually think writing Tweets is incredibly difficult, but a poet friend of mine is a master at it. Maybe our meta-living depends on genre?

Q: So would you say that the function of metawriting alters with genre?

A: I do think the function probably alters depending on genre. I'd say as a reader I'm much more tolerant of metawriting in fiction. In nonfiction, where the "meta" feels so much more self-conscious, I believe the trick of it is harder to pull off. It can so often seem like only a gimmick, not essential to the emotional thrust of the piece, and at its worst, "meta" can feel self-congratulatory or pretentious or condescending. But maybe I'm speaking more about my own limitations as a writer. I've only ever tried incorporating the "meta" explicitly once in an essay, and even then I was writing in the second person, so there was some remove. A great example of an essay that uses "meta" to its full potential is Cheryl Strayed's "The Love of My Life." In this meditation on grief, she discusses the expectations of narratives and stories, and how our most raw, emotional experiences can't adequately be shoehorned into them, but of course, she's discussing all of this in an essay, with a story and a shape. It's incredible.

Q: Yes, Strayed's comments regarding story versus essay thrilled me the first time I read them. You're referring to "If You Knew Then," an essay that first appeared in *River Teeth* and has been anthologized. Another piece of yours, "First," appeared in *The Best American Essays 2009*. Final question, in honor of the self-conscious nature of this anthology: those essays were chosen after you had written them, yet "I Was There" was written for this anthology (thank you). Did that alter the writing, and if so, how?

A: I'm still such a school nerd that I like getting assignments like these. While I might have several ideas for projects in mind at any given time, an assignment like this one (with a deadline) gives me something concrete to work on. Tackling the "meta" aspect of the assignment was challenging, but having certain limitations in writing frees you in other ways. For the same reason, I give my students a lot of prescriptive assignments in creative writing classes. As limiting as they can be, there's also a kind of comfort in having a few of the doors closed off from you, because then you have fewer places to wander to and get lost.

"Okay, let's say that a metamove or metagesture is when the author intentionally draws attention to a work's genre, its very existence as fiction or nonfiction."

Genesis; or the Day Adam Killed the Snakes

ADAM AND EVE live in a farmhouse surrounded by apple orchards. One spring day, Adam pokes his head into Eve's study. "What are you doing?" he asks.

"Working," she says.

"Oh. I'm going to the attic to bring down the air conditioner," Adam says.

"Great," Eve says into her computer screen.

He waits. "I might need you."

"Uh-huh." Her fingers fly across the keyboard.

A few minutes later, he calls out. "Come here! I want to show you something."

Eve snaps her laptop shut. She never gets any work done when Adam is home.

In the attic, Adam points to an abandoned cot. Two black coils bask in the light coming through a dormer window.

Yes. Adam and Eve. Apples and snakes. Snakes with tongues that flit out to greet her.

"Oh my God," Eve says.

"Five feet long," Adam says a little proudly. "Maybe six. They're big fuckers."

In the last few months, they've found plenty of shed snake skins on the attic stairs, in the basement, hanging from tree limbs. Snakes slithering across their gravel road, and once, she almost ran over one with the John Deere. When they have friends out for sunset drinks on the long porch, Adam and Eve bring out the skins—long strips of dry paper. But they have never actually seen a snake in the house. And now, here are two.

Eve tiptoes back downstairs and goes to her study. Adam finds her at her desk, staring at the ceiling. "They're right up there," she says, pointing. "How can I write thinking about them above my head?"

Yes, Eve is a writer. Adam is too, but this isn't important until later.

Adam crosses his arms. "I knew I shouldn't have shown them to you."

"They must move through the walls at night," Eve says. "How can we sleep?"

"I knew it!" He stomps downstairs and returns a few minutes later with a shovel, the one they've been using to plant perennials in the front yard.

"What?" she asks.

"I have to kill them."

"No," she yells. "That's too dangerous. Can't we just capture them and put them back outside?" He gives her his "I-can't-believe-you're-so-dumb" look, and she remembers the mice. That winter, they used a humane catch-and-release trap until Eve said, "I might be crazy, but I think it's the same mouse." Adam marked an X on its back with a permanent marker, and sure enough, they caught the same mouse again a few days later. So they switched to the death traps. Adam baits them with peanut butter, and at night, Eve hears them snap shut in the kitchen.

Armed with the shovel, Adam trudges into the attic, and a few minutes later, Eve hears him whacking away. Soon he's screaming, "Stupid motherfucking snake! Die! Die!" She wonders if the snakes are poisonous, if she should help. But help how? She doesn't move from her desk until he yells, "Open the door!" Adam has bagged one of the snakes. It writhes on the shovel scoop, red innards bulging like sausage in its casing. Adam drips snake blood on the floors, the rugs, all the way to the front door. Tossing it far into the yard, he marches back inside. "The other one," he spits, slamming the attic door behind him. More whacking. More motherfucking. More blood spots down the stairs.

Eve finds Adam standing in the front yard. He's breathing heavily, leaning on the shovel, staring down at a black and red pool of snake. Eve squats down to get a better look. One of the snakes opens its fleshy white mouth wide, like it's screaming. "Careful," Adam says. "They aren't dead yet."

He tells her they wedged themselves in a corner, where the angled roof meets the floor, so he couldn't just chop off their heads. Instead, he had to poke and beat the snakes to death—or to this near-death. He brings the shovel over his shoulder like a spike hammer and finishes them both, pounding their tiny heads over and over with the curved underside of the shovel. Then, Adam carries the snakes toward the weed-choked sluice that feeds their pond.

After, they sit quietly in their matching Adirondack chairs on the porch. A few days from now, Adam will discover on the Internet that he's just killed two nonvenomous black rat snakes (*Elapheobseletaobseleta*), praised by area farmers as better mousers than barn cats. He'll read the on-line article out loud to her, pausing after this sentence: *Although it is one of our most valuable snakes, human fear and prejudice against all snakes often result in this shy and beneficial species being killed on sight.* But right now, Adam and Eve are still sitting on the porch, free of this knowledge. Right now, Adam has just done a brave, brave thing. Eve touches his hand and says, "I love you," because she is so grateful, and Adam says tiredly, "I love you, too."

From the porch, Eve notices that services are over at the little stone church up the road. Yes, this story takes place on a Sunday, and yes, there's a church, and yes, there are snakes, and yes, they live in an apple orchard, but there are no actual apples yet. It's spring, you see. The trees bear pink and white blossoms, and the orchard hums with millions of bees. The world looks like Oz, like it just snowed flowers. Eve loves this place, and she believes their finding it is a sign that her life is exactly as it should be. Some nights, Adam and Eve sit on the porch with martinis and talk about getting married in the little stone church, but neither of them ever uses a word other than "someday," although they have been together for six years.

That night in bed, Adam is quiet for a long time. Finally, he tells her that he had to swear in order to work up enough hate to finish off the snakes. "They've probably lived in this house for years," he says. "Longer than us." He says, "I'll never be able to get those images out of my head. I can't believe you made me do that."

"I didn't say to kill them," says Eve.

"No, but you said you couldn't stand them being over our heads."

"Well, could you?"

He rolls over. "I could have lived with it."

"Bullshit," she says. "You just feel bad, so you want it to be my fault."

There is a long silence, and then he says, "It is."

In the weeks that follow, Eve feels less certain about her future with Adam, as if the snakes have left a curse on the house. Adam and Eve fight about very stupid things like eggplants, *The Andy Griffith Show*, and bath towels. For the hundredth time, Eve asks, "What's wrong?" and for the hundredth time, Adam says, "Nothing."

A few months later, during summer's long green stretch, Adam invites a colleague and his wife over for dinner. While Adam and his colleague are casting lures into the pond, Eve gives the wife a house tour. In the study, the wife pauses for a second and looks up at the ceiling. "Something's happened up there. I can feel it. I'm a little clairvoyant." Eve tells her about the snakes, and the wife nods knowingly, like she already knows how this story will end.

After the colleague and the clairvoyant have gone home, Eve sits on the porch and thinks, *Maybe I'll write a story about the day Adam killed the snakes*. She's been thinking about it ever since it happened. Actually, she was thinking about it while it was happening. Writers are weird that way. At the moment, Eve has no theme in mind, no point to make. Just images in her head: the black snakes, their white mouths, the pink and white blossoms, the blood blooms Adam scrubbed furiously from the rugs.

Adam is inside doing all the dishes because she cooked the big dinner for four. That's the deal they've struck, so that everything's equal. Eve sits on the porch with a drink, listening to the thrum of pond frogs and the buzz of cicadas, remembering the white noise machine she and Adam used in Chicago, how they preferred the "Summer Night" sound, a recorded loop of what they now have for real. Maybe she'll use that detail in the story she will write about the day Adam killed the snakes. Maybe she'll change their names to John and Mary. Before they go to sleep, John and Mary will argue about whose fault it is that the snakes are dead, and then they'll have sex, the kind that's more like hate than love.

Eve's not sure what happens next or how the story will end, but this doesn't worry her. She's also well aware that just because something really happened doesn't mean it will work in a story. A story can't hold apples and snakes and sex and Sunday and church and a psychic. And won't one snake do as well as two? And shouldn't she move the snake from above her writing desk to above John and Mary's bed? Isn't that more potent, especially when they have angry sex there later?

The truth is: Adam and Eve have never made love in anger, but it seems appropriate for John and Mary to do so, and certainly better than admitting that Adam and Eve have not touched each other—except by accident—for a long, long time. These days, living with Adam reminds Eve of college, of politely sharing space with her roommate Penny. Every Friday, Penny left to visit her boyfriend Harold, and every weekend, Eve had the room to herself. She always felt a little surprised, even a little resentful when Penny returned from Harold's on Sunday nights.

Sitting there on the porch, Eve listens to Adam washing dishes and keeps thinking about her story. Maybe she'll write a scene in which a worried Mary snoops through John's briefcase, afraid she'll find love letters from another woman or downloaded porn. Instead, she finds a poem typed on John's office letterhead, a poem in which he imagines them as an old couple, sitting in rocking chairs. This poem makes Mary cry, but not for the reasons you think. Mary cries because John has crossed out every word and scrawled "stupid" next to them. *What is stupid*, Mary will wonder, *the poem or the thought of us growing old together?*

You think this happened, but it didn't. Harold wrote the poem to Penny, and Eve found it once (free of edits and self-loathing) in her roommate's jewelry box. No, Adam never wrote a poem like this. In fact, he hasn't written anything but to-do lists for years. Lately, whenever Eve publishes a story, Adam will congratulate her and then shake his head, saying, "God, I hate you." This is a horrible truth, but Eve would rather use the fictional "stupid" poem to represent Adam's frustration than the fact that he often—and quite literally—beats his head against a wall.

The real truth is: when Eve snooped through Adam's briefcase, she didn't find any poems at all. Just the porn. But she can't bring herself to put this detail in the story she will write about the day Adam killed the snakes. She would look bad, invading his privacy like that. Besides, Eve promised Adam she'd never reveal his secrets in her stories—that he once threw a cat off a roof to see if it would land on its feet, that his swimming coach fondled him when he was eight, that his parents have never, not once, said that they love him. So she'll change all the real details, omit all of his secrets, but Eve knows that the story will hurt Adam anyway. There's no way around it.

Adam has gone upstairs, but Eve still sits on the porch wondering, "What is this story about anyway?" She won't know the answer for another two years. When Eve finishes the story about the day Adam killed the snakes, she'll know it's a story about the day she knew she could ask him for anything—to kill a snake, to marry her, to give her a child. The day she knew that everything would be fine as long as nothing went wrong. It's a story about the bad days that always come, Adam holding out the shovel scoop full of dirty diapers and overdue bills and unwritten poems and ads for jobs he'll never have and houses he'll never own, telling her "Look at what you made me do." The story will be about the day she knew in her heart (but not in her mind) that she would leave him.

But try to remember that Eve doesn't know any of this yet. She's sitting on the porch, watching fireflies blink across the lawn, waiting for Adam to fall fast asleep. Maybe you think she's sitting there because it's such a beautiful night. That's true. Maybe you think she's sitting there because she's avoiding sex. That might be true, too. But here's what Eve thinks: that once he's asleep, she can sneak upstairs and write without him knowing, without making him feel bad. She doesn't yet see this as an important detail in the story, but she will. The story is forming inside her, and someday, when she's ready, she will write it.

Q: Cathy, I'd like to start with a comment you made in a *Ninth Letter* interview. You referred to the shock you felt "sitting in a darkened theater when Ferris Bueller broke the fourth wall and spoke directly into the camera" as akin to your experience reading Tim O'Brien's metafiction *The Things They Carried*.

A: I have always loved metagestures, going all the way back to *The Monster at the End of This Book*, which I read over and over again. Grover from *Sesame Street* told me not to turn the pages, and when I inevitably did, he'd yell, "You turned the page! Stop!" A book that knew it was a book. Brilliant. I like it when art presents a paradigm shift, when it forces me to confront my assumptions, when it asks, "Why this way and not another way?" We begin our lives as readers by buying into the idea of willing suspension of disbelief. We say to ourselves (without really saying) that we are willing to believe that the fictional world we're entering is real, to a certain extent. We must believe this in order to enter Gardner's vivid and continuous dream, in order to "lose ourselves" in the act of reading. But metagestures, like those in *Ferris Bueller's Day Off* and *The Things They Carried*, remind us that we're reading or watching something that is not real, that has been created. There's something even more "real" than the carefully rendered reality we're being presented with.

Q: First, *Ferris Bueller* and *The Things They Carried*, and now *The Monster at the End of This Book*. You had me at Grover. A terrific book and one that offered me, a reclusive girl who talked to her dog Skeeter and spent most of her time in a yellow room singing into a Donnie and Marie microphone, the chance to be a part of a book. O'Brien implicates us as readers, too, particularly in "How to Tell a True War Story," because he is writing about how to write and how to read. I'm drawn to this idea of "meta" allowing a work to be more real. If in fiction we enter John Gardner's dream and a metafictive piece wakes the reader from that dream, what are we entering in nonfiction, particularly the personal essay or the memoir, or both? And how do you think metamoves alter (enhance) nonfiction in different ways than they do fiction?

A: Okay, let's say that a metamove or metagesture is when the author intentionally draws attention to a work's genre, its very existence as fiction or nonfiction. And let's say that fiction and nonfiction aren't categories, but two poles on a spectrum called "narrative" or "story." If a story is presented as fiction, then a metamove brings that work toward the middle of the spectrum, toward nonfiction. If a story is presented as nonfiction, then a metamove brings that work toward the middle of the spectrum, toward fiction. A metamove is an intentional one. But that's not the only way nonfiction writers move toward the middle of the spectrum, toward fiction. They do it by conflating or reordering events. Creating a narrative persona. Dramatizing scenes the writer didn't witness. Re-creating dialogue. Revealing the interiority of their subjects. These commonly practiced techniques of creative nonfiction are fictional techniques. It's the practice of literary realism used to bring the reader into the story that's being told, to show instead of tell, to make the story more readable. In *How Fiction Works*, James Wood says that since Plato and Aristotle we've been talking about mimesis. What is "real" and how should fiction represent it? What I'm saying is that I was always taught that mimesis or "showing" is better or more like real life than diegesis or "telling," but I don't really buy that anymore. Raymond Carver famously said, "No tricks. . . . I hate tricks. At the first sign of a trick or gimmick in a piece of fiction, a cheap trick or even an elaborate trick, I tend to look for cover." I firmly believe that that sound bite, those two little words *No tricks*, have done more harm than good since Carver published them nearly forty years ago in the *New York Times Book Review*. "No tricks" became a maxim in creative writing classes, an unbreakable rule of the discipline, a way to prohibit work that wasn't straight-up realism. It made the job of teaching creative writing easier. "No tricks." But Carver also said in that essay that "real experiment in fiction is original, hard-earned and cause for rejoicing." Everyone seems so determined these days to separate fiction and nonfiction, to define them in opposition to each other, but I'm interested in that place where they overlap, how they hang out and talk to each other.

Q: Do you see metawriting as a trick? Or as a tenet of postmodernism? Or as something else entirely?

A: No, it's not a trick. Carver called it "extremely clever chichi writing." What could be more real, more sincere, than acknowledging that something is indeed made-up? And I don't think you can call this impulse postmodern anymore. We live in a world of "truthiness," where so many things are "faux real." Young people get that. They live it every day. There's a new literary magazine I'm quite fond of called *Artifice*. They like work that's aware of its own artifice. They say, "We're done with 'No tricks.' We want to see what comes next. Which is to say: we want tricks. Not cheap tricks. Deeply moving, deeply felt tricks. Committed tricks. Compelling tricks." I really like that.

Q: Might you point to some of your favorite examples of writers exhibiting either "truthiness" or a penchant for metawriting that you admire?

A: I've always been intrigued by Maxine Hong Kingston's memoir *The Woman Warrior*. Personally, I think this book can be read as either autobiographical fiction or as nonfiction. Aleksandar Hemon's work also exists in that murky middle between fiction and nonfiction, especially his novel *The Lazarus Project*. Lorrie Moore's short story "People Like That Are the Only People Here" is another example of what I'll call "nonfictional fiction." I respect these two writers immensely, but within the last year, I've heard both Hemon and Moore publicly denounce nonfiction and proclaim fiction as the nobler genre—interesting coming from two writers whose work edges toward the nonfiction end of the spectrum without actually going there. Alice Munro's short stories "Menesteteung" and "Friend of My Youth" are both metafictional, as is Rick Moody's "Demonology," a piece that is sometimes published as fiction, sometimes as nonfiction. Going further back, check out Sherwood Anderson's story "Death in the Woods," which was decidedly metafictional long before there was such a term. Consider this line, which sounds like it's straight out of *The Things They Carried*: "The scene in the forest had become for me, without my knowing it, the foundation for the real story I am now trying to tell. The fragments, you see, had to be picked up slowly, long afterwards." Another throwback work of metafiction is Norman Maclean's autobiographical novella *A River Runs Through It*, which contains one of my favorite quotations:

> "You like to tell true stories, don't you?" he asked, and I answered, "Yes, I like to tell stories that are true."
> Then he asked, "After you have finished your true stories sometime, why don't you make up a story and the people to go with it?
> "Only then will you understand what happened and why."

Ultimately, I call most of what I write fiction. There is an inherent contract between the reader of a nonfiction work and its author. That contract says that the author has done everything in her power to tell the truth. Fictional techniques may have been used, but the reader can trust that the work is truthful. Since I am almost never able to abide by this contract, I submit my work as fiction and check the "fiction" box, when it's necessary to check boxes.

ANONYMOUS

"Fiction is a wonderfully flexible form, a capacious means of exploring psychology and possibilities, but when it comes to bearing witness to the troubled world in which we live now, I turn to nonfiction. When life grows stranger than fiction, nonfiction is hard to resist."

The Facts of the Matter

HERE IS HOW IT HAPPENED: the door to the suite was open that night when I walked past and saw her splayed across a couch, one foot on the floor, one leg hooked over an arm rest. I was coming in from a party. Two AM, or three. The fabric of her skirt curled around her legs like smoke or like the drapery in Bernini's "Ecstasy of Saint Teresa," which I'd seen just the week before in Vincent Scully's art history class. I stepped in—to see if she was all right. That is what I told myself. Her head was canted back at a disturbing angle against the cushion, it looked as if her neck might be snapped. I touched her leg. Said something, maybe asked if she was okay. Got no reply. I set my hand on her calf, intending to wake her, but she didn't wake and something about the smooth skin under my palm made me sit down and leave my hand there. And then, because I knew she wouldn't mind, because I knew she wouldn't *know*, I stayed.

These are the facts of the matter: twenty years ago—because the opportunity arose, because no one would know, not even the girl unconscious on the dorm room couch—I took advantage of a girl I liked. At the time I didn't think of it as rape—. I thought that things had gotten a little out of hand. There had been a party at the Taft Hotel that night, hosted by a popular history professor, and someone had seriously spiked the punch. We were all pretty smashed, in her case to unconsciousness. She was a gorgeous girl, someone I knew only slightly, from a huge art history lecture course and our residential college. We had not spoken at the party that night, though I'd seen her there; she was the sort of girl you noticed across a room, beautiful that way, what my Dad liked to call "a long tall drink of water." In the convoluted logic of the drunken and ashamed, the fact that we had not spoken at the party made what happened seem more acceptable, because it was more *remote*, not something I had anticipated or worked to further. The act itself was fast and furtive as porn.

"DON'T TELL ME WHAT YOU FEEL," essayist Barbara Hurd has said, "tell me what you think." So I am thinking about the facts of that night, and whether facts matter to a story such as mine. Were I to tell you details—her hair color, the color of the couch, its texture (which I still recall, as, curiously, I still recall the poster over the couch), would that matter? Were I to tell you that we were both in Davenport College, known at the time for housing wealthy heirs to vacuum and candy fortunes, legacy kids, which I was not, would it change how you'd read this and me? Would this become a "class narrative," an account of a scholarship kid's misguided effort to exorcise his rage?

Would it matter to know my name, my race, or hers, or is a piece of nonfiction more potent for *not* knowing who I am, for not being able to make this personal, singular, *my* problem *not* yours? Is it discretion not to reveal more of the facts, protecting her identity, or am I merely protecting my own? How telling is a factual tale, and how much telling is too much? (Does it matter that I've never told anyone this?)

TWENTY YEARS LATER, I am a professor at a good writing program in the Midwest, and though I do not often think of it, I do—sometimes— imagine fucking one of my students. It happens only once or twice a year. I consider this a modest achievement. Friends at other universi- ties—GW, Harvard—tell me about wanting to fuck their undergrads all the time. These are guys a decade or two older than I am, in their fifties and sixties, who mistake the innocent flirtation of nubile twenty-year- olds for erotic interest. (I have a seventeen-year-old stepdaughter, so I know better. She talks about skanky old guys who hit on her and her friends.)

I feel attracted, sure, but I wouldn't act on it. It's not done anymore. But I understand why it once was. These girls are smart and eager, and even if what they are eager for is life, approval, knowledge, *not* sex, the buzz can feel the same. I know one guy—famous fiction writer—who says that in *his* day, there were certain undergraduates who considered sleeping with a professor part of getting a liberal education. Who am I to disagree? (Though I do note that he was asked to leave his last tenured post on account of having taken one too many students up on this, so perhaps the interest was not always reciprocated.)

I know plenty of smart, well-educated, sensitive guys, *good* guys, who talk about women as cunts, about booty calls and getting pussy. They are, in all likelihood, overcompensating for having been nerdy skinny guys in high school and college, as I was, but still. These are the facts.

IT'S BECOME FASHIONABLE lately to question the *importance* of facts in works of creative nonfiction: "In our hunger for all things true," David Shields says in *Reality Hunger: A Manifesto*, "we make facts irrelevant." Given that any narrative involves a selection of details and thus a distortion of sorts, *facts*—so the argument goes—aren't important. As long as an account tells the *truth*—psychologically, emotionally—facts aren't required.

The thoughtful, erudite writer Robert Atwan, series editor of *The Best American Essays*, recently questioned the necessity of facts to creative nonfiction at a conference in Manhattan, where he spoke in praise of "the literary art of fabrication," noting that great novelists (Maugham and Nabokov among them) have often composed novels in the guise of first-person memoirs, making "us aware of how indistinct the boundaries between the two [forms] can be." Atwan asked his audience, "Is it possible that a piece of personal writing can be grounded in fiction and still be considered an essay? If some determined graduate student conclusively discovered that [E. B.] White never owned a pig, should we consider [White's essay] "Death of a Pig" a short story? . . . Is all that separates an autobiographical essay from a story fidelity to fact?" For many, facts are not crucial to a work of literary nonfiction: "Even if [the facts are] invented," Atwan asks, "what difference would it make to the reader?"

I COULD LIE AND TELL YOU that I'm sorry about that night; I could tell you that I think about the girl on the couch with regret, or something like it. Would it matter if it were true? Would it matter if I accurately recalled for you the split-level apartment at the Taft Hotel where the party was held, the enormous arched window that looked out on New Haven Green, the Jim Dine painting that hung above a staircase (of a red coat floating eerily on a black background), or the way the early morning air felt against my face and hands as I walked home along Chapel Street, back to our residential college, where I'd find the girl on the couch? Would it matter if the salt tang of the air that morning seemed to contain within it youth, with all its promise and untarnished expectation for the future? Would it matter if I saw her the next day at Wawa's—the corner grocery—but pretended not to? She looked pale in a navy pea coat and her hands shook when she emptied coins onto the counter, though maybe I misremember this and am conflating someone else's hands with hers (I couldn't have been close enough to see her hands—I kept my distance among the racks of chips and candy, the enormous pickle barrel). Maybe the hands I'm remembering are my own.

LATELY I NOTICE MY STUDENTS struggle with certain parts of speech; they have trouble with conjunctions, prepositions, and certain verbs. Not one or two students, but en masse, as if it were a flu going around. A particularly virulent bug.

They have particular difficulty with the verb "to lie," which confuses them: *I lay* (past tense); *I laid it on the table* (transitive); *they had lain together* (past participle).

They no longer seem to know how to use conjunctions, those small but useful parts of speech that clarify the relations among people and things (*and, but, or, on*). Increasingly, I find myself correcting prepositions in their papers—not just obscure ones (for example, *enamored of*, not *enamored with*), but the more common and obvious and crucial. (A movie marquee in my college town last year advertised Tarantino's "*Reservoir Dogs* showing *at* Nov. 11"—as if time were a place.) Though small, prepositions matter: to laugh *at*, as any child knows, is not the same as to laugh *with*; to *experiment with* is not the same as to *experiment on*.

I wonder what it means, if anything, that we've lost the knack of conjunctions, prepositions, and how to properly employ the verb *to lie*. I wonder about the significance of such lexical slips—what, if anything, it signifies that as a culture we seem collectively to be losing our grasp, losing our footing, to have come unmoored in language.

To say, "I lie *with* you" is not—after all—the same as to say, "I lie *to* you."

HERE'S THE THING about that night: it did not change how I saw myself. (Gordon Lish used to ask his students to describe a moment when their behavior changed who they thought they were; to my surprise, that night did not.) Maybe it should have affected me more, should have been a "decisive moment," to borrow Cartier-Bresson's phrase. I do not know how it affected her, the girl on the couch. I rarely saw her and only later heard that she dropped out of Yale at the end of sophomore year; she has become one of those whom even Google cannot recall from obscurity. Perhaps she married, changed her name. I can say—because I can say it anonymously here—that it was a pleasure. Strange. Rare. Like fugu. A risk that leaves the lips tingling.

I have not repeated the experience. Nor would I seek to. Nor, evidently, am I alone: "In one influential American study," writes University of London historian Joanna Bourke, "one in every three men attending college reported that they would rape a woman if they were guaranteed that they would not be caught. One in every four admitted to actually having made a forceful attempt at sexual intercourse that caused observable distress (crying, screaming, fighting, or pleading) to a woman."

I find these statistics disturbing, and comforting.

IF AN ACCOUNT PURPORTS to be true, *does it matter* if it is?

It matters to some: in July 2010, the *Guardian* newspaper reported that a Palestinian man in Israel had been convicted of rape after having had *consensual* sex with a woman who had believed him to be a fellow Jew. The accused man was sentenced to eighteen months in prison after the court ruled that he was *guilty of rape by deception.* There was no question that the pair had engaged in consensual sex; *the crime was that he had lied to her about who he was and what he wanted.* When the two met in Jerusalem in 2008, the man said he was a Jewish bachelor seeking a serious relationship; he turned out to be an Arab from East Jerusalem. When the woman discovered the truth, she filed criminal charges for rape and indecent assault. In a plea bargain, the charge was changed to rape by deception.

A lie can be a violation, a forced entry, a kind of rape.

Of course, you could read the story in other ways: *politically* (as indicative of the oppression of a minority at the hands of a majority); *conventionally* (as affirming, with a new twist, that old saw, "Hell hath no fury like ..."); or *psychologically* (was she was angered by his misrepresentation of identity or by his misrepresentation of *intention*? He said he wanted a *serious* relationship ...). But what interests me is the larger question the story raises: does it *matter* if what gets us into bed (or into a book) is a lie? If the *factual* story we're being told and sold is not, in truth, *fact*—but a fiction?

I am struck by the language of Judge Segal in the case, which—if one considers the bond between reader and author to be as intimate as that between lovers—seems relevant to the debate over facts in literary nonfiction as well: "The court is obliged to protect the public interest from sophisticated, smooth-tongued criminals who can deceive innocent victims.... When the very basis of trust between human beings drops, especially when the matters at hand are so intimate, sensitive and fateful, the court is required to stand firmly at the side of the victims—actual and potential—to protect their well-being. Otherwise, they will be used, manipulated and misled."

IT IS INTERESTING THAT WRITERS of creative nonfiction have become so at ease with lying, so uninterested in truth, at a time when our government is obsessed with obtaining the truth through increased surveillance, interrogation of suspects, data mining. "Credibility assessment" has become a watchword in the paranoiac post-9/11 era, a governmental goal, while artists—at least in the realm of literary nonfiction—seem to be increasingly sanguine about lying. I would like to imagine this is a response to government surveillance, resistance to the loss of privacy, but it seems instead to be a shrug. A capitulation. Truth is left to those who want to make use of it. We are happy to play with our words. Indifferent to the facts of the matter.

OF COURSE, ROBERT ATWAN is right that we have at our disposal a wide variety of literary forms—the short story, the novel, the yarn, the tale, the sketch—that offer us a chance to represent *as* fact that which has been imagined. And certainly one may "essay" a subject without recourse to fact, since to *essai*—to return to the word's French root—means simply *to weigh* or *test*, thus describing an *action*, a mode of thought, not an obligation to factuality. But when we call a literary work *nonfiction*, no matter how heavily we lean on that modifying adjective *creative*, we are trafficking in facts, or claiming to, and to pass off fiction (as fact) is a lie. I can't help but wonder, who is served by such uncertainty, by flexibility when it comes to the facts?

IN THE SEVENTEENTH and eighteenth centuries, English novelists often toyed with the boundary between fact and fiction by prefacing their novels with claims about their factuality, asserting they were only editors of someone else's papers, journals, or oral histories. It was common to disguise a fantastical account (*Gulliver's Travels*, say) as factual. Politically, things were dicey. Criticism of those in power could get you thrown in jail or worse, so critiques of the powerful often took fictional form to protect their authors from retribution.

It wasn't until the revision of the Stamp Act of 1724 that factual news—which was taxable—was officially distinguished from untaxable fiction. I like to think there's a connection between the growing awareness of the *difference* between fact and fiction that opened the eighteenth century and the democratic revolutions that closed the same age. I like to think that literature might have that much power, and that a frank naming of the facts proved decisive, a turning point, giving rise to previously unimagined liberty.

NOT LONG AFTER I graduated from Yale, I moved to New York City, where I attended a show at the Whitney on the subject of rape. I went with my then-girlfriend, a woman I wanted badly to marry. One of the young female curators of the show wrote in the exhibit catalog (in the marvelous mandarin fashionable at the time in literary-critical circles) of the trouble of writing subjectively about rape, the danger of sensation-alizing one's story, of re-inscribing what she called the "rape-ability of women" by narrating one's own survival of assault. The curator did not say whether she had herself been raped. Instead, she wrote of how the artwork selected for the exhibit allowed women to bear witness to the act of rape without personalizing (potentially trivializing) it. She wrote eloquently of the pieces on display.

But what has stayed with me from that show was a collaborative piece in which viewers were invited to participate by reading and writing—on notecards color-coded for age and gender—their own experience with rape. I wrote on a card and placed it in the Plexiglas box for others to read. Not knowing who, if anyone, would. Then I got up and walked away. I did not look back.

WHEN REPORTS BEGAN filtering out of certain villages in the Congo (in early August 2010, of gang rapes of women, girls, and boys by members of the Rwandan rebel group the FDLR)—just twenty miles from a UN peace-keeping mission—the stories were hard to believe: "We thought at first he was exaggerating," the program coordinator for the International Medical Corps in North Kivu Province told the *New York Times*. The numbers—some reports claimed 136 raped in a single village—strained credulity. Old women and young boys were said to have been raped; wives were raped in front of their husbands and children. Some victims were raped by six men at once.

Could these really be the facts?

A month later UN investigators discovered that the incredible stories were true; although the numbers were inaccurate, they were not inflat-ed—the actual tally of rapes in the region appears to have been around five hundred—and some 242 people were raped in a single village in just four days.

Perhaps it is only those who are not subject to the consequences who can afford to say that facts don't matter.

I WONDER IF SHIELDS AND ATWAN would be so cheerfully flexible about the facts if the nonfictions were of another kind, if it were their doctor's *unfactual diagnosis* (appendicitis, say, that led to an unnecessary surgery)? Would they be as easygoing were it an unfactual accusation that prompted their incarceration for an indefinite period in an undisclosed location by means of extreme rendition? Or a fanciful assessment of an oil spill, disguising vastly greater damage? How about an insurance adjustment that insouciantly undervalued a home destroyed in an all-too-factual fire?

And if they would *not* find such nonfictions acceptable, I wonder why they (and we) tolerate the unfactual passed off as fact in our nonfiction art? Is it because we believe that art—that compass of the culture—doesn't *matter* as much as medicine or insurance? Or is it because we—like the powerful in the seventeenth and eighteenth centuries (who couldn't bear to read a frank assessment of their failings, prompting social critics to couch critiques in fictive terms)—cannot bear to *face* the facts, to look in the literary mirror and behold ourselves honestly, truthfully, portrayed. Has creative nonfiction become a form of cultural cosmetic surgery, helping us hide our flaws from ourselves, convincing us that the facts don't count?

DOES IT MATTER, in an account such as mine, who was raped, under what circumstances? Does it matter if there was a girl, a couch, if there *could* have been? Would it change things to know that the girl on that couch got pregnant that night (a fact I would only learn years later from her close friend)? Would it matter if (in fact) the girl were conscious; if when she woke, he finished and left her there and never spoke of it? Would it matter if *I* were that girl?

IT SEEMS TO ME a simple matter, this matter of facts: if we fail to recognize a distinction between fact and fiction at this crucial juncture in our American history, when we are still the most powerful nation ever to have existed on earth (if arguably in decline), if we fail to recognize that there are facts (global warming, extreme rendition, gang rape, torture, "collateral damage," civilian casualties, "friendly fire"), if instead we capitulate to the logic of the PR man and maintain that a *convincing* story is as good as fact, that personal or aesthetic truth is equivalent to a factual account, and that facts are (in fact) rather old-fashioned, distastefully earnest (or as David Shields would have it, "irrelevant"), we will be, it seems to me—like that girl unconscious on that couch so very many years ago—fucked.

Q: In the December 2010 issue of the *Writer's Chronicle*, in a piece titled "Tratteggio in Creative Nonfiction: How Jon Krakauer, Maxine Hong Kingston, and Helen Fremont Fill the Gaps," Susan Detweiler points out, "To create a nonfiction narrative with an emotional core and truth about human nature, missing pieces often must be subtly added to fill in where memory lapses or the knowable ends." While "The Facts of the Matter" focuses on facts and truth, it also raises issues of "what is known" (and not known, I might add). A passage from the piece reads, "though maybe I misremember this and am conflating someone else's hands with hers (I couldn't have been close enough to see her hands—I kept my distance among the racks of chips and candy, the enormous pickle barrel). Maybe the hands I'm remembering are my own." This passage points out such a gap in memory, a misremembering, and the only time in the essay in which the concept of remembering is directly raised. If facts matter, what is the role of memory in nonfiction?

A: Memory is a fountainhead for creative nonfiction, of course; it's the root of memoir, as the word implies. But memory is inevitably fallible, so many of our best memoirs recognize that fact and strengthen the work by exploring memory's failings. Mary McCarthy's *Memories of a Catholic Girlhood*, for example, makes memory's faults a structural feature of the book, alternating chapters in which childhood is recalled with italicized chapters in which she points out how the prior chapter's memories falsify the past.

Wanting nonfiction to hew close to fact is not a matter of being priggishly punctilious (Thou Shalt Not Falsify), but rather of recognizing that the richness of nonfiction comes of the rigorous effort to find meaning in what actually happened, what's actually recollected, not—as in fiction—from making stuff up. When we start making stuff up in nonfiction, we're often doing it for the sake of convenience—to make a better story, to make a buck—rather than doing the hard work of making meaning from what is. Of course, memory's faults are part of "what is," so a lot of good art can be made from foregrounding the fact of its failings. Mary Karr's *The Liars' Club* does a beautiful job with this as well, commenting on memory and its gaps and tricks; and Nabokov's *Speak, Memory* is arguably a portrait of consciousness as much as anything.

At the same time, there's plenty of room for invention in nonfiction—and often such invention is necessary, if we're to grasp the full meaning of a story—but the writer owes it to the reader to signal when we've entered the realm of fiction. Hong Kingston does this brilliantly in *The Woman Warrior*, where she narrates her childhood as the mythic warrior FaMulan and later imagines a whole chapter about her mother's effort to track down an aunt's husband. But Hong Kingston is honest with the reader: she lets us know that she wasn't along for the ride to track down that husband, that she made up the story from a single line her brother told her. And the fact that she confesses this—letting us in on the "facts" of the tale—makes it all the more powerful, letting us see the role imagination has played in her life. She is true to her psychology—portraying truthfully how her mother's voice and stories eclipsed her own—while still making use of meaningful invention.

Another great example is Lee Martin's memoir *From Our House*, in which he makes poignant use of imagination to describe how his father lost his hands to a corn-shucking machine before Lee was born. Martin needs to represent the moment because it shaped his father's life and therefore his own, but he wasn't there. So he does the simple, honest thing and signals the reader when he leaves fact behind: "I'm free to imagine the day any way I like," he writes, before launching into a powerful scene of the accident that took his father's hands. It's a brilliant moment and made more powerful—not less—by the candor with which he acknowledges that he was not there to save a man he loved.

If we turn to nonfiction for the bite of reality, we are inevitably disappointed when it's falsified—I think we sense it, even if we don't know why we're disappointed. And if art is the compass of a culture, as I believe it is, we're in serious trouble when artists working in nonfiction start confusing convenient stories for actual facts. When this happens in art, it's inevitable that it will happen in politics, and we know from recent history that's a hard road to travel. Soon politicians are telling us we have to go to war on the basis of fictional yellowcake uranium finds, and guys on Wall Street are happily telling us that securitized subprime mortgages are AAA-rated investments.

My rule of thumb is simple: if you wouldn't lie to your lover or best friend about what happened to you, don't lie to your reader. If you wouldn't invent a moment or memory for the sake of convenience when confiding your most intimate history to your beloved, don't lie to us. The relationship is equally intimate.

Q: Reading your answer, I cannot help but think of the imploring Blanche DuBois in *A Streetcar Named Desire*: "I never lied in my heart." What other "rules of thumb" do you have as a writer?

A: I don't think of fealty to fact in creative nonfiction as a "rule," more like an obligation, a meaningful constraint. I mean, why balk at an expectation of facts in nonfiction? It's sort of like complaining about the necessity of meter when writing a sonnet. That's simply the challenge of the form. If you're going to claim the heft and authority of fact, you have to deal with the challenges that come with that. If you want to make stuff up and pretend it's true, you've got a form for that: it's called fiction. I find it bizarre that there's actually debate over this—how very seventeenth-century of us.

As for "rules," I have a few:

Don't bore the reader.
Write every day.
Read everything.
Don't believe what you're told, which of course includes what I'm telling
     you now.

John McPhee puts it far better than I in regard to that cardinal rule of creative nonfiction (don't lie to your reader): "Things that are cheap and tawdry in fiction work beautifully in nonfiction because they are *true*. That's why you should be careful not to abridge it, because it's the fundamental power you're dealing with. You arrange it and present it. There's lots of artistry. But you don't make it up."

Q: I'm thinking of Vivian Gornick's categories of *situation* and *story*. Situation: the literal context or event. Story: the emotional truth of it. She claims that the strength of her personal narratives derives from her "[scrupulous] faithful[ness] to the story, not the situation." How might situation and story work within the context of "The Facts of the Matter," in that you create a persona and then reveal that the persona has been a construction (as they all are, really) and that the victim of that narrator may indeed (I say, may, see your above answer), in fact, be you?

A: I agree with Gornick that an accurate account of events is not enough: we must make meaning of events if we're to make art (or even simply artful nonfiction). Fealty to emotional truth over facts is fine in nonfiction, as long as one signals the distinction to the reader. But Gornick's argument assumes that there are "facts," that there is a "situation" to be artfully manipulated. The trouble with our contemporary contempt for facts in creative nonfiction is that it opens the door to nonfactual accounts, to fictions that are loosely based in fact but are not factual. Which ultimately undermines the power of nonfiction and our ability to act.

In "The Facts of the Matter," both situation and story are complicated, because we can't get a purchase on what's true here. We don't know what the situation is: is the narrator an insouciant rapist, or a woman long ago raped, or neither? And if we don't know that fundamental fact, then can we trust the other "facts" in the piece—the eighteenth-century history, the account of rape in the Congo? Ultimately the real victim here is neither the narrator nor the possibly fictive young woman who was raped; it's factuality itself, and the reader, who is played by a piece that engages us in a story of rape but may be simply playing at it.

It's worth noting that the details recounted in "The Facts of the Matter" are all "true"—I know men who have said each of these things and women to whom this precise rape has happened—but it's not clear whether I am that man, that woman, or neither. So the victim here is fact itself, which is undermined by such indeterminacy.

When the stories of mass rape first started filtering out of the Congo, no one took action because they assumed the stories must have been exaggerated, fictions of a kind. It was only after the facts were confirmed that action was taken to prevent it from happening again. Our contemporary fashionable indifference to fact in creative nonfiction encourages just such paralysis and indifference. If nonfiction is just another literary performance, pretending to recount facts that matter, it needn't engage us deeply or move us to action; such feints encourage complacency instead; fictions passed off as facts incline the reader to treat even factual accounts as mere entertainment.

And when we cease to command the facts (or care about them), especially in a democracy, we are all—as my piece concludes—fucked.

Q: I like the implications of the term *artful nonfiction*. What writers do you think perform nonfiction in an artistic way, and how? And what do you see as the distinction between nonfiction and literary nonfiction? Is artful nonfiction a category all its own?

A: A student of mine put it beautifully, I think; she said that when you're working with fact—whether as a reporter or a literary nonfiction writer— the facts are like clay. You mold the factual material and shape it. If you're a reporter, you then work to wipe away the fingerprints, to remove your personal mark. But if you're a creative nonfictionist, you leave those fingerprints, because they're part of the art you're making. Your imprint on the factual material—your sensibility and mind—are part of what makes it artful nonfiction. It's how one particular mind makes meaning of the actual.

In my experience, it's this mark of the self that makes for art—when I look at a painting by Francis Bacon or read Virginia Woolf or listen to Bach or REM or Vampire Weekend, what I respond to and am transported by is meeting another mind transposed to another medium. Briefly, you get to see through other eyes. Briefly, you get to give yourself the slip, which is what we aim for in prayer, in love, and in art (I think).

There are so many nonfiction writers whose work I admire. I'm a huge fan of the great literary journalists: James Agee's heroic lyricism in *Let Us Now Praise Famous Men*, which both documents and anthemizes the rural poor, forcing the reader to see these workers as worthy of art, and to see their plight as tragedy; and also the magnificent reportage of Joan Didion in *Salvador* (to take one example), which takes us into the hallucination that was El Salvador in the 1980s and U.S. policy in Latin America. She saves politics from the dull drone of Washington bureaucrat-speak and gives it the visceral power of nightmare, which seems a far truer portrait. I adore Lillian Ross's wry, deadpan reports ("The Symbol of All We Possess," for example), in which she hovers over events, self-effacing, but shaping, like an angel visiting the living, tenderly, mockingly observing. And of course David Foster Wallace's heartbreakingly lucid and relentless dissection of all we do not want to think about in the Information Age. I love James Baldwin's work, Maxine Hong Kingston's, Ondaatje's lyric memoir *Running in the Family*, which creates a polyglot form that beautifully enacts the hybridized sensibility of the expat, the postcolonial. Really, there are too many to name: among essayists, Mitchell, White, Woolf, Hazlitt, Joy Williams, M. F. K. Fisher, Anne Carson. I love the elliptical insights of Lia Purpura, which often register in me like snapshots (I experience them as if they were photos I'd seen), uncanny and beautiful, often sad, a bit like Diane Arbus's work; Eula Biss's illumination of the familiar, whether telephone poles or a doctor's pain scale, is wonderful as well. I'm taken with Ander Monson's play with information and technology (the whimsical hypertext), which seems to befriend what otherwise might seem a dauntingly antiliterary realm. For memoir, I return again and again to Harrison's *The Kiss*, Karr's *The Liars' Club*, Slater's *Lying*, Spiegelman's *Maus*, Bechdel's *Fun Home*, Flynn's *Another Bullshit Night in Suck City*, Audre Lorde's *Zami*, Merton's *Seven Storey Mountain*, Fox Gordon's *Mockingbird Years*, and Mandelshtam's *Hope Against Hope*. To name a few.

All of these are artful, most of them are art.

Q: Leaving fingerprints: I had never thought of it before, but seeing it here in your answer makes me consider its application to metawriting. Because you write fiction and nonfiction, I'm interested in how (or if, or when) you know a piece of writing is going to be fiction or nonfiction. In other words, what creates an E. J. Levy short story versus an E. J. Levy essay, and is that writer the same? Is that writer you?

A: It's hard to resist turning the question back to you: would it *matter* if I were E. J. Levy? Do such facts matter to a piece of nonfiction, and if so, how? Does it alter how we read the piece to know that I may be a woman—to know that, if I were a woman, I likely didn't commit that rape, though I might have been raped in that way. (In fact, I was neither rapist nor raped in this way: a friend's sister was.) For me, nonfiction almost always involves bearing witness in some way; perhaps this is because I came to fiction from journalism. Fiction is a wonderfully flexible form, a capacious means of exploring psychology and possibilities, but when it comes to bearing witness to the troubled world in which we live now, I turn to nonfiction. When life grows stranger than fiction, nonfiction is hard to resist. But it's precisely because we want to know that the strangeness is actually out there—*not* a convenient fiction or device—that it's important to cleave to the facts when we claim the authority of nonfiction.

I almost always know before I settle down to write whether a piece will be fiction or nonfiction. I enter each differently, as if by separate doors. Fiction just feels different to me—as if I'd been tapped on the shoulder and directed to bring something into being, it feels oddly external and often arises from items I've read in the news, strangely enough—whereas nonfiction usually involves turning inward, tilling some inner soil. Often I turn inward in response to something that has disturbed me—the rapes in the ironically named Democratic Republic of Congo, or the current fashion for labeling fictions as fact—but the process is more internal, more intellectual, and for me more arduous. I suppose I'd say that I feel tethered by facts in nonfiction, whereas in fiction, I feel as if I'm in one of those dreams where you have the power to fly. I feel released.

Released from the lifelong fiction (or is it nonfiction) of being E. J. Levy.

Q: You might think this is a strange question, but I'd like to address any potential concerns you might have (as an academic) of "your" admission that you think about sleeping with your students. This is the line: "Twenty years later, I am a professor at a good writing program in the Midwest, and though I do not often think of it, I do—sometimes—imagine fucking one of my students."

A: Strange indeed. I appreciate your smirk quotes there; it's after all a persona piece—I don't mean that I have wanted to bed my students, anymore than I mean that I long ago raped a peer at Yale. The speaker of the piece is an invention (a composite of things others have told me and my own observations and life—in short, it's a fiction), a fiction intended to suggest the trouble that comes of making stuff up in nonfiction. The

ANONYMOUS

reader is all too likely to mistake such fiction for fact, whether we're talking about sex or WMDs. And I think—as a culture—we need nonfictions to lead, not mislead, us. (Or at least to acknowledge when a piece ventures into fictive terrain, as this piece does, so that the fiction is a meaningful part of the nonfiction, rather than simply an attempt to pass off invention as fact for the sake of borrowing the latter's power.)

"Every time you examine yourself you're someone just slightly new."

The Girl Is a Fiction

ONCE A PERSON has been a girl, it's hard to write about the subject.

The other day, as she walked the long hallway lined with etchings and lithographs, she saw a teenage boy lounging against the dais of the central atrium's sculpture. She observed him from above and at high speed, often her condition when she is busy, has somewhere else to be, but even from that perspective she could tell many things from his haughty posture. Foremost, he knew he could be seen. She didn't suppose he knew she, in the actual fact of her body and mind, was hurrying above him down the long hall, nor did he seem to consider the janitor guiding an industrial waxer over the concrete floors behind him an appropriate audience, but it was clear the fact of his visibility, his display, his own body pompously wasted and arranged in broken angles, weighed heavily on his mind. Secondly, he did not appear to believe whatever he had been told about the sculpture that thrust up toward the skylights, throwing a shadow across the top of his head. The sculpture was hewn from a variety of exotic woods (rosewood, spicewood, mahogany, walnut, others besides—more unusual ones) and was carved, polished, and pegged to form nebulous nodes, shapes like pseudo-pods that rose from their round base to varying ascendancies. It is called "Lust," or "Envy of the Body," or "A Human Amongst Others of Its Kind," something of that nature. Though the sculpture is the centerpiece of her and the teenage boy's shared institution, and thus highly valued, she has never paid it much specific attention. The janitor dusts the tops of its pegged and polished nodes with a soft rag affixed to the end of a very long stick.

What would she have thought as a teenage girl arranging her artfully wasted limbs against the dais of a highly conceptual sculpture?

She was fourteen when she had sex for the first time, though she told the boy it was not her first, that she had had sex (phrased in that fashion it sounds even more like consumption—she had a burrito, she had a piece of watermelon candy) many times before with her previous boyfriend, who was older. She didn't lie this way because she was nervous about the physicality of sex. She was a teenager in the very last gasp of the twentieth century. She was a girl who knew how to analyze the febrile lushness of Gap jean ads and the ripe heft of Calvin Klein underwear models, who was in fact taught something of this nature in school but was still titillated in a vaguely sinful way by the lyrics to Marky Mark and the Funky Bunch's "Make Me Say Ooh." Which is neither to quantify nor to antiquate her childhood. Rather, look at her: a girl who discovered her father's *Playboy* collection in the basement workshop (every issue since the month her sister was born) and found the erect penises entering stage left into the sexy office scene whimsical and rapscallionly. A girl whose mother told her not only to have sex before marriage, to test out the waters, but also about the abortion they, her parents, had decided on when her sister was six months old, a dinner table scene that is for some reason related in her memory to the image of a vast whirling cosmos sparking blue gases against the nimbus of the Milky Way. A girl who once wrote in her journal, "Jesus is reading this over my shoulder," but whose conception of religious faith was based purely in the superstitious, the wild order, the natural world. A born pagan hedging her bets. She lied about her virginity not because she was scared of sex, but because she knew the boy she was about to have sex with—a scarred, vicious boy, a violent boy, a smart boy sadistic in his emotional intent—and she didn't want to give him any power over her. Should she stop to think about it, the emotions she associates most clearly with losing her virginity are curiosity and anger. Curious, curious, what *does* this feel like? What does it feel like to him? His penis so slim and pale it was like nothing very much to her, no pain, no real hint about adulthood. And anger because, of course, he had been given a power. Afterward, lying in a slick made by their bodies, it was clear from his attitude that he had done this to her and she had done nothing to him. How could this be? She was beautiful and knew it, all angles, her only flesh her little breasts that perked from hard-laddered ribs. And she had lied, with her mind and her body. Bucking, moaning, arching, it had been a wonderful show and yet there, smoking cigarettes in her forget-me-not-papered room, it was clear he had won. She had given him nothing, but there was still something of her he had taken and would keep in his mind, an image he could turn to, an understanding she had not forged. She was furious. She rose over him and punched him in the stomach—untended, unprepared— with not inconsiderable force. But because his father also punched him and his mother once told him she wished she had aborted him when she had the chance, he only laughed and asked if her parents kept liquor in the house. After that, she was in love.

The sculpture is supposed to represent human community. Its abstract shapes yearn toward each other, and the negative space they cradle is contained, harmless, an object lesson for the health of the democracy. If the sculpture is called "Lust," its subtext is not yearning. If it is called "Envy of the Body," its subtext is not control over the body. The sculpture is inherently romantic because it abstracts and yet demands a concrete rendering. It generalizes its subject, but associates itself with a specific tradition (public art, civic pomp) that seeks to define not space, not the artist, but those who have bought and placed it. The purchaser asks, do you see what we value? Could you tell us what it is? There are sheets of stiff construction paper tented all along the dais that read: "Parents! Keep Your Kids Off the Sculpture!" But the boy's elbows are firmly planted, his buttocks hooked over the pristine mahogany ledge, one sneaker propped and strutted against the fine-grained concrete platform. The signs clearly do not apply to him. He has not thought enough about them even to disregard them. From where he stands, he can see both the school's glass-fronted doorway and also down the passage to the orange cinderblock barrier that guards the girls' bathroom. Is he waiting for someone? She doesn't think he is. Is he spying on someone? Not that either. He is waiting for nothing, for what comes. He is adrift in a very large space and is trying to claim it with his body.

As a girl, she was often overwhelmed by art. She sought it out in the public museums of the city and wrote about her reaction to it in journals. El Greco made her cry—the enormity of his vision, the pale lengths of his bodies stretching toward a sky that was only canvas. A god that was only the artist, imperfect and splattered. Mondrian made her angry. She considered his movement away from the organic deformity of his windmills to the geometric precision of grids and boxes as a kind of selling out. In his later works he was thinking of his audience, its reactions to his innovation, and not his subject, is what she, who considered her audience in all her actions, surmised. She hated him—this dead artist, this forever-irretrievable stranger—with the kind of fervor she reserved for the boy in her school who had grown a bristle-brush mustache, played on the soccer team, loudly asked his friends in the hallway if under her jeans they'd find a prick or a slit. Both, she wanted to tell him, and wildly, fiercely, blood-thirstily, she wanted that to be true. It would be like having a pet, a little snake: friendly but dangerous, tame but unpredictable. Under my jeans, she wanted to say, I have a snake and a cat, a fist, a ruler, a spoon, a scream, a box, a bowl of oranges, a sword, a shell, a suit of armor, a windmill. "Fuck you," is what she did say, and he and his friends laughed.

As a teenage girl arranging her artfully wasted limbs against the dais of a highly conceptual sculpture, she would have thought, "Fuck you." She would have wanted to burn the place down.

She is still young, but so removed from the girl she was that she has a hard time imagining her. The girl is. She can see her, feel her—she is her and no one else, but she is also beyond imagining. Poor girl, every time she dresses her in memory, the girl roils with embarrassment. The girl would disown her adult self, she's sure of it. She's neither hard enough, nor fast enough. She has constrained her spirals, driven off nothing. She is happy. In her early twenties, she heard from the boy she lost her virginity to. He was also in his early twenties, living in Boston to be near his mother— who spoke in an exotic Russian accent and had impeccable calves—and working for a currency exchange making more money that she had ever bothered to imagine. At the time she was writing stories, though never ones about girls, and he had found some of her work on-line. In the particular story her long-ago lover read, a woman shoots her boyfriend in the throat and watches him bleed to death on her kitchen floor because they both know there are lusts more primal than the ones that live in the body. The lust for death, for example. The lust to do harm. Other things happen, but this is the gist, and this is the part the boy most admired. "You're really doing it," he wrote to her. "You always said you would." She knew from a mutual friend that he left his college ahead of his expulsion. A rape charge had been leveled against him, and one night he had been beaten over the head by the alleged victim's friend, who was wielding a fire extinguisher. It had knocked him out, split his scalp. Even now, her computer screen casting cold blue light onto her face, she pictures him lying in the dim hallway of his dorm, blood seeping into the institutional carpet. She remembers his brutal cheekbones and bad teeth, the stupid, aggressive strut of his chin, and she is curious, curious. That is what he is to her. Violence and curiosity. She supposes there are worse combinations. "I still have a lot of problems with my parents," he wrote, and she pictured his father reading the paper at the kitchen table in an undershirt, the china cabinet behind him stuffed with delicate objects so jumbled they were unrecognizable. She pictured her own father, recently divorced and assiduously labeling the boxes he would store in his new garage. She pictured herself, the angry girl purposefully smearing her makeup in front of the mirror so it looked like someone had punched her in the eyes, and herself just the night before pushing her boyfriend's shoulders back on the bed, holding his hands up to her hips or her breast, saying: hold me here, hold me harder, pinch me, make it hurt.

Once a person has been a girl it is hard to ever be anything else, but one cannot talk about it. She cries all the time. There is a television commercial for a phone company in which a girl loses her dog and finds it again. "Sarah!" the television girl says, her voice breaking on the name, "You're home!," and every time, no matter how often she sees it in a night, long, extravagant tears leak down her cheeks. Her father goes into the hospital with a reaction to an antibiotic—nothing serious, nothing more than uncomfortable—and she stands in the kitchen shaking, digging her fingers into her eyes. "Stop. Please stop," her boyfriend says, and probably, if she applied herself, she could stop, become a harder person again. But she won't, because right now it feels like everything is art, everything is sex. Everything overwhelms her and she is baffled, battered, whaled about like a node, a pseudopod, plankton trailing phosphorescence deep in a crowd of identical others, trilling, sparking, anonymously tiny but making with her shape the outline of something larger. Something that passes through.

Inside of her, there is a romantic space and it is empty. El Greco would have seen that and stripped it naked. Judy Chicago would have tried to feed her papier-mâché. This could go on: What would Louise Bourgeois do? What would Foucault? Who would look at her, mummify her, fill her, fuck her, spindle her into gold? She is not a virgin, but she is still vestal. What matters the absolute least to her is herself. Sometimes on weekends, she goes into the mountains to take a walk along the ridgeline. Stretched below her she can see the valley in which she lives, but from that vantage she recognizes nothing. A band of steam rises from a gap in the trees. It might be a river or a road. She stands for a long time considering it. This has nothing to do with art. At last. At last. At last.

INTERVIEW

Sarah Blackman, author of "The Girl Is a Fiction"

Q: A line from the close of your essay reads, "This has nothing to do with art." I was once at a film conference, and an audience member asked the panel on history in film how the presenters viewed the distinction between art and history. Given that your writing involves a personal history, how do you work with(in) or against that relationship?

A: This is a sort of convoluted question to answer, because it involves a lot of layers of individuated definition. History (with a capital H) for example is not, I don't believe, different from personal history. We understand History and, particularly in this country, are taught History, through the lens of our personal experience. Thus, again particularly in this country, subject as it is to the rampant predominance of a culture of advertisement, it is very easy to fashion our experiences, even as we're having them, as part of a more or less entropic timeline that will lead to some neatly encapsulated experience. In other words, big-deal events (such as losing one's virginity or seeing an Abstract Expressionist painting for the first time) are not really experienced publicly. They're a big deal because they are so intensely private. But because we understand History as a human endeavor, there is an assumption that, even as we wonder, "Is that all?" or break down crying in the lobby of the museum, that somehow whatever we're doing or feeling is being recorded. For posterity. Even if we're the only one doing the recording.

By "we" I mean "I," of course. From a very young age, I've been drawn to and sort of hysterically affected by art. I grew up right outside of Washington, DC, and used to skip school way too often and go to museums—particularly the Hirshhorn. Once, I even took the train up to New York in the morning and spent the day at the Museum of Modern Art. When I got home late that evening, I told my parents we had been on a surprise field trip to a waste management plant. I guess, to answer the question, I've always felt drawn to visual art, painting in particular, because it seems both a captured moment of big-deal personal experience (the inside turned outside and put on display) and also a manufactured part of History. The self of the artist defines how that self is going to be perceived by whoever comes next. I think that conflation is a very generous and productive one, but it can become problematic when it replaces the experience as it happens. Instead of holding on to the boy's shoulders or probing the canvas, you start thinking about what is going to come next, and then what is going to come next, and what would sound pithy as a final line.

Q: So in your life, you eschewed the demanding narrative to create your own, and then you offered an alternative narrative for an audience. Interesting. I used to tell my parents I was going to the movies, when I was really out in the back of some guy's pickup truck in the new subdivision, drinking Purple Passion out of a can and smoking unfiltered Camels. Not as classy as the Museum of Modern Art, but still a false narrative that provided a more real experience. I still recall having to re-create the plot of *Pretty in Pink* at the dinner table the next night from what I knew from the trailer alone. I see, through the lens you proffer, that we also create our own history, and for me, the stories I have told, true or not, I consider to be part of my history.

Let's shift to the concept of the "self of the artist" replacing the experience as it happens, imagining what comes next and the final line. First, I want to ensure I'm with you here. Do you mean persona? Or something else? And is this replacing and imagining something you do in your life? Or do you reserve these metamoments for your art?

A: Oh, there were plenty of boys with cars and cigarettes too. I'm just telling you the fancy parts.

I don't think I mean a persona exactly, or at least not a conscious one, although the idea of using a persona as a mouthpiece to express an experience that wouldn't be as believable or as present from a third-person authorial perspective is kind of close. I mean rather that people who make things (painters or potters or writers or basket weavers, whatever) are very aware of narrative. Not in the sense of plot construction, or not primarily, but more in the sense that they are aware of themselves at a particular place in a timeline that not only will continue after them but that also has existed well before them. They are aware of braiding themselves into that timeline with what they are making, what will outlast their corporeal selves. To discuss it in a less grand sense: sometimes, and this is part of what I'm exploring in my essay, that awareness of the "time-that-will-come-when-I-am-not" takes precedence over the pure experience of the "time-that-is-right-now-when-I-am." Or at least it does for me, and I find myself telling the story of myself experiencing whatever rather than really experiencing whatever. It can create a lot of anxiety. I remember quite distinctly being about eight years old and telling Bubba Tex (our mean-spirited orange tomcat) the story of Santa Claus, knowing as I told it that this was too precious, was not even a story I had any present emotional investment in, and that telling the cat that the sound of my dad hauling boxes up from the basement was really an elf, with reindeer, beard, and the rest, was falsifying the experience instead of living the complicated moment of feeling superior (I knew something my sister didn't), sad (I didn't want to know something that lessened surprise in the world), and guilty (I was lying to the cat who was always so painfully honest with me). But I kept telling Bubba Tex the story of Santa Claus because preserving the narrative was more pressing and more comforting than living the experience without a narrative to structure my understanding. Of course, I didn't articulate it like that at the time. I was a neurotic kid, but still a kid.

Probably everyone feels this way, actually, and some people just think about it too much.

Q: I want to avoid the question of writers you admire, but your essay's consideration of writing an "as-is" versus a potential "is-no-longer" leads me to ask you which writers do that well—in both fiction and nonfiction. Or, perhaps, which writers' narratives have "structured your understanding"?

A: I think there are a lot of writers who do that well through their own lens (really any writer who is doing something well is doing that well!), but the ones that really feed me and make me want to write myself are Kathryn Davis and A. S. Byatt, who both have such fearless intelligence in their work, such a sense of the self diffused through totally individuated characters; Kate Bernheimer, who fully inhabits the dream; Gaetan Soucy, who fully inhabits his reader's dream; and, to go back a few years, D. H. Lawrence all the way. They all write fiction, but in nonfiction I would say the seminal practitioner of navigating between the "is" and the "will-not-be" is John Berger. He's a fiction writer too of course, but even his purely critical texts are infused with a sense of both loss and experience. I particularly love *And Our Faces, My Heart, Brief as Photos*, which is a distillation of all his modes. A beautiful, terribly present book.

Q: This anthology seeks to explore various levels of metawriting, and in our discussion, you have raised issues of the self as artist, the awareness of narrative, and, in "The Girl Is a Fiction," the conflation of experience and representation or art. How do you see "The Girl Is a Fiction" as fitting into the context of metawriting?

A: Originally, I wrote this essay in the first person, but even though I wrote the whole piece this way and its final form hasn't substantively changed, the first person seemed false and strained to me. In the first person the piece seemed too aware of itself as memory, even if partially speculative memory. It seemed self-indulgent. Perhaps it still seems self-indulgent, but when I changed the point of view the whole essay came into focus for me. Perversely, it actually seemed less distant in the third person, more immediate. I think for me that is what I like most about writing a piece that might be termed metawriting. When I abandon the attempt to relive the experience, abandon the pressure of the authenticity of the moment and instead allow myself to conflate what I remember about the time, what I might have thought about the time, with what I think now into an interwoven whole, the results feel more true to me than the literal truth. Everything I wrote about in that essay actually happened, but I don't care if it did or not. Which for me is the real joy of writing without worrying about genre, literary or otherwise. The girl is a fiction because I am not her anymore, when I was her I was heavily invested in creating another kind of her, and the self that is both me and her has always hated and reacted violently against being told what I was. This is probably why I started writing in the first place. My writing is often very heavily invested in memory, fully inhabited by memory, but I don't think memory actually exists without the tool of invention. There's no way to know the self without simultaneously creating a new version of the self. Which feels disingenuous and flighty. Which messes people up, because it makes them think there's some "real" self in there they haven't seen yet, that they have to work harder to uncover. It shouldn't really be that hard, because, in a very small but maybe the only available way, that's a kind of immortality. Every time you examine yourself you're someone just slightly new.

DAVID LAZAR

"The essay is by its nature a self-reflective fo[r]
self's prism considers the world."

a Saturday"—I h[
may regret tha[
nauseating, [
married, [
many [
ma[

On Dating

LIKE MANY PEOPLE MY AGE, after a few forays into dating in high school, my social life became a kind of "falling into" with more and less significant others. I spent a lot of time in schools and academic settings, time in cities and college towns, and you were around people, and if you and they were available, you kissed in dark corners, or lived together for several years, or fucked and battled until you exhausted each other psychically and moved on, or dallied and flitted about . . . but you didn't exactly "date" in the conventional sense. You didn't participate in that social ritual of calling and meeting up with someone you didn't really know, fumbling around with your social self, your ego, your desires, that our culture seems to depend on for a large part of its mating ritual. I was always grateful: it seemed like something exotic birds or squirrels did, that severe checking out of potential partners. But I was also a bit curious. And postmarriage, if predivorce, in a new city, I wanted to meet someone, create some kind of intimate connection. I was bored and lonely, and I've never liked being alone, never bought the whole "solitary-life-as-good-for-the-soul" ideology. I like being partnered, like the dialectic, the friction of two people together. There have been times in my life when, rather obviously, I've stayed disastrously partnered rather than be alone. Oh, call me irresponsible! But anyone who has been alone for long enough inside of a marriage understands the pent-up desire to explore the world of available boys or girls when the curtain falls on the girl or boy one has gone kaput with.

I hooked up with a couple of the on-line services, since that is apparently the only way anyone meets anyone now: Match and JDate (I thought it might be interesting to go out with a Jewish woman again after a thirty-five-year gap, even if my own ironic sense of identity made me a bit queasy—"CurlyNeurotics.com," "Kvetch and Kiss," "Never on

…d my own euphemisms) were my preferred organs. I … word. The idea of my family's projected joy was startling, … somewhat horrifying, though. I started dating while I was still … still cohabiting, in fact, which was, I understand, not the path … would take. I was, however, not exactly emotionally pining for a … riage that had any green left in its leaves; I had just had few friends … nd was switching off nights on child care. I was spending a lot of time at the movies. I'm willing to see almost anything, anytime. Want to drag me to a camp horror film? Not my primo genre, but okay. Certainly any noir, any musical, anything Warner Brothers, obscure melodramas, Almodóvar, Woody Allen—I don't care if they're subpar. I'll run out to see the new Aki Kaurismäki, and if you want company for the Korean film festival, give me a call. J'aime la vie cinématique!

But, to paraphrase Groucho Marx, even so, I like to take myself out of the theater once in a while. And I started using dating both as a distraction, almost a kind of hobby, and as an emotional distraction from the turmoil of a divorce that I came to call the Divorciad.

I'm going to tell you a story, of course. And it will be funny. Anecdotes are like essay candy. They're your reward for listening to me, to the essayist, talk. But I'm always a bit fraught when it comes to narrative. There is no denying the illustrative power of story and our primitive desire for it. Of course, stories themselves aren't usually what interest me most. What most engage me are questions, extrapolations from experience, ideas that shake the warp and woof of my experiential bearings. But autobiographical narratives have also served me as fodder and as the building blocks for extending speculations on what I think I'm doing in the world, how I think I'm generally misconceiving things, which I think is a generally more interesting path than trying to prove why your equation is sound math.

One of the things I gathered early on in my dating escapade (which makes the whole thing sound more madcap than it was, as though I was some Mack Sennett character crashing through the window of a sushi bar) was how deeply the years of attending to myself, for example writing essays, exploring the nature of my selves through time in linked narratives, had affected my presentation of self. I was somewhat taken aback to find, with Lamb, "how art thou changed, Thou art sophisticated!" I was smooth and controlled—somewhat polished, even—in my social demeanor. I was extremely effective at establishing a kind of intimacy very quickly, partly by asking questions, and gently probing, partly by what I chose to reveal, and partly through tone, which was warm. Let's say an oboe. All of this was very revealing, since my self-image, the last time I had dated, had hovered somewhere between Eddie Bracken in *The Miracle of Morgan's Creek,* Lou Costello, and Leo Gorcy.

I have to stop here and elaborate, because I realize I'm in danger of sounding like some kind of dating lounge lizard. I don't mean that at all. I mean instead that years of writing essays, talking about autobiography, years, in fact, of being in therapy, of adopting a largely psychoanalytic way of considering most situations, years of second-guessing myself, considering and reconsidering my motives, playing with the language of memory, trying to understand the implications of memory and the metaphors we use to consider it (those rooms through whose windows we're simultaneously looking in, looking out), years of thinking about myself in rooms full of strangers, backing myself into corners, literally and figuratively, as I overthought the painful complexity of saying "hello" to someone I didn't know, years of talking to students about their most revealing and painful experiences and how they might render them, how they might honor them, how they might, if the circumstances fit, go at them like a mad dog, years of walking down streets by myself at night (looking in clothing-store windows, shops of bric-a-brac), thinking that making a fundamentally beautiful and lasting connection with a partner was impossible on the level of the charged, trusting connection I wanted, as though what I was looking for were just short of incest, a kind of siblinglike, playful, supersexual, utterly trusting, joined-at-the-hip-across-a-crowded-room thing that still didn't involve some kind of nasty mirroring of the self, because who wants to have that ding! ding! sensation with oneself, I mean, as if you couldn't tell, I like my company, but I get awfully, awfully, awfully tired of myself sometimes. So, what I mean to say is that by the time I started dating, I could communicate my sense of self clearly and vividly to the person opposite me. I was used to drawing other people out. And I had a well-developed affective vocabulary. Which is to say, women tended to like me fairly well, those who didn't find me too short.

One thing that hasn't changed much about me over time is that I prefer to be somewhat passive when it comes to my initial interchanges with women in any kind of mating ritual. While I couldn't go out with everyone who contacted me (the twenty-two-year-old in West Germany was an avid chess and beach volleyball player, and I'm not that big on chess), I did go out with a lot of women. And did have some reasonably odd experiences.

One woman who seemed very interesting was a Jewish high school Latin teacher. She taught at a large Chicago Catholic high school, and I was really intrigued by what her cultural milieu was like, and how she pulled it off. I spent my childhood in the suburbs of Our Lady of Grace, in Brooklyn, and a part of me has always looked over the cultural fence; the wife I was Homerically divorcing (note, Goddess, the price of attorneys) was Catholic, at least on Easter, after we separated, until the 5 PM transition. I thought my date might be like some undercover Jew, some Jew under duress. I had visions before the date of taking communion with her, after a drink or two. You know, she would show up to work in some Jewish trench coat that hid the Jewishness underneath. All day long she was afraid her Jewishness would show. But her superb Latin kept her safe, as long as no one, no jealous yenta from the Jewish community center, made an anonymous call to the principal saying, "There is a stranger amongst you." That sort of thing. She was a pleasantly attractive woman, very thin, almost a kind of wastrel, really—wan, with soulful, slightly mad eyes that seemed to be looking inward, searching for something unsurely. After some pleasant conversation at the bar of an Italian restaurant, she asked if she could hold my hand. She smiled sweetly at me, in a way that was genuine, endearing, kind of nuts. I thought she was kind of interesting, and was halfway through a second gibson, and so agreed. I seemed to remember we spoke about declensions and dogs; she said her entire neighborhood hated her dog, and she didn't know why. The dog had nearly bitten another dog once, but it was all a big mistake. I spoke a bit about moving to Chicago, a bit about my situation. It seems interesting now, looking back, how unconcerned most women were about the fact that I was cohabiting with the wife I was separated from and in divorce proceedings with. I can't say, in similar circumstances, I would find that very reassuring. I was a bit like a teenager who could never take a date home because he had a deranged mother sitting in the living room, knitting. I'm not sure what to make of that, other than that perhaps I was very convincing, I was taken as trustworthy and sincere about the finality of the marriage emotionally, and that logistically, the legal part would end (bellow, Goddess . . .) before, I thought, the next cicada life cycle had run its course.

Sincerity is an interesting quality to talk about, to isolate, both in non-fiction writing and in person. It's quite different, after all, from honesty, even from trustworthiness. Conventionally, I think, we understand sincerity to mean conveying truth of feeling, genuineness in conveying what the speaker or writer believes or thinks. We feel we are being spoken to in the moment without duplicity when we experience sincerity. But sincerity can be complicated by self-deception and time. We've all had the experience (have we? haven't we? do I overgeneralize?) of passionately or hypercritically arguing a point as though there were virtually no other way to see it, think it, feel it, only to find ourselves later having had the graceful experience of actually listening to someone else and realizing that our position, our thoughts, our feelings, weren't the white-hot lightning

DAVID LAZAR

bolt of truth they seemed in the moment . . . sincere, but a flawed line of reasoning, something we now wanted to disown. Again, sincere. Sincerity and trustworthiness can also be mimed, of course. Or can be so fleeting as to be virtually useless. It is as a longer-term extension of character, or over the course of a body of work, that we get a clearer idea of a person's, a writer's, sincerity as a deeper quality, as part of an ethos, and not of tone. Sincerity as tone, is how one appears over a drink, what one might reveal in a paragraph. Sincerity as character, as ethos, is the ability to construct a consistently trustworthy self over the course of multiple works, or the work of relationship in its many forms.

That was about as eventful as the night got. I dropped her off and bid her adieu with a chaste tap on the cheek. She called me up a few days later and asked me to go to dinner and a movie. She was lovely and sincere, after all, despite being somewhat overzealous. If she were grabbing at men's hands impulsively, and not just mine, considering my need for engagement that didn't cost four hundred dollars an hour (I'm talking about attorneys, not women paid to hold hands), that didn't seem a far stretch. But our second date was inauspicious. She had the sniffles, and over a bowl of excellent Vietnamese consommé at Tank Noodle asked me to skip the movie and come back to her place to meet her dog, which I agreed to innocently, having nothing else to do, though conversation had lagged at dinner, both of us seeming to find the other a bit elusive. I've often wondered about the nature of this invitation, if it were actually some kind of euphemism that slipped by me years ago: come back to my place, and, you know, "meet the dog." Hey, Dave, did you "meet the dog"? "Hey, fellas, what a night. You know, I 'met the dog.'" I don't know. If it is, it's obscure, or some Latin translation from the Hebrew, some idiomatic blip or something. I thought that when I lived in England and got "put the kettle on," I was all set. In any case, we did go back to her place and met the dog that the neighbor hated. It was a very big dog that didn't bark so much as moan in a sing-song way when you got close to it. It made me a bit sad. The first thing Charna did, after dogs and humans were introduced all around, was open the sliding closet doors to show me the cats, and then close the sliding closet doors. I'm not sure why there were cats in the closet. Nor do I think this was in any way a symbolic gesture.

Charna sat on the couch and I sat on a chair and we had a desultory conversation I don't remember about what. She seemed to grow sadder and more distracted and I grew increasingly bemused by exactly what I was doing—I really didn't have a clue, or rather I was clearly not terribly interested in Charna at this point, though I wasn't at all unhappy about sitting there, somewhat disengaged from any real social involvement, and considering her furniture and her, considering myself and what a general idiot I was in so many ways, how odd, disastrous, unpredictable, and lonely my life had been, despite lovely relationships with friends. It's nightmarish to think that the thing that saves me from moments of despair—sitting in a slightly shabby apartment in Chicago at the age of fifty in the middle of (pipe down, Goddess) a divorce during a date that was veering toward a combination of David Lynch and Pee Wee—the ability to stop and pull inside, to try to be the person upon whom nothing is lost, to look around and see where I am and how I'm situated, is also the reason for where I am and how I'm situated. In other words, the reason I was okay in that crazy situation, and am now spinning out what may or may not be an entertaining paragraph about it, is what put me there in the first place: a kind of adaptable interest in the world and seeing myself in it. I'm terribly polite and very adaptable socially, because there is such a well-carved self inside, a self that started taking notes when I was twelve or so because it needed a bit of distance, some ballast from the unkindness of its world, which never seemed to fail to point out how weak, how gross, how underachieving I was. As much as I feel generally like a Montaignean, in this respect I suppose I'm Baconian. I keep my counsel, even when I play the neurotically revealing Jewish New Yorker. Though I also have a deep desire for revelation, honesty, and trust. I am speaking about moments that are liminal, times when I am in the gray areas of real intimacy, mock intimacy, trial intimacy, public gatherings, and new acquaintance.

And the reason I write essays is to try to find moments, sincerely, when I press myself, press the advantage of my own controls to the point where I learn something a little bit new. For instance, I think my politeness, which I've always thought of as a bit old-world, is useful to me in a limited way. It gives me pleasure, for one thing, because it's attached to gestures and language ("I beg your pardon"; "it would be my pleasure"; "you're too kind"; "it was a lovely evening, and it was charming of you to have me") that I associate with an earlier age, that of my parents, of the films of the 30s and 40s, of phrases heard in elevators in Manhattan as a child. I'm dating myself. But my politeness is also a kind of courtly persona that I can adopt with a well-used ease, at this point. It isn't that I'm not being genuine when I'm being polite (or is it?), but that I'm conveying an attitude more than something personal. Though it's a sincere attitude.

In any case, at Charna's apartment, I was reasonably comfortable in an uncomfortable situation because I didn't want or need anything particularly more than what I had at the moment—a place to sit and think. And she perhaps had more pressing needs: a greater intimacy, a fine romance, opening and shutting the closet with cats. I cannot speak for her, and

DAVID LAZAR

should not. But after some longueurs that seemed long even to me, she announced, "I'm going to walk the dog, and then the date will be over." Reader, do you do internal double takes? I said, "That's fine," and began to parse the sentence. It was clear she was ending the evening, now that the canine introduction, euphemistic or not, had been performed and had turned into a desultory affair, and I felt dismissed, the way you feel you have been less than amusing, less than ingratiating, less than sincere, in the presence of someone you had been observing, perhaps even tolerating. That Charna's end-of-the-night signal (I was sure that "walking the dog" was not another euphemism) was absurd made the acknowledgment that she was no more interested in me than I was authentically so in her an excellent, mirroring reminder that the years I spent achieving a measure of social equanimity, which is to say the ability to exist in a state of relative ease in a social situation in which I wasn't completely comfortable without experiencing the compelling desire to sprint for the nearest elevator or window, didn't relieve me of the need for empathy.

Am I being empathetic to Charna even now? Or is she just a foil for my quixotic, ever-present need to pull myself, my own motives apart? At what point does the desire for self-knowledge actually slide into something more narcissistic? Charna: I chose a satirical name for her, Hebraically dark, or burnt, the narrative sacrifice to . . . what? My need to amuse, to rope in the reader with something entertaining to wrap around the notions of the remembering self? Lazar, my own name, has ancient etymological connections to blackness. Is this my subconscious connection to self-mockery? My unconscious connection to . . . connection?

We all know that the motions of confession can be as canned, as predictable, as epiphanies. And that sincerity is a fraught, even a dialectical quality. Public sincerity is not necessarily private sincerity, and we may in fact as post-Rousseauians be relying on our private selves as keepers of the most sincere part of ourselves, or the most real sense of sincerity we experience. Trilling of course has much to say in *Sincerity and Authenticity* (which was required reading when I was in college) about the growth of autobiographical works of literature and the development of the sincere self and its replacement by a struggle for authenticity. Inspired, no doubt, by Montaigne's sincerity ("My imperfections will be seen here to the life," "To the Reader"), Hamlet says, "To thine own self be true," the aphoristic commandment of sincerity, one would think. But as Arthur Melzer suggests in "Rousseau and the Modern Cult of Sincerity" (*Harvard Review*, Spring 1995), sincerity may have devolved into a quality of self-disclosure, "an adherence to the self" that eschews other qualities, such as honesty, truth, or plainspokenness.

I don't want you to think I felt terrible that night, or that I'm feeling now some self-lacerating guilt. That would be insincere. But I think it wise to question, considering the depth of my observing self, the relationship between the observing selves I live, the observing selves I remember, and the observing selves I write. Untangling them is impossible. And to look at the nature of self-disclosure in the way, for example, when I began dating (shhhh, Goddess), I did so within the limits of decorum, so naturally, so sincerely, but with an edge of performative skill. I've spoken enough to and about the self over the years to be able to put mine over with some alacrity, I think. I have a self that I can perform, that is familiar, that I can make exist in prose. The question is, so what? It is a dangerous quality, because it creates a false, or shall we say, an intensified sense of intimacy. Do I talk about myself too easily now? This can be a problem when meeting people you have no desire ever to see again, to whom self-revelation creates expectancy, intimacy. And it should. And in fact, in the rest of my life, it does. But it was strange to see that what had become one of my self's processes, one of my habits of being, to paraphrase Flannery O'Connor, had also become, or was in danger of becoming, a tic, a habit performed without sufficient due process of empathetic concern. Look, it isn't as though I were talking to a mirror, or that my interest in my companions for the evening were feigned. It's just that as I did my analyst/analysand number at this or that bar, or this or that restaurant, what I probably wanted most was for someone to find me fascinating and irresistible, and self-disclosure was my instrument. And I'm sure everything I said, or almost everything, was sincere. Speaking about myself falsely is like being made to eat a food I've cooked, and detest. I don't really see the point. Why bother creating a false idol of oneself, since you know you're going to have to throw the tablets down at some point anyhow?

You may wonder why I didn't just try more assiduously to make friends in the months of painful cohabitation. You may wonder why I didn't just buckle down and spend the time more usefully alone. You may wonder how I could spend so many nights rehearsing myself with different women, presenting the self, presenting myself in semihopefulness that some connection might be made, only to hear the vague hissing of air escaping. You may wonder how anyone can begin the process of courting while their marriage is in the process of legal dissolution. Some of these questions are worth essays of their own, some will be dispatched by certain readers with knowing recognition. I'll just say that my own—choose your frame of reference for this moment in this essay—set of needs, neurotic makeup, sense of liminal necessity, emotional philosophy, or pathology, or ideology, seems just about to demand the idea of romantic love,

DAVID LAZAR

the sometimes-labyrinthine or perverse pursuit of coupling. Blame it on Fred and Ginger, blame it on the family, blame it on the troubadours, or blame it on a fleeting glimpse from our family's Buick of a couple walking in Central Park on a fall day in 1965. They were wearing lambswool sweaters and jeans, holding hands, and talking. I think they were talking to each other about themselves. Both had glasses. Is that why I can't seem to stop talking about myself, writing about myself?

Is every essay I write a date, and is the date really with myself?

INTERVIEW

David Lazar, author of "On Dating"

Q: You once wrote, during one of our e-mail exchanges regarding metawriting in essays, "all good essays are, in a sense, meta-essays." I thought here would be the perfect place for you to expound on that statement.

A: The essay is by its nature a self-reflective form, a form through which the self's prism considers the world. Montaigne's essays are full of the discourse of the essay, because in discussing the self, creating the self through which one essays the self, one essays one's essay. If that sounds like some kind of mad chiasmus, it's because the essay is an exercise of and in self and sensibility. As Lukács writes in "Soul and Form," "The essay is a judgment, but the essential, the value-determining thing about it is not the verdict . . . but the process of judging," and one of the things the essay is constantly judging is itself, its assumptions, its biases, theoretical foregroundings. Lydia Fakundiny writes at the beginning of her anthology, "Essays, it seems, insist on being thought about only in essays." The reason for this is that, when essaying, we can't help but call attention to what we're doing. We digress, lose our way, and frequently come close to losing ourselves, if such things even quite have form. Having form. That's perhaps the point—the tension between self and persona, craft and whatever escapable ideas we're chasing—it pops up in the inevitable question as we write essays: what am I doing here, what do I want, what can I say, *Que sais-je . . . ?*

Q: The types of essays you mention are what I consider essays in their purest form, Montaignean in the self as subject, with essayists setting out to settle some question without insisting that we do. So if Montaigne tells us in "To the Reader," "It is myself that I portray," what happens when the self's prism reveals itself as writer? Or can we, as essayists, ever leave that writer back at home while we go out, wandering Woolfean streets?

A: I wander the streets all the time as a father, or a boyfriend (I still like that word, it makes me think of the Shirelles), or a shopper, or a flaneur, but the writer is usually there somewhere, but she or he's been there since I was a kid. Here I'm loath to overgeneralize. . . . I've been writing in my head ever since I can remember, forming paragraphs, engaging in dialectical experiments, challenging myself, flirting with taboos to see if they felt too scary or just right. I don't think self necessarily reveals itself as a writer, as in "Ah-ha!" It's inextricable. But I do think some essayists are more writerly, more self-identified. I don't particularly like writing about writing, ironically. I tend to run screaming away from poems about poems. They tend to have a self-haloing effect, a seeking after aura. But the essay's struggle is more about meaning than about being a writer, about the difficulty of finding and articulating, of unraveling and exploring whatever it is that's creating the necessity for the essay.

Q: In *Truth in Nonfiction: Essays,* an anthology you edited, you contribute a complex piece, "Occasional Desire: On the Essay and the Memoir," in which you explore the occasions of essay, autobiography, and memoir, highlighting the interrogatives lurking beneath and between the lines of essays. In that piece, you argue a justification (occasion) for autobiographical prose to be less "because it was, or because I am" and more "because I am because it was." Is there an occasion for metawriting? And if so, would "because" be a part of it?

A: The occasion for metawriting is, "Who cares?" The occasion for metawriting is, "Do I really think this, or am I going through the motions of what I have always thought?" The occasion for metawriting is, "How can I test what I'm thinking and saying in a way that scares me?" The occasion for metawriting is, "What would I think if I could actually change, and not just pay homage to the idea of it?" The occasion for metawriting is death. The occasion for metawriting is a deep distrust of the self. The occasion for metawriting is a yearning for the perfectly flawed sentence that is the comet's tail of an idea.

Because language is the lady in the lake. And the essay is the trial we self-administer.

Q: "The occasion for metawriting is death"?

A: Of course. Death is the mother of self-consciousness. And essaying, we inscribe the self, briefly, in time, ours, in space, who knows? Montaigne's "To the Reader" states, "Having lost me (which they must do shortly) they may recover some traits of my conditions." We're always essaying, at least I'm always essaying, with the idea that the idea I'm threading around myself leads from nothing to nothing, except that it has, perhaps, some witnesses.

Q: You write in the title piece of your 2003 memoir *The Body of Brooklyn* that essayists are "a kind of secret society of neurotics, compulsives, obsessive self-examiners" forming a "kind of literary fraternity." In keeping with that metaphor, what ensures an autobiographical writer's membership in this House of Essay (Are the Fictions chatting him up, too? What about those terse Poets? Why "Go Essay," as the t-shirt from Rush Week might brag?), and what missteps do you see fledgling pledges, ranging from *The Best American Essay* to beginning creative nonfiction recruits, commit?

A: It sounds like quite a party at my house. No wonder so many of my friends are therapists. House of Essay sounds a bit like House of Usher, and I like the idea of the gothic essay, though I'm not sure that part of the genre has been completely fulfilled yet. Nevertheless, we're all a bit gothic in the terror and pleasure that reside in the self's architecture we construct and walk around. And isn't the psychological element in gothic literature, the necessity of deconstructing the doppelgänger (essayist and persona), somewhat similar to that of the essay? I digress.

Nothing ensures membership in the Essay Club (the House was foreclosed) other than being interesting, having ideas, writing prose. And even then . . . the connection with poetry has always been strong, but not terse. The essay is by its nature both a lyrical and an expository form. And one need only look to the eighteenth century—Sterne, Swift, Addison and Steele, Fielding—or, more recently, to W. G. Sebald to see the ways fiction essays fictively or uses the essay essayistically in a fictive context.

As for "Go Essay," I'm all for it, though it sounds a bit threatening, a bit too postal. There is so much interest in the form now. "All I have is a voice," Auden writes in "September, 1939," and that is the basis of the essay, the personal, critical voice of sensibility, in essays, blogs, in fragmented, lyrical, longer and shorter forms. The urge to speak across and combine forms is indelibly powerful now. And that's heartening in a time that seems morally windswept frequently.

Missteps: the self that forgets the big wide world, the essay without questions, the avoidance of conclusions where conclusions are, in fact, possible, even in an open form. The idea that images are always substitutes for declarative sentences. Forgetting that writing is as severe a craft as painting, sculpture, or architecture.

Q: Actually, I think you're on to something with the idea of an essayist's doppelgänger, especially given the concept of "On Dating." However, I want to return to language, which you mentioned earlier as the lady in the lake. (And I have to ask, bewitching Arthurian legend or Raymond Chandler femme fatale, or both?) You use the phrase "the language of memory" in "On Dating," which calls to mind a claim made by Pam Houston in an e-mail exchange with me regarding the fiction-versus-nonfiction issue: "I don't wholeheartedly believe in language's ability to represent the world as it really happens." Of course, she's addressing story versus essay, something you allude to in "On Dating" when you note our "primitive desire" for narrative, yet you display an imperative desire for questions. Is not "the language of memory" an interpolation embedded with questions? If so, how well do you trust language (your "well-developed, affective vocabulary" notwithstanding) to ask questions, explore their instigations, and, as you note, when the conclusions are there, answer them? That is to say, if language may fail to capture the (writer's) world as it really is, what chance does "the language of memory" have?

A: (The femme fatale is the lady in the lake. Thus, Chandler's own. But Viviane, or Nimue . . . they can help or hurt us depending on where the mirror is, our angle of vision, how good we are at displacing our displacement, and how well we embrace the death wish, I think.)

I'm not sure I wholeheartedly believe in anything other than trying to take care of children, but so what? We have the language we have (like our mothers, our sons, and daughter) and the language we make. What is the world as it really happens? This is less important to me than reflective attentiveness, and I suppose to that extent I'm more of a casual phenomenologist. I think we've worn out certain Lockean platitudes and Platonically utopian desires for art's ability to represent. The essay enacts, radically; it's about process. The essay is perennially about to start and about to end, but not about to copy. I don't think essays represent. They present. That's one difference between the essay and fiction.

About my trust or distrust of language—I think language is horrifyingly full of mines—each word or two urges me to digress, to lament, to underscore and explain, to clarify, to stop in exhaustion and spit at the impossibility of getting past the cultural, historical, and personal encrustations in the words that I use, my personal level of ignorance, my sweet and beguiling syllabically enchanting ladies of the lake; I think language beautifully full of the poetry of immanent clarification of some small pinprick of what living might mean. Fuck. Why else would anyone care to spend a life writing sentences? What chance does the language of memory have? Memory is the language that subjectivity gives to experience. It exists in a combination of image and words. It exists outside of chance; I

DAVID LAZAR

think the question that resonates for me in writing is how to keep memory from being falsely reified into a static set piece. How to, instead, prod remembering into a dynamic process that includes multiple subjectives. Memory is dynamic, unstable. Radical, and radically useful. And potentially frustrating in its complete escapability.

"I think the metaessay makes more moves to bring the reader directly into that process. Using small but powerful phrases such as 'I would like to believe . . . ' It's a subtle distinction. In a traditional essay, the essayist seems to take a more distant stance; maybe you might call it 'disembodied,' while a metaessay has a more naked, physical quality to it."

The Dog at the Edge of the World

I'VE BEEN LOOKING FOR ONE of my favorite Franz Marc paintings called *The Dog at the End of the World*. At least I *think* that's what it's called; I had the image on a postcard I gave away, and I've never been able to find it again—not on-line, not in an art shop, not in my book of Marc paintings. I gave away this card to a man I'd been dating only a short time. I gave it to him because he had an unruly dog he seemed to love despite her flaws, and I tried to love her so he would love me. But that dog was incorrigible, a thin black lab so excited by any glance of attention that she jumped on laps, peed on floors, turned herself inside out in her devotions. None of it worked, not her pleas for love, not my own dog-as-cupid matchmaking, this love by proxy. Shortly thereafter, the man broke up with me—in a way that was so passive-aggressive I didn't quite realize I'd been dumped, and so I kept calling, kept leaving messages, kept torturing my girlfriends with my distracted ramblings about him at breakfast—and so I've never seen my *Dog at the End of the World* again.

Now, years later, I don't want the man back, but I do want the postcard, my dog at the end of the world. Maybe she was called *The Dog at the* Edge *of the World*. Either way, I remember her as a small white dog, sitting with her back to the viewer, dwarfed by a vista that stretches out vast and light and covered in snow. This dog does not seem dismayed to be at the edge of such blankness, such unknowns, nor does she seem eager to go out into it, to tip over that edge and explore. No, the dog is merely—as my remembered title suggests—simply *at* the edge, content to be in the space between the known and the unknown. I think she even rests her head on her forepaws, eyes half-closed in contentment.

Maybe this picture doesn't even really exist. Perhaps I've conflated several different Franz Marc paintings to create this one resonant image of a dog immersed in a landscape broken into Marc's characteristic shards. Marc painted animals of all sorts: cows, chickens, deer, cats; dogs are by no means his favorite totem. In another painting, *Deer in the Monastery* (this one I can find with no problem), he paints the faint outlines of one resting deer emerging from swaths of green, resplendent in a single ray of light. The deer looks so restful, so at peace, her head tilted up, bathed in the last rays of sun that find her here, deep in a garden tended by the careful hands of monks. I imagine she's a fawn, with faint polka dots of infancy just fading into the tawny fur, the skin taut, not yet pitted by age. She rests, legs folded, accompanied by a chorus of strange birds who, until this moment, have not known how to burst into song.

PERHAPS I'VE FIXATED on the dog at the edge of the world because I'm just now beginning to understand what Winston Churchill called the "black dog" of depression. *This* animal, I know now, has been at my heels for years, an unstinting companion. Perhaps I see Marc's white dog as a kind of redemption, how she sits so restfully on the dangerous precipice. And I want to grab that animal back from my fickle lover's hand, have this white dog returned to me: this animal he couldn't have really understood or loved the way she deserves.

As it turns out, Marc himself suffered from severe anxiety and depression. He escaped on the night of his first marriage, in the throes of an anxiety attack that would lead him to Paris, into the sanctuary of the paintings of Van Gogh, Cézanne, and Gauguin. His anxiety, as he put it, "numbed the senses," and he came back to his senses by studying those artists who amplified the world, made it brighter, more intense. These artists studied the natural world, knew it intimately, and through this intimacy could carry out acts of profound transformation. In one of his letters, Marc writes: "I am trying to intensify my feeling for the organic rhythm of all things, to achieve pantheistic empathy with the throbbing and flowing of nature's bloodstream in trees, in animals, in the air."

Marc found his subject in animals, and he became an expert through careful observation. He kept himself afloat by teaching animal anatomy classes in his Paris studio, showing others how an animal's body can only be depicted in abstraction after you thoroughly understand the primary reality of muscle and bone. His animals gradually transformed from realistic renderings to the faintest suggestion of animal forms emerging from a chaos of color.

I stare at one of his more famous paintings, *The White Dog* (this image you can find everywhere): a sleek white dog, asleep in a patch of snow, so that it becomes a study in repose, in calm. The dog gradually merges into the landscape—the white fur, the white back, echoing the white of the snow. It's a close-up, the rest of the world cut out of the frame so that our eyes fill only with sleeping dog, a dog that must be inured to the cold. I briefly wonder if this is my white dog, just so my search can be over, but something about the animal isn't quite right. I think *my* white dog must be more complex—both afraid and content, holding many opposing emotions at once—while this white dog has found his place too easily, can lie down in the snow and think nothing of it.

AND NOW, THROUGH another brief foray into Internet circumnavigation, I've found it, my white dog. But it turns out not to be a dog at the end of the world, nor a dog at the edge of the world, but *A Hound Before the World*. A hound, and he looks it, much bigger than I remember, squatting on his large haunches, ribs clearly visible in his barrel torso, bulbous forelegs muscular as a weightlifter's. His ears droop down to either side of his jowly face, and his black eyes look out onto the world with an expression I can't quite articulate: certainly not the calm I remembered, more like bewilderment. Before I found the painting again, my dog was just a pinpoint on the horizon, but now here he is, large as the world, which shatters in pieces of blue and red and yellow and orange, not monochromatic at all.

I don't know what to do with him, this hound. He's too big, too goofy, too . . . how do I put it . . . too *male*. He doesn't know or understand that he's a dog at the edge or the end of the world; rather he's *before* it, a stance that, to me, feels completely different. He's paused momentarily between past and future; he's not invested in what lies across that divide. He's got a master, no doubt. He's got someone who's about to call him back, throw him a bone, bring him home.

I want my own white dog back, the one I fabricated, the one who led me to the edge and allowed me to sit still, showed me how to be alone with no need to either leap into the abyss or back away. The little pill I take now for depression really does the same thing: it allows me to stay a little bit longer at the edge and observe, often with bemusement rather than despair. Like a tourist lured by a roadside attraction, I stop at this handy viewpoint, read the interpretive signs, perhaps buy a postcard to remember the vastness of a landscape normally viewed at a squint, too close to really understand.

When I travel I often send home postcards to myself, cryptic messages that urge me to remember my best self. These aren't missives meant for public consumption, carefully crafted and literary. No, I say stupid things like, "Remember this, floating in the warm waters of the Adriatic and being completely yourself," or "Remember that full moon? Remember that feeling of being at peace in the world?" Always these postcards—when they arrive in my mailbox after I've returned home—take me by surprise. Always I forget that I've written them, so that when a colorful, slick card falls out from among the bills and advertisements, I get a momentary shock of recognition when I glimpse my own handwriting. I take the card inside before reading it, turn it over carefully, curious but a little afraid to see what I have to say to myself. Always, the message begins with "remember."

Maybe that's what healing is, a kind of remembering. An ancient remembering that can't be done with our misfiring brains alone, our faulty intellects. No, there's something animal in it, insight that can't necessarily be translated into human words. I think that's what Franz Marc's animals did for him: they aroused the discerning part of his brain, nudged new circuits to fire, told him which details matter and which do not. He remembered the animal parts of himself, and these transformed on his canvas in the form of red horses, leaping cows, recumbent deer, and sleeping dogs. Sometimes the animals are dead, and sometimes they are bewitched. Oftentimes they are solitary, but sometimes they jostle against one another in a field. In one of his later works, *The Fate of the Animals*, Marc paints wild horses and deer in a furious composition: heads flung back, necks exposed, sharp planes of color jutting in every direction, animals accosted by light.

Three years after *The Fate of the Animals*, Marc died in a World War I battle at the age of thirty-six. In a last letter from the front, he wrote that "nothing is more calming than the prospect of the peace of death. . . . It leads us back into normal 'being.' The space between birth and death is an exception, in which there is much to fear and suffer. The only true, constant, philosophical comfort is the awareness that this exceptional condition will pass and that 'I-consciousness' which is always restless . . . will again sink back into its wonderful peace before birth."

Peace before birth: perhaps this is what I seek out in my white dog. That is what I read into the posture of her small but regal back.

I suppose I'll need to paint my own *Dog at the Edge of the World*, or put her together through mosaic, placing a broken bit of tile here, a fragment of blue glass there, her white back a crescent of an ancient teacup. I'd put in a bead of a black eye, positioned just so, to make that sidelong, beckoning gaze I remember so well. I'll work on the perspective, adjust as necessary, make her small enough to show the enormity of the landscape at her feet. But not too small. She is not overwhelmed; I have to remember this. She may not know where she's going, but she understands where she's been. It might take a long time, this dog at the edge of the world: there are so many details to get right, so many small and infinite gestures.

BRENDA MILLER

Q: *The Best Creative Nonfiction* series, edited by Lee Gutkind, in which the third installment features your essay "Table of Figures," includes a preface to each essay in the form of a paragraph of metawriting (how the essay came about, how the author defines or extols creative nonfiction). In your preface, you mention writing "the hermit crab essay." Would you explain the concept, and how you were initially hesitant to do an exercise you had done so many times before?

A: When I was writing *Tell It Slant* with my coauthor Suzanne Paola, I was trying to think of ways to describe the kinds of pieces that take on forms that already exist out in the world, such as the how-to article (Lorrie Moore's stories in *Self-Help* are excellent examples of that voice), a recipe, a list, and so forth. I had written my own "How to Meditate" several years earlier, which is a highly constructed narrative about my experience on meditation retreats. Whenever I had tried to write this material in traditional narrative format, in the first person, it felt trite and forced; once I hit on the voice of the how-to article the writing emerged so easily that I completed the essay in one twelve-hour writing stint. As I tried to describe this process, I remembered the hermit crabs you see in tide pools around here; they are crabs born without their own shells, so they have to find abandoned shells to inhabit as their own. They animate these shells, make use of them, to protect their soft underbellies. This seemed like a fitting metaphor for how these types of essays work. The form itself enables you to write about material from a completely different vantage point, and so you can often really delve into material that has eluded you otherwise.

With "Table of Figures," I was running a workshop at the Rainier Writing Workshop on the "hermit crab" form. As I always do, I have the students brainstorm the kinds of forms or voice one might appropriate. We write them on the board; there are always dozens. Then I ask them to make a private list of subjects or memories they have either been reluctant to write about or had a hard time writing about in the past. Then, of course, I ask them to dive in, take one of those subjects, pair it with a form, and go! Students always write amazing things, even in just the fifteen minutes I give them for the exercise.

On this particular day, I was feeling lazy and wasn't going to do the exercise, since I had done it many times before. But it gets boring watching other people write. So I looked up on the board, chose a form at random—table of figures—and just started writing without thinking about it too hard. The word *figures* reminded me of bodies, so that's where my mind went, and I ended up writing the first three sections of that essay in about ten minutes. This experience reminded me that it's always good to write with your students, as it reminds you what obstacles they'll run into as they're writing, and how the process might be going for them. I think it's also important to be a good role model in class, to show that you too believe in the power of in-class writing. It's actually how a majority of my essays get started.

Q: Is your piece "Artifacts," featured in *In Brief: Short Takes on the Personal* (Norton, 1999), a "hermit crab essay" or something else, in its fragmented collage of objects (angel, shell, unearthed crystal, dead people's things, empty vessels)? In it you write about forms that keep changing: "One moment they are clearly containers; the next moment they are contained by what surrounds them." I'm thinking of the relationship between form and content in writing, which you seem to foreground. Why do you think that is?

A: I would classify "Artifacts" as more of a collage essay than a "hermit crab," as it gathers together many diverse fragments and holds them together with the title. The title acts as a kind of glue to fasten all these pieces together in one essay, and it provides the metaphorical underpinnings of the piece. For me, it's an example of how important the small structural details are when writing in lyric forms; you have to give your reader clues (even subtle ones) that will nudge them in the right direction. In my lyric essay class, the students catch on quite quickly to the fragmentation part of lyric essays; what's harder to learn is how to hold them together. Sometimes the simplest thing is the title.

For me, as my writing has evolved, form cannot be separated from content. The forms are what allow the content to emerge. I hadn't realized I was writing about form so early on in my career, so thank you for pointing out those lines to me. Seeing them now, they seem prophetic.

Q: This anthology in fact explores the concept of form as genre, fiction versus nonfiction, but also the ways in which writers are self-consciously writing in a certain form. In her interview in this anthology, the fiction writer Cathy Day asks, "What could be more real, more sincere, than acknowledging that something is indeed made-up?" This concept brings to mind your essay "The Dog at the Edge of the World," in which you prefer the image you invented (misremembered?) to the one that exists, and in which you close with the idea that "there are so many details to get right, so many small and infinite gestures." You have created a nonfiction work that raises the issue of memory versus invention and (re-)creation, which I find fascinating.

A: Yes, I think that has become the richest area in my writing process right now. I don't worry about the "real" so much as my *perception* of the real, and it's in the working out of the discrepancies between the two realms that a different kind of truth emerges. I can't seem to stay rooted in fact (too boring) or invention (too ungrounded), but instead inhabit that space in between, where anything can happen. I think it does speak to a kind of sincerity on the part of a writer, when you are willing to let the reader in on your thought process and do not rely on presenting something fully formed.

Q: I tell my students that a good essayist must first be a good thinker, as the essayist is following, as Phillip Lopate describes in his introduction to *The Art of the Personal Essay*, "a more intuitive, groping path." To that end, as readers, we are observing the essayist's thought process. So if that is the case, how might you distinguish the metaessay from the essay? Or do you?

A: I think the metaessay makes more moves to bring the reader directly into that process. Using small but powerful phrases such as "I would like to believe" or "perhaps," or even that miniscule workhorse "maybe," invites the reader to mull with the writer, to imagine, to dwell in uncertainty rather than to imbibe certain facts, histories, or information. It's a subtle distinction. In a traditional essay, the essayist seems to take a more distant stance; maybe you might call it "disembodied," while a metaessay has a more naked, physical quality to it.

Q: You mention nakedness, which makes me think of vulnerability, a tender and necessary element of the essay and one present in "The Dog at the Edge of the World": "The little pill I take now for depression really does the same thing: it allows me to stay a little bit longer at the edge and observe, often with bemusement rather than despair." Such moments go beyond mere confession; they imbue the writing with connection. Though such disclosure is not for everyone. What in your person(a) do you think invites such exposure? And to what end, do you think, does vulnerability work in your, or others', writing?

A: As I mull over your question, I've just come from a rehearsal for the Threshold Choir, a group of women who sing at the bedsides of the terminally ill and dying. I suppose there is no place as vulnerable as this one—so near to the edge of mortality—and yet the singing these women do makes that vulnerable place so tender, so alive, so vibrant. Even though this was "just" a rehearsal, we could all feel it in that room: a kind of portal to the unknown, welcomed with these joyful and compassionate voices. I would like to believe my writing—and the writing of those I admire—is this kind of singing, a way to embrace vulnerability, transform it, revere it.

In a world where we must be so armored most of the time, I think writing (or any other art) must be the place where we let down that guard. If we don't, then what are we doing there in the first place?

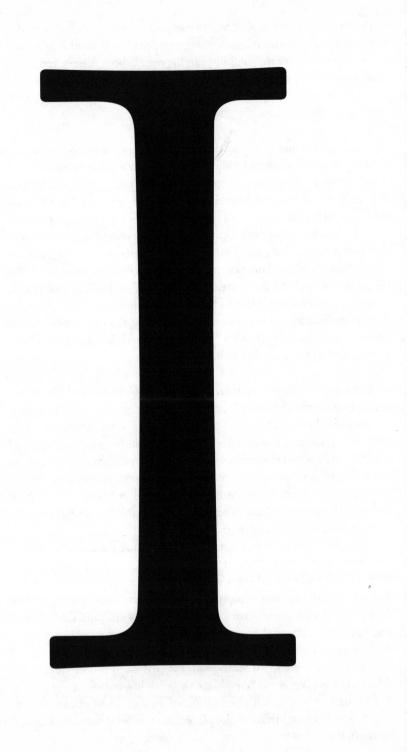

"Yes, what's most important is the art, is the artifice, but finally we live in a world that demands that art come from an artist, and who that artist is, for worse or for better, matters to a whole lot of people, which means it probably ought to factor into our thinking on the subject."

Facing the Monolith

DID I FORGET TO MENTION IT? It's submerged in every sentence, diphthong without which it's hard to go for long (ask the Oulipo). It, a tic, a blip, the Goodyear blimp, an exclamation point without a dot, you can't avoid it, those *I*'s, somehow American, always thinking, being, wanting to find our way to something biggie-sized and tasty, always gerund, processing, grinding up an *us* into component bits of light, but at the bottom of the can of *us* there is just *us*. *Us* as selves displayed via memoir, via reality everything, via the move to the more real.

The world is filled with them, jutting, jousting, rutting, roasting them on television cooking and other shows. Sometimes it's easy to believe that without *I* there would be no world. As you may know, the word *Internet* should be capitalized. The Internet is not the world, though some days it seems like it; it is another space in which we can separate our *I*'s from our bodies, let them erect themselves, let them do their thing.

I, receiving sexts from senior citizens concerned about our eroding communications standards, our sagging breasts, the proliferation of poetry, and the increasing use of the emoticon and the word *like*, which is unstoppable, but which I like. I may lament dropped apostrophes in e-mails, television ads, possessives repossessed by teens who think of everything as theirs, including memoir, including technology, the world's best worlds, including individual experiences that may seem idiosyncratic but are not.

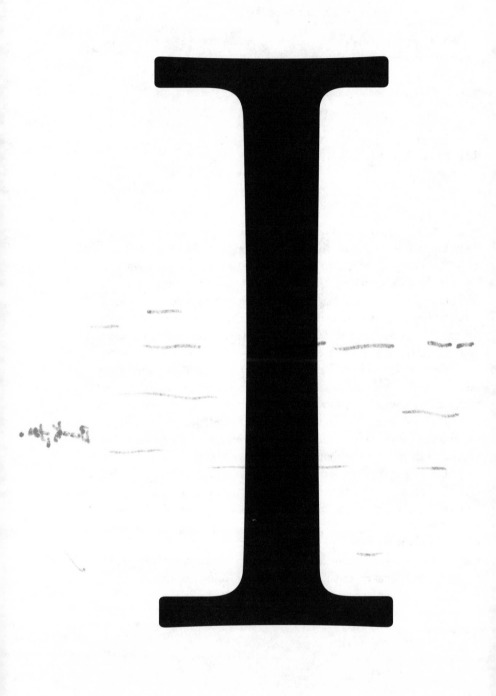

WHAT MAKES AN *I*? What makes us display our *I*'s? Why can we some-times not believe our eyes? And what good are eyes, are *I*'s, if we can't believe them? Is the self an atom, indivisible without catastrophe? Or a conglomeration of unlike parts, a rebuilt Hardy Boys jalopy? (The Hardy Boys novels were not written by an *I*: their "author," Franklin W. Dixon, like Carolyn Keene and plenty of other "writers," is a construct, a conve-nience, a conglomeration of nameless ghosts.) Is it a bunch of flowered turn-ons, measure-ments, and pet peeves? Is it a wiki? A palimpsest? A set of Russian nesting dolls?

Obviously we believe in *I*. We have to believe in *I*. We decide to believe in *I* in this culture. But I can't shake the feeling that *I* is only a shared and useful assumption.

And well, yes, part of my interest in memoirs, in YouTube, in personae, in the public display of *I* is that I envy them, unrepentant, unashamed displaying themselves—live! nude! girls! real! wild! hot! authentic! living! life!—for you.

I can't imagine a life in which I was not too self-conscious to try to tell my story unmediated. I've tried to be a good midwesterner, raised sort of Protestant (which is to say Protestant) and filled enough with shame (and thereby its opposite, pride, and its accompanying exhibitionism, that sud-den panty flash, that taboo zest, that rush of *yes* and more than *yes*), that I just cannot imagine myself into that kind of consciousness at all. That self-consciousness is a big part of what separates the celebrity from the noncelebrity, studies show.

Like any other neurotic, I become necrotic with time. The half-life of *I* is such that it decays into dandruff serif flakes, skin cells, yesterday's brains, who we used to think we'd be.

TALKING ABOUT *I* is an undertaking, meaning talking about decay, the inevitable end of each *I* back into the flatness and underneath of the caverned earth. It is talking about shame. It is talking about voice. It is more than that, sure. It's also about eye and pathways of brain, and where the brain directs the eye to look, and then what the eye filters to the brain: the raw optical data of seeing becomes processed, constructed, becomes what is perceived, which is to say a fiction. There are many minds devoted to this processing and perception. But for now, I must simplify: the expressed *I* is a function of voice.

Isn't that what writers are instructed to be in search of? Isn't that what blurbs and reviews laud? A wholly original voice? *Sui generis*, godhead, in italics? You know, amazing and different, but still not so unlike the others as to make us unduly uncomfortable.

Students in creative writing programs are toiling by the thousands trying to find their voices. Meaning, partly, trying to select their voices from the thousands of voices they encounter in books, in life, in workshops, at readings, in songs, at bars, chat rooms, on-line. What is the range from which they might choose? How new can you be and still be intelligible or interesting?

Then there are those self-styled writers who claim they don't read because they don't want their voices to be influenced or curbed. Indeed. Though when confronted with a strong enough voice, it does happen. I read DeLillo, I write a DeLillo-ish story. Same with DFW. Kincaid. Didion. D'Agata. We become possessed, *we* no longer *I* but a kind of nested *us*. Isn't that what we're after? If we want to learn how to possess, we must first be possessed.

CONSIDER THE CASE of musician Tom Waits. His voice is a unique one, is it not? A signature style? He has developed it over his years of songwriting. Like Dylan, or Springsteen, his is distinctive, unmistakable for any other.

(He might be faulted for the overmythologization of his voice, but that's another argument.)

He refuses to allow his songs to be licensed for use in commercial advertisements (unlike many contemporary musicians).

Does he believe he does not want it diluted?

Does he not want it to endorse? To condone?

Waits has often been asked to license his songs for ads. Several times, after his refusal, ad agencies have used soundalikes singing jingles sometimes very similar to his songs. Waits successfully sued Frito-Lay for this practice after they used a Waits-ish song for a SalsaRio Doritos commercial. He successfully sued Levi's for using a Screamin' Jay Hawkins cover of one of his songs in an ad. He sued European car manufacturer Opel. He successfully sued Swedish car manufacturer Audi. Also MP3.com and the company Third Story, whatever they do or make.

The idea behind the lawsuits is that an artist is entitled to the right of publicity, to not have her identity associated with a product as an endorsement without her approval. The Frito-Lay lawsuit was won on the basis of "voice misappropriation."

According to the judges' written opinion on the unsuccessful appeal of the lawsuit, "The defendants argued at trial that although they had consciously copied Tom Waits' style in creating the Doritos commercial, they had not deliberately imitated his voice." In their minds, *style* is not protected, but *voice* is. The judge didn't see the difference, affirming the legal protection of a voice (in California law anyhow), citing a previous judgment in a lawsuit by Bette Midler: "What is put forward as protectable here is more personal than any work of authorship. . . . A voice is as distinctive and personal as a face."

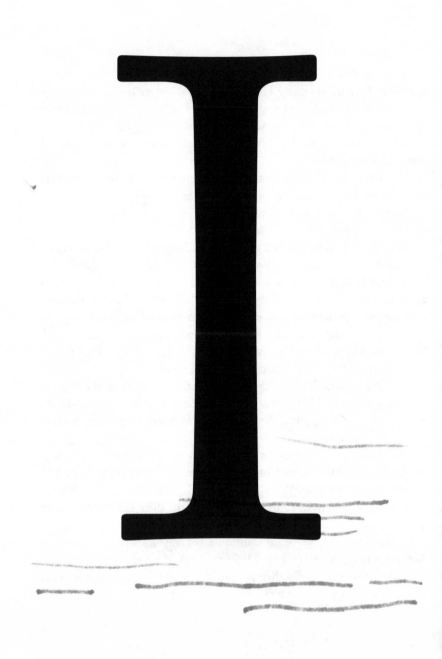

WE ARE UNDER NO OBLIGATION to consider legal definitions of either style or voice when we're talking about *I*, but it's useful to think about them. The court deems voice to be unique to an individual, a function of the physical person, which is therefore protected. In prose, when we say *voice* I think we mostly mean *style* as it shapes and is shaped by content—the two a strand of DNA, inseparably wound.

If you add up enough elements of style, don't you end up with a voice? It's not as if Waits is the first singer to sound rough and worn (try listening to some blues), but part of what makes his voice distinctive is how little it is like those of most popular musicians in the era of autotune and multitracked, overdubbed production.

One of the more entertaining facts of this case is that the song Frito-Lay had tried to license was "Step Right Up," a song that Waits says is "an indictment of advertising." Of course advertising is excellent at divorcing surface from content: witness the country cover (note the change of style necessary to change the context of the song) of Morrissey's apocalyptic mope "Every Day Is Like Sunday," used to promote the NFL's *Sunday Night Football*. Or consider the public misunderstanding and misuse of Springsteen's "Born in the USA," or the use of Iggy Pop's "Lust for Life" in an ad for Carnival Cruise Lines, and I'm sure this list goes on and on, and this is all highly entertaining for those of us with a deep appreciation of irony, which is partly an understanding that voice is a doubled thing with an edge, not always directly aligned with lyrical content.

Content is protected by copyright, probably a little too rabidly for my taste.

Not that many of those unread undergrads are producing any original content either. Not that any of us are.

And what does "original content" mean?

But I will give them this: these humans proudly displaying their *I*'s are definitely not self-conscious.

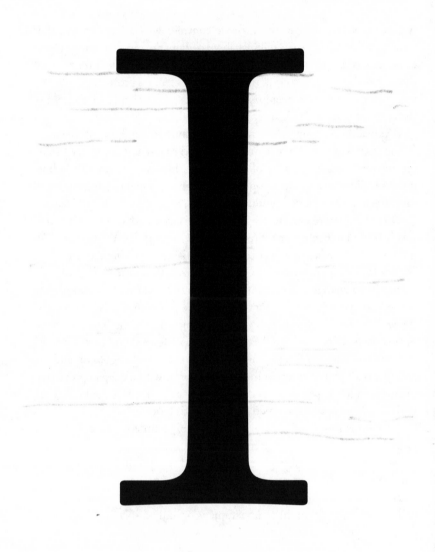

THOSE OF US WHO cannot live the unexamined life find it hard to imagine.

And it is easy to see another's failings, which is why it can be such good TV. Not so much our own.

Perhaps we envy that which we cannot attain: exhibitionism, youth, the experience of growing up with no expectation of privacy and what that does to an *I*. Maybe we should all pop a bunch of Prozac and feel better about ourselves, our porous boundaries, and our civil liberties. Or we should shut the fuck up and write, and not worry about it, until late at night when our brains recycle all of our many flaws in our nightly mini-memoir wherein we tell stories to ourselves about ourselves and our days.

Either way, here's what I believe: the way to talk about *I* is to talk about world, not (just) to talk about *I*. *I* sees world through eye. And what we see and say about the world says a whole lot about ourselves.

I think it says enough.

World includes *I*, after all.

EVIDENTIAL LANGUAGES embed how things are known into the way they're told: when I say I know that the Teddy Bear Cholla can put the hurt on you quite speedily, an evidential language would embed how I know it into how I say it. I know because I have stumbled or was thrown into a cholla (By the way, that hurt, Dad! Enjoy the public spanking in the memoir ...). Or because I saw it happen to someone. Because I heard it happen to someone. Because I read it in an essay, and we now know reading is a kind of simulation. Because I ran a simulation. Because somebody Tweeted it. Sent it through the filter of the telegraph or the telephone that trims the extreme upper and lower frequencies from our voices before transmission. In English, we might say, "I heard that x," or "It seems that x," or "I saw that x," or "I concluded that x," but it is not required, so mostly we don't if we can avoid it. We just say *x*, and doubt and cry, accuse, investigate.

I, THE NINTH LETTER, missing, buried neck-deep in the strata: its stately Ionism, its appealing pricklike jutting. As you know, *I* can mean a number, *i* another. Imagine. I mean anything could be buried in its crypt. Memory, sure. Fantasy, sure. Maybe even fact. The stories we tell ourselves about our past, from which we construct self and what we call the future. "We think of our future as anticipated memories," says behavioral economist Daniel Kahneman. Experience is not what we think it is. Or, it is, actually. How it's remembered matters to the brain more than how it was. This is why we're storytelling-special. We examine, reconstruct, pump it through the algorithm. We think: we make it so.

THE MORE YOU PRESS ON IT, think about *I*, about what we present as our individual pieces of *I*, the smaller it gets. You start shaving away elements of style, grammar, repeated content, genre, learning, shared linguistic tics. You shave away bits of individual experience that, it turns out, lots of people share: alienation! depression! desperation! repression! frustration! salvation! You peel away layer after layer of shared intellectual pretension.

Lots of people played Dungeons & Dragons. Lots of people had a dwarf character. Lots of people had a childhood friend die. Fewer had a childhood friend murdered. Lots had a parent die when they were young. Fewer haven't been to a funeral since. Lots of people like the band Low. Lots of them like the Sisters of Mercy. Lots like (or liked, at any rate) the Spice Girls, for different reasons.

Are we a confluence of events? Of likes? Of fanboy crushes? Are we defined by our dislikes? Our moral objections to sleeping with students? Our high horses? Our creepy lusts? Our desires to increase our busts? Our deep hurts? Our dirt? Our handfuls of untold secrets? Our aversions to memoir? Our obsessions with our mothers? With the glorious mishmash of the word *motherfucker*? The library of books read, video games played, songs listened to, drunken conversations had? Our constellations of pornography? Our friends on Facebook? Our Netflix queues? Our scattered cell phone conversations? Our vocal tics? The people we always dreamed of sleeping with? The people we slept with? The people we sleep with every night in body or in dreams? (And is that *sleeping with*?) The people we regret we slept with and won't admit to if pressed?

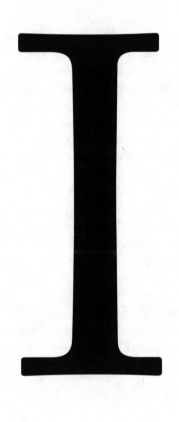

THIS LAST WEEK I have been in residency at the Atlantic Center for the Arts, in New Smyrna Beach, Florida, teaching nonfiction to teens. The complex is cut out of some prehistoric woods, three master artist cabins, a gallery, several art studios, and assorted other buildings, all connected by boardwalks like a spider web or a map for brainstorming ideas, like the kind we were told to make in school, if seen from above. The buildings are mostly locked. There are two kinds of locks on the buildings: the key lock and the keypad lock. Everyone here knows the keypad code, so all involved—master artists, students, staff—can open the buildings that are not locked with keys.

A few buildings are locked with keys: the black box theater, the sculpture studio. There's no reason we should be in these buildings, we're told, but if we need to, they'll unlock them for us if we ask. Half the time I spend here I am wandering around, checking buildings to see which I can get inside of. It's as if I were in high school again, stealing master keys, trying to access any kind of space that I see is beyond my current level of authority. Same with my behavior in video games. You get acclimated to checking every door, talking to every non-player-character (NPC), trying to pick up every object, trying out each fork of the skill tree, the conversation tree. This is how you find new things in games, how you learn what is allowed and what is not, which is what we all want to know about the world. Every step here I am in a game, I am that game—*I*, isometric, wandering, accumulating.

I LIKE IN VIDEO GAMES with diverging plotlines, eventually we return to the same fork, in which we find ourselves between them, these *I*'s. Like pillars in stories they rise on either side of us. We are diminished. We creep as if spies among the spires. Isn't that the effect we were looking for, to triangulate our selves in the trough between the two of them, this book, that one, this brain, that one, this fool, that dumb-ass one, and by looking up and seeing something recognizable and recognizably outside of us, we are reassured?

I'M SERIOUS. This is serious stuff.

Pressing on *I*—interrogating it—is a valuable task. So we should laud our memoirists, our personal essayists, our vulnerability artists, the kids in their bedrooms filming themselves for webcams or YouTube, for their attempts to get at what *I* is or can be or might be, what it might look like anyhow, or what they want it to be at the least, even if by omission, by incorrect assumption, by unsupervised play.

I as playpen.

I as boundary.

I

WHEN *I* IS THE SIZE of a colossus and a long way off, as it is when we are teens, it's smooth and huge. Get closer and we can see the cracks in its base, its many pockmarks, the scars from zits or asteroid hits visible in the high-def. Others have been here before, we understand. They have been hurt in this space before. They have spray-painted their names on the column. They have nicked off chips to take home, to remember. A souvenir, they think. Like the tourists who cut off a piece of the Humongous Fungus, the world's largest contiguous living organism, in Michigan's Upper Peninsula, and by so doing, reduce its size a little bit. The more tourists come, the smaller it gets, until it will become too small and lose notableness, and tourism will then slow, and then it will grow again. There is an equilibrium point between shrinking and growing, between being remembered and forgotten, that defines its constant size.

So you look up at it. It's natural. We're in equilibrium. You should take a chip home, have a story to remember this. Perhaps if you plug your story into the world it will grow into a monster if you give it long enough and feed it well enough.

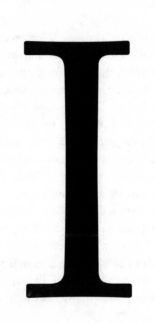

SECRETLY WHAT I FEAR, and maybe what we all fear about pressing on *I*, is that if we push it too hard it might disintegrate. If these *I*'s turn out to be fiction (entirely possible), then what is to say we have an *I* at all?

And where does that leave us? Not anyplace good.

If we can't conjure an individual brain, individual experience, with language, what good are all these lines?

What if *I* turns out to be not a self, but, like Franklin W. Dixon, a ghost collection, a grab bag of tics and tricks? So much for originality. So much for the idea of the author. So much for genius, sui generis.

It's instinctual, I guess, that we're made to recognize ourselves in the mirror. Looking good, I think: slimmer, fitter, a little balding, maybe, but also maybe more memorable, bigger, puffy like a thrush or heffalump. In that moment we are aware of *I* but also of context, background. World and *I*, we think, and that implies a self, a mechanism for seeing and being able to recognize both World and *I*. Then: this isn't always very helpful.

THE HUMONGOUS FUNGUS is believed to be the biggest individual organism in the world. It is 1,500 to 10,000 years old. It covers thirty-eight acres, mostly underground. It weighs at least one hundred tons. Going to see it is tricky, since the vast majority of it (as with many plants and fungi) is underground. You can only see tiny "offshoots that poke through the surface in the fall, edibles commonly known as button or honey mushrooms" (according to the Web site for the Humongous Fungus Festival in Crystal Falls, Michigan).

I've actually never seen the fungus though it's not far from my hometown. I spent a week working at a Bible camp just outside of Crystal Falls one summer, where I pretended to be the brother of a woman I might or might not, in retrospect, have been lusting after (so I could show up at the camp and get some work, which consisted mainly of maintenance, torching hornets' nests, and, for some reason lost to me now, shellacking a dead squirrel we found on the side of the road and mounting it on the hood of the camp truck). Oh *I*, you ass, your wacky stories, your delinquency.

WELL, THE HUMONGOUS FUNGUS *was* believed to be the world's largest (and oldest) living organism *as of 1992*. About eight years later another claim was made in Washington. And two years after that, another, larger one was discovered in Oregon's Blue Mountains. The science behind determining what constitutes an individual is probably not worth going into:* suffice it to say that this is one massive thing, and suffice it to say that what was once a true statement ("fungus believed to be the biggest organism") is no longer a true statement, so its truth value is at least partly temporal, contextual.

The world changes around you quickly if you let it, even if you don't notice.

———

* "All the vegetative isolates had the same mating type, the same mDNA restriction pattern, and had the same eleven RAPD products and five RFLP-based markers, each marking a heterozygous locus." (Tom Volk, glossing the paper by Myron Smith, Johann Bruhn, and Jim Anderson published in the journal *Nature* announcing the find.) If you are down with this, you're a smarter woman than I.**

** "I could never be your woman." ("Your Woman," by White Town, good song.)

I

"YOU'VE CHANGED" is what my friends say when they see me, my new configuration of facial hair, my new and fatter ass! My new dentistry. No longer do my front teeth define me in their flaws, I think, though I don't know whether anyone else ever cared, and my self-consciousness about it always pushed me to look at the teeth of others when I talked with them, and I bet it made them self-conscious, too: Is there something in my teeth? Are my teeth fucked up? Who is this fuckup who's looking at my teeth? Or maybe he's thinking about my mouth in a more sinister way, or doesn't want to look me in the eye, and what is wrong with me so that he won't look me in the eye or think about my mouth in another context? My thinning hairline (sad but true, especially sad since I've really liked my hair for as long as it's lasted), my settling into the outlines of my own body. But, wait, what changed? Am I not the same? Am I still who I was? Or do I contain that old layer after layer, like wallpaper? Perhaps we should go to the yearbook? Or perhaps we won't. (What's a yearbook, Dad?)

I

EVEN THE PALMS in my front yard, beautiful and majestic, have been shaved, like a long-haired cat for summer heat. They look like *I*'s, these palms that sound like the sea when they sigh in the wind. These palms that rise from the ground and serif out into the Arizona sky, deckling its edges. A guy came to the door today and offered to shave them for twenty-four dollars each. In truth, they have needed shaving for a long time, their fronds spilling over onto the yard where I would have to pick them up when the wind shook them down.

Now I know that palms, though beautiful, are barbed. (Try transplanting one, like my friend Jon and I did: enjoy your injuries.) Everything in the desert is dangerous. The tiny fronds are spined to keep animals from eating them. They drew my blood, Jon's blood, and who knows, we might be accidental blood brothers now, part of each other now, as we carried the plant and its root ball to my truck.

The sun and wind here will grind nearly anything down to nothingness in time.

Every plant in my yard draws blood, as if to say, "Who is landscaping whom?"

I

I UNDERSTAND THE TERM is *manscaping*. I had been watering the palms. I'm trying to be a better American male, responsible by unwritten social contract for yard work, hair, and trash removal. Because in Tucson, Arizona, we have (mostly) given up lawns (reason to move here: how I hate a lawn), this project is easier for us allergic asthmatics, us Morrissey-loving wilting lilies in the year-round sunstruck heat. Still, I am called to cut the plants back, or else we won't have a yard but a collection of plants. All world, no us. We need some semblance of control. We need another hero. The electric hedge trimmer fills me with the sound and authority of the chain saw, the authority of the image of the Big Daddy, shirtless and glistening, tending to his yard, authoring a novella in Norwegian about hunting, and in this way we all want to become our fathers, even if we lost them, forgot them, or had them killed. Even with the trimmer, the project, like most involving self-discovery, is painful. It's loud, cutting back the bougainvillea in the side yard, and thorns fly everywhere. A face mask is required. Goggles. Heavy shoes to withstand the thousands of thorns flying in all directions. And even then I will have to remove a dozen later from my body, saying, "You are not of me; I do not need you."

I

EVENTUALLY WE'LL HAVE the palms skinned (in the context of palms, this means trimming them all the way down to the smooth-looking bark). They too will be *manscaped*, golf-clapped, shaved, fresh smelling, and ready for their dates.

(These are not date palms, however.)

I

YOU SHOULD NOT SKIN a palm all the way up to its blossoming top. You need to leave a foot or so of outgrowth to catch water and channel it down into the trunk, so it can do its desert-survival thing, so it can grow. Don't water palms or their bases will rot, and they will soon be pulled down and become horizontal, fallen like the sky. They store their own water. They are desert plants. They are rooted against wind or monsoon storm.

I

WHATEVER YOU WANT to say about the self, it is persistent. It will do nearly anything, anyone, anytime to survive. Our *I*'s are built, or grown, or designed, or evolved, whichever you prefer, to withstand storm, to withstand a storm of attention and excavation, erosion. These caves go on forever, or close enough to forever that it might as well be forever, since we are not big-brained enough to comprehend it all. This must mean that either (1) there is something essential there or (2) there is nothing essential there at all, but the complexity of the network is such that it is permanently (we can only hope) beyond our ability to unravel.

AS PROMISED, we are shrinking, you and I, this *we*, this collection of organisms, palm, lichen, plant, animal, individual, formerly indivisible. There is almost nothing left. (There is something left; even in the midst of all of this erosion, there is always something left. I have to believe there is something left.)

Q: I'm intrigued by your concept of "pressing on *I*." Will you press the concept and discuss how it works in your writing? As well as in other venues?

A: Quite a lot of my work is interested in pressing on the concept of *I* and individual experience. Nearly all of my poems are in some way dramatic monologues. Most of my fiction is written in the first person and is in some way aspiring to a representation of an individual consciousness. Nonfiction is, of course, a more direct way to get at these questions in that the protagonist of the essay is (some version of) me. That makes it a much riskier endeavor, but also one dearer to my heart. The essay, for this writer at least, is the best way that we have of simulating consciousness, the curlicues of brain synapse and missed connection, the constantly shifting and redirecting lines of thinking. Of course the finished essay is a fixed thing, so it's only an approximation. (Thankfully, we all say, as we breathe a sigh of relief: if we could really exist entirely on the page, then we'd have made ourselves redundant.) But even if I'm not writing first-person work, even if I'm writing fiction or poems, I'm still the one processing, editing, selecting, framing, representing. Which is one reason why readers automatically connect the artwork to the artist, the individual brain (they presume) behind the art. It's impossible for us not to do this: we want connection, we want identification. Which partly explains the appeal of creating authors such as Carolyn Keene, who was of course a bunch of anonymous writers writing things under the authorial mantle of the Nancy Drew author. Edward Stratemeyer, the brains behind the popular book series (as well as the Hardy Boys series and many others), correctly understood that readers demand an author, and provided a fiction in its stead, with great success.

Q: Robin Hemley, a fellow contributor, points to the interrogatory nature of the essay, so, if I may place that along with your *I*, would this be correct: *I?* Or does it go beyond inquiry?

A: All forms of art are, I hope, interrogatory. A good bit of the writing process is trying to suppress conscious thought enough that you can allow some of what's beneath to bubble up and make itself manifest in the world. I don't believe that good art can come from a place of conscious thought or intention. It comes from someplace else, someplace darker. Then once that thing gets halfway into the world, our job is to apply conscious thought and craft to allow it to take its best and most interesting shape. But essay is a little different from story. Because of its greater conflation of the *I* with the authorial *I* (though they are not one and the same, the distance between them is shorter in the essay than in anything else), the essay is the best platform for that overt process of discovery and self-interrogation. As Hemley says, we read essays to read thinking (or a kind of approximated thinking: thinking crystallized in a fixed form is a formalized sort of fudge, the best we can do, so we'd better be satisfied). So the finished form of the essay can best accommodate process. But when I am talking about pressing on *I*, I'm not just talking about interrogating myself when I'm writing but about pressing on that very idea of selfhood that seems so sacrosanct in Western, particularly American, culture. Of course the best laboratory in which to play with this pressure is our own selves, whatever that is, since we have a lot more of ourselves at our disposal than we have of others'. And it makes easier questions of disclosure, and how much right we have to write about others. Not that this gives essayists a license to ignore anything beyond the self (good luck with that). We perceive the self through its contrast with the world, so the world quickly must become an essential subject in any essay worth its salt.

Q: Collectively, your responses lead me to think of the early twenty-first-century spate of superhero films that devote a significant part of the narrative to the human behind the superhuman. There seems to be a great need for contemporary readers to lift the mask, peel off the suit, in order to expose the Whys and Hows of a Peter Parker or a Bruce Wayne, and even those of their respective antagonists. I noticed this recently in a nonfiction class I taught as we studied Truman Capote's *In Cold Blood* (1965). The students, unprompted, devoted a great deal of time to "finding the author" or questioning the truth, due to the author's absence from the page. "How would he know?" Even though I worked to emphasize the nature of the nonfiction novel, the fictional elements blended with reportage, the students were more prone to point out where they felt Capote showed through the narrative, where his façade of using others to tell and see the story that he saw or heard fell away. Their insistence on author hide-and-seek intrigued me. Imagine how Capote's masterpiece might be a completely different kind of masterpiece if he had allowed himself to indulge the *I* of the world he encountered in Holcomb, Kansas, in the prison, and in the writing of it all.

A: I think readers have always read books to find the author in books, but the advent of mass-squared media (mass media has, after all, been around for a while, but it's hard to think that it has ever been nearly as *mass* as it is now) combined with the general sense of depersonalization that most people probably feel in the world today, has made us hunger for individual human stories. In spite of all the talk about Western individual-ism, I don't know that we've ever been as marketed to and case-studied, as pigeonholed, classified, data-mined, overheard, watched, and sold to as we are at this very moment. Grocery megastores track our purchases and use facial-recognition cameras to track the route we take through the store. Our IP addresses are logged as we surf for porn, punching in our credit card numbers. Our on-line selves are combinations of products, collections of consumer preferences, which Justin Bieber song we like or dislike, or if we don't talk about Justin Bieber at all, then we're one of *those* people, and aren't we too cool for school? So it's no surprise, in this miasma of con-struction and fiction, that readers—and people of all sorts—crave personal, individual, emotional connection. We crave authority and a sense of surety. We crave the power and personality of the author, the solid physicality of the hands behind the artwork. We do this to a fault, obviously, since it's so easy to dupe us with faux memoirs and overtly "autobiographical" nov-els. And we like the duping. So readers are going to read the *I* into any constructed piece of writing, regardless of how much the author is appar-ently present in the writing, or how obvious and powerful the absence is. It comes with the territory. Authors have authority. We are legally and personally liable for our works in a variety of ways. Those contracts we sign for our books indemnifying the publisher against legal action—they mean something. Yes, what's most important is the art, is the artifice, but finally we live in a world that demands that art come from an artist, and who that artist is, for worse or for better, matters to a whole lot of people, which means it probably ought to factor into our thinking on the subject.

Q: So it seems that metawriting may satisfy an urge that readers have, whether it be conscious or not, to know the Who, What, Why, and How behind the work. What, in turn, might urge the writer to do it? Why do you?

A: I don't know that metawriting is any more interesting than other sorts of writing in terms of readers' desires to connect personally with the artist behind the art, or with another human being's human story, especially since metawriting can pretty quickly devolve into a recursive spiral of self-consciousness and neurosis, which is usually a frustrating and uninteresting reading experience. I think the challenge for the writer (any writer) is to make this self-examination, this inwardness, lead to actual human emotion. Which is a way of saying that (meta)writing ought not to be (merely) an intellectual exercise. I feel that way about writing and art in general. All art's an experiment. The successful experiment does more than make you think: it also *moves you* and reveals something about the mystery and par-ticularity of what it is to be alive. Which is what we're all after, isn't it?

"We read the essay to see a mind at work on the page—or at least that's why I read. That's one of the hallmarks of the essay. It's a constantly questioning and recursive form. So it's natural that an essay would concern itself with its own form and ask the question, 'Why do I exist?' in much the way its author asks the same question."

The Pickpocket Project

"It is far better for the profits of our purse to be taken from us than to be robbed of the riches of our minds and souls."
—CARSON MCCULLERS, *The Heart Is a Lonely Hunter*

IT'S MY FIRST FULL DAY IN PRAGUE, and I desperately want to find someone to pickpocket me. I put my wallet in my back pocket, ride the elevator to the reception area of the Pyramida Hotel, and set off for Wenceslaus Square with my wallet sticking out ever so slightly from my back pocket. Can any pickpocket resist this? But there's a problem. My wallet does not seem all that enticing, or all that visible. There isn't much *in* the wallet besides two letters taped together and a one-hundred-koruna note, so it doesn't make much of a target. Likewise, the wallet keeps slipping further into my pocket and presents hardly a bulge. A pickpocket would need X-ray vision to pick this wallet.

I take the 22 tram to Malostranska and change to the subway. A middle-aged man rides the escalator down in front of me, dressed in a cream-colored shirt and matching pants, a big fat wallet sticking out of his back pocket. He must be Italian. I don't know why. This is just how I am. Like most humans, I jump to conclusions, though I am always ready to be disabused of them. I can't believe he has his wallet right there, a prime target for the clumsiest of pickpockets. Are there really people like this? Or is he too conducting an experiment? What is the advantage of putting your wallet in your back pocket? It strikes me as strange and uncomfortable. I find myself acutely aware of the wallet rubbing against my butt, and odder still, I worry about that moment when, inevitably, someone will bump me and it will be gone. Wanting to be pickpocketed feels viscerally anti-intuitive. I don't want to be pickpocketed. Yes I do. No I don't.

In fascination, I watch the Italian tourist descend on the escalator. How easy it would be to bump him, to reach out and gently tug the wallet from his pants. I tentatively reach out my hand. An experiment. Nothing more. Then I pull it back and stick it in my front pocket where it will cause no one any trouble.

At Mustek, I leave the train and walk around Wenceslaus Square, slowing when I see a group of teens or young men who seem as though they might have nothing better to do than to pick someone's pocket. But apparently they do. No one comes near. All day. I return to my room at the Pyramida. Obviously, I will need to reevaluate my project. I will have to find a way to make myself more visible, more of an obvious and easy target.

WHEN I MENTIONED my project to Hana, a native Czech and one of the coordinators of the Prague Summer Program where I was teaching, she was leery. "You know, Robin, your project makes me quite uneasy."

"Why?" I asked. "For safety reasons?"

"It's not that," she said. "Would you do this in your hometown?"

Ah, was I offending her? I saw her point. I guess I could be seen as making light of a serious problem. Who goes out and purposefully tries to be pickpocketed? Just some American fool who thinks it's funny.

Sure, there's a healthy sense of irony involved, but that isn't my sole motivation. My friend Jack Myers was pickpocketed right in front of me on the Prague subway last year and lost about a thousand dollars, mostly his winnings from a good night at the casino the night before.

What's simultaneously good and bad about me is that I have an insatiable sense of curiosity. I love to board trams and buses without knowing where I'm going and let them carry me away. I like to pick up real estate books and imagine what it would be like to live wherever I go. So this is about curiosity, but it's also about imagination. Can I engage imaginatively with a pickpocket? Can I turn his or her manipulation of me around and manipulate back? I half-remember a Hitchcock film, *To Catch a Thief*, I think, in which the burglar sneaks into the store to grab something. He's dressed in black. The store is in shadows. Stealthily he crouches, moving swiftly and silently, when outside a pair of headlights sweep through the store. A police cruiser passing by. He freezes and so do we. Hitchcock has caught us. We are the thieves. Because of the camera angle, the music, the situation, we, who would never be caught dead robbing a store, sympathize with the burglar. We don't want him to be caught. It's all a matter of perspective, of course.

I want to get the stories of the pickpockets, to see who they are.

"I can tell you who they are," Hana said. "If you want their stories, I can give them to you. In fact, maybe I should pick your pocket. How much are you giving them? A hundred dollars? I think the only thing they should get is a pair of handcuffs."

She went on to share how she has confronted them in the past and how she has put herself in danger because of this. One pickpocket yelled at her when she told a woman on the tram whom he was targeting to close her purse. She has witnessed many people have their belongings stolen.

Her response was sobering to me, but not deterring. I'm still intrigued: that doesn't mean I approve of them, but the only way I can get them to tell me their stories, I think, is to offer them money.

And so I have composed a letter to the pickpockets. It reads:

Dear Pickpocket,

Please read this entire note if you would like to receive one hundred dollars.

I apologize for tricking you with this mostly empty wallet, but I offer you this small amount of money in the wallet as a token of sincerity.

I am a writer and you are a pickpocket.

I am curious about you and would like your story. Not your whole life story, but one thousand to two thousand words of it. I would like for you to write about your life as a pickpocket, and I would like the right to publish it, edited or not, in any form in the world, including on my Web site. You do not have to use your real name. You may write your story in Czech (or any other language with which you're comfortable), and I will have it translated. Or you can write in English, which would be easier for me. If I decide to use your story, I will wire you one hundred dollars through Western Union, and you can pick it up at any location in Prague you wish. My only requirements are that you keep the piece between one thousand and two thousand words and that your piece be believable. If you agree to this, you may contact me at my e-mail address and ask me any questions you wish about my project, or you can skip that and simply write your story. In either case, please use the special code I've supplied at the end of this letter so that I know that you have indeed picked my pocket and not simply heard about this from a friend. If you have found this note on the ground and are not a pickpocket, please let me know the circumstances of finding this note and write five hundred words about your life. In return, I'll give you fifty dollars if I decide to use your story. I should add that if I think you are lying to me, I won't pay you. (I'm a fiction writer as well as a nonfiction writer, so I know a few things about lies.) I realize that you might think there are easier ways to get one hundred dollars, but I imagine that you might enjoy telling of your prowess as a pickpocket and that you probably enjoy a challenge, considering the line of work you are in. Thank you. I hope to hear from you. My e-mail address is robin-hemley@uiowa.edu. Your special code is Pick This44! This code may only be used once.

Despite her misgivings, Hana translated the letter into Czech for me:

Vážený zloději/zlodějko,

Pokud si chcete vydělat $100 (sto amerických dolarů), dočtěte prosím tento dopis až do konce.

Omlouvám se, že jsem vás nachytal na tuhle skoro prázdnou peněženku, ale ten drobný obnos, který v ní je, vám nabízím jako důkaz, že to myslím vážně.

Já jsem spisovatel a vy jste kapesní zloděj(ka), ale nepochybně jste i něco víc, stejně tak jako já jsem nepochybně něco víc i něco míň než spisovatel.

Zajímáte mě a rád bych znal váš příběh. Ne celý váš životní příběh, ale to, co se z něj vejde do 1000-2000 slov. Rád bych, abyste mi popsal(a) svůj život kapesní(ho) zloděje/ky a udělil(a) mi právo zveřejnit tento záznam, ať už upravený či neupravený, v jakékoli formě včetně umístění na mých webových stránkách. Nemusíte použít své pravé jméno. Můžete svůj příběh napsat česky a já si ho nechám přeložit, nebo ho můžete napsat anglicky, což by pro mě bylo jednodušší. Pokud váš příběh shledám důvěryhodným, pošlu vám prostřednictvím společnosti Western Union (http://www.intercash.cz/; několik desítek poboček po celé Praze) $100 (sto amerických dolarů), které si budete moci vyzvednout na kterékoli pražské pobočce. Jediným požadavkem je, aby váš příběh měl délku 1000 až 2000 slov a aby byl uvěřitelný. Pokud na tento návrh přistoupíte, můžete mi napsat na mou e-mailovou adresu a položit mi jakoukoli otázku týkající se mého projektu. Nebo nic takového ani dělat nemusíte a můžete se rovnou pustit do psaní. V obou případech prosím nezapomeňte uvést speciální heslo uvedené na konci tohoto dopisu, abych věděl, že jste mi ukradl(a) peněženku. Pokud jste tento dopis našel(la) na zemi a nejste zloděj(ka), dejte mi prosím vědět, za jakých okolností jste ho našli, a přidejte 500 slov o svém životě. Na oplátku vám pošlu $50 (padesát amerických dolarů). Musím vás ovšem upozornit, že pokud budu mít dojem, že mi lžete, nic vám nezaplatím (nezapomeňte, že kromě pravdivých příběhů píšu i beletrii, takže o vymyšlených příbězích něco vím). Asi si možná říkáte, že existují i jednodušší způsoby, jak získat sto dolarů, ale třeba byste mi rád vyprávěl(a) o své zlodějské zručnosti a navíc vzhledem k vašemu povolání odhaduji, že se rád(a) potýkáte s neobvyklými situacemi. Děkuji a doufám, že mi napíšete. Moje e-mailová adresa je robin-hemley@uiowa.edu. Vaše speciální heslo je Pick This! Toto heslo může být použito pouze jednou.

S pozdravem,

Robin Hemley
robinhemley.com
robin-hemley@uiowa.edu

Before my trip to Prague, I purchased six cheap wallets at Walmart. My plan was to distribute them to the participants in the Prague Summer Program administered by Western Michigan University for the past fifteen years, where I had been a faculty member the previous year. Richard Katrovas, the director of the program, ran the idea by Western's lawyers. They wanted nothing to do with it. What if the students found themselves in a dangerous situation? What of the liability? This all sounded reasonable to me, but Richard liked the idea and saw no reason why faculty members, acting on their own, should not participate. So that's my plan: distribute the letter and wallets to various interested faculty members and then see what happens.

But I'm concerned that a pickpocket finding the letter and an empty wallet might be angered and simply toss the wallet away, or perhaps be suspicious of some kind of trick. So I taped some money to the letter so that a pickpocket would at least be intrigued and have some kind of reward. Hana thought my initial offering of fifty koruna (a little under three dollars) would be seen as an insult. "They won't think anything less than a hundred koruna is serious money."

So that's what it was. A hundred. I printed out Hana's translation and my original, taping them back to back. "You know," she told me, "they might not all read Czech. They're not all from here. In fact, a lot of them are from other places. Albania. Russia. Some Roma, and oddly some Bulgarians."

I didn't ask why Hana thought it odd that Bulgarians would pickpocket, though I suppose I should have. I was just a little befuddled by this, which struck me immediately as something quite true and obvious. Of course they wouldn't all be Czech. Prague is known throughout the world as a tourist destination, and so it must also be known by pickpockets as a destination too. What would stop an enterprising Russian from traveling to Prague to ply his trade? I thought of pickpockets as men, though I supposed this was sexist. The person who had pickpocketed my friend Jack, we both agreed, was a woman, or at least she had been a distraction, part of the gang. A very tall woman, she had pressed close to me and tried to step in front of me as I waited to enter the train at Mustek with Jack and our other companions. When we entered the crowded train, I found a seat. Jack and his wife Thea stood, and the tall woman stood next to him, with some of her male friends (they seemed together) beside her. She stood, almost blocking my view of Jack. I offered Jack my seat. Although he had been battling cancer and is about fifteen or twenty years my senior, he declined. When we got off the train, Jack and Thea lagged behind, searching for the wallet that was now gone, filched from his fanny pack right in front of us.

Something about that day stayed with me. I don't think of myself as a control freak. In fact, most of the time, I feel a little out of control. Perhaps that's why pickpockets intrigue me, how in control they are. I imagine them as simultaneously confident and desperate. Of course, they probably do not see themselves as in control at all, but as victims wanting to get control over their lives and ours. I imagine them to be something I am not, or maybe something that I am and can't admit.

But admit I must. Like most humans, I can be both victim and perpetrator:

When I was seven years old, I started a pickpocket ring at my summer day camp as an alternative activity to swim period. For about a week, my little group of thugs operated under the radar, mostly snatching combs from back pockets, but other things as well, until we were finally busted and our ring broken up.

When I was twenty-four, I lived in Chicago near Wrigley Field. One day, I was riding home from work and the El was packed. I had my wallet in my left pocket, my Walkman in my right, and my headphones on. (These were Walkman days.) I was dressed in mid-eighties regalia, linen pants with elephant legs and a pastel-striped shirt; my hair, though naturally curly, could have been permed. I was listening to the Talking Heads' "Burning Down the House" and swayed my shoulders in a stiff, white-guy way when I felt a tug—my head jerked to the side and I heard someone nearby exclaim, "Damn!" I guess I was lost in the music and didn't wonder why my head would have been tugged to the side. About thirty seconds later, my head jerked again, this time violently to the side, and I put my hand on the Walkman in my pocket.

"Damn!" I heard again through the Talking Heads, and now it finally dawned what was happening. I removed my headphones. In the packed El, I couldn't see who the pickpocket was—I could barely reach my hands to my pockets to keep hold of my wallet. But I did the best I could until the

ROBIN HEMLEY

train reached Addison. I knew that pickpockets love exits and entrances, anywhere people crowd around and jostle one another, so again I kept my hand on my wallet as I exited the train onto the wooden platform. Much of the train left with me. The Cubs were playing a day game against the Cardinals, and the train platform was awash in fans with blue hats and red hats, blue t-shirts and red t-shirts. I made my way down the stairs with the crowd and then to the exit. As I approached the turnstiles, the man in front of me, a young guy in a White Sox cap, definitely out of place, bent down as though he were going to sneak out of the El. I had seen guys jump a turnstile to get into an El station, but never anyone try to sneak out of one. It was free to leave. I put my hand in my pocket and felt another hand there, but only for a second.

"Damn," someone said behind me.

"Hey," I yelled, finally finding my voice. The guy in front of me took off running one way, while the guy in back ran off toward another exit. These were the types of pickpockets who rationalized their crime by seeking only the dumbest, most oblivious people they could find. People like me. What was I going to spend my money on anyway? More Talking Heads? More elephant pants and pastel shirts? I'm sure I looked like I could easily replace what they took. The problem was that no matter how hard they tried they couldn't take my money, and that just made *them* look stupid. Obviously, I had completely pissed them off. Even if they had succeeded in snatching my wallet, they would have been disappointed. Maybe I looked like a rich kid from the suburbs, but I made all of two hundred dollars a week, and in my wallet were a measly five dollars and one credit card with a twelve-hundred-dollar limit. Still, I sensed that there was more involved here than money.

A few years ago, the day after I had arrived in the Philippines after a twenty-four-hour trip, I let someone hold the door open for me when I exited a taxi. A few seconds later, my cell phone had disappeared. I hadn't felt a thing.

And this, the most difficult admission: ten years ago, when I was going through my divorce and was strapped for money, I found a wallet in the seat pocket of the plane I had just boarded. I looked through it and saw that it belonged to a Japanese man—his identification and credit cards were there, as well as seventy-five dollars. Ninety-nine times out of a hundred times I would have told the flight attendant about the wallet and turned it over. I have done such things in the past, many times. But not this time. Why didn't I at least take the money and leave the wallet in the seat pocket? I could have taken the seventy-five dollars and left the rest where it would have been discovered by a more honest passenger, or a flight attendant. I'd like to say I was insane. But I knew what I was doing, though perhaps not completely. Maybe I wanted power over another person's life even as mine was falling apart. I didn't know what to do with the man's wallet so I kept it. All of it, including his identification. Every few months I would come upon the wallet, sort through his cards, and stare at him. "Who are you?" I asked the photo, but I might as well have been asking myself. On many occasions, I wished I could give him back his money and the many hours (of worry, of canceling cards) that I stole from him.

If you ask me what a pickpocket looks like, I will be forced to answer, "C'est moi." In French, it takes out some of the sting.

A SUDDEN STORM BURSTS outside my hotel window as I get ready to attend an evening reading. The day has been sunny, but now the rain slashes sideways and people below dash for cover. The storm lasts fifteen minutes at most, and the sound of the rain is replaced by sirens. I ride the elevator down to the lobby and walk to the tram platform. While I wait for the 22, I notice two likely pickpockets, though in thinking this, I realize that if taken too far this game could be an exercise in stereotyping and poor judgment. But what choice do I have? Looking for a pickpocket when you really want one is harder than it might seem. The two men seem in their forties, hard-bitten with sallow complexions. One is short and wears a black beanie. The other is taller and wears a jeans jacket and paint-splattered pants. I edge closer to them, backward, so they can see the bulge in my back pocket. I feel like some horny barnyard animal trying to get other animals to notice my butt. They look at me in that uninterested way that people who are interested in you look, and converse in Czech or another Slavic language.

On the platform, the short man in the beanie speaks in soft tones to the taller man, his companion, who digs in his jeans jacket. He withdraws a cigarette pack, almost empty, and doesn't offer his friend one, but puts a cigarette to his lips and mumbles something. He holds the cigarette in his mouth without lighting it.

Pickpockets tend to work in small gangs. Two together and two off to the side, who pretend not to know the other two. You can spot them if you're looking. There are not so many of them really. It's a turf thing. Each gang has its own territory. Or so I've been told.

I don't like to earn anyone's disapproval, and though I don't know Hana well, she seems to regard me with an ironic smile when we meet. This is the difference between us, I think a little sadly as I watch my two pick-pockets on the platform. She has an ironic smile but is sincere while I have a façade of sincerity, and inside, well, I don't know.

I wait an unusually long amount of time on the platform, more than fifteen minutes, and there is still no sign of the 22. The crowd at the stop grows, which under the circumstances seems promising. The more pressed-up against my fellow passengers I am, the more likely I am to succeed.

I notice another man on my other side, dressed much like my two conferring pickpockets. He watches me, too, his mouth hanging slightly open. After twenty minutes, a lone 36 tram trundles up to the platform and two of my pickpockets get on, the tall man with the dangling cigarette and the man with his mouth open, who closes it and waves good-bye to a family, two children and his wife most likely, all of them speaking Italian.

That leaves only the man in the beanie who I'm certain now is no pickpocket at all, but simply a man, an ordinary man whose story I will never be privy to, because of the language barrier, because he will hop onto the tram and be whisked away to another life entirely, an honest life, no doubt. I regard him and his black beanie, which is the most curious thing about him, a cultural marker with which I am unfamiliar.

He and I wait side by side for ten more minutes without a tram in sight. Nearly half an hour has gone by when normally the trams run every seven or eight minutes. Finally, the 22 rattles toward us, but from a direction it has never come before. The road in front of the Pyramida is wide and straight and you can see the trams a quarter of a mile away as they approach, but this 22 has appeared unpredictably from tracks along a small side street. I regard the red and white tram warily. Should I board? There doesn't seem to be much of a choice. No other trams in sight. I step into the car, and the man in the beanie follows me. The doors close and he sits across from me, looking out the window.

Before long, I notice that the 22 has taken a turn, well, for the worse. It's following the route of the 36. The conductor made an announcement in Czech when I boarded the tram, and it certainly explained all, but my Czech is limited to a few words. As we head away from the direction I want to go in, I hear the steady peal of sirens and my imagination starts firing. An ambulance flashes by, then another, then a police car, and then a fire engine. I have no idea where I'm being taken or what's going on in the city, but surely something out of the ordinary is taking place.

BEFORE CLASS THE NEXT MORNING, I stop by the Prague Summer Program office on the first floor of Charles University to arm my fellow faculty with wallets. There are only two people in the office, located in a spacious if somewhat dilapidated building catty-corner to the Rudolfinum and near the banks of the Vltava. Richard Katrovas, in frayed jeans shorts and a black muscle shirt, sits at a desk in the middle of the room filling out forms. Hana sits at the farthest end of the room at a computer; she gives her ironic smile when she sees me, and a small wave.

"How's it going, buddy?" Richard asks. I sense he wants to call me "little buddy." "Any luck getting your pocket picked?"

"So far, no. I'm here to make some more wallets up." I tell him about Hana's reservations, which he dismisses. "The difference is that Prague is a city with a history of crimes of stealth. In the United States, it's brute force."

"So you want to help me out?"

Richard laughs. "Sure, I'll take one."

I'm not sure what I'm thinking. No pickpocket in his right mind would dare touch Richard's pocket. Built like a wrestler, Richard is also a black belt in karate, and not "this Tae Kwon Do shit where they give a black belt to practically anyone who can wave. Back when I did my karate training in Japan, a black belt really meant something."

There's tape on the table near Richard, so I attach the Czech and English versions of the letter together, back to back. I'm out of one-hundred-koruna notes, so I ask Richard if he has any. "I promise I'll pay you back," I say, feeling vaguely suspect.

Richard looks only slightly skeptical, but he hands me the money. I approach Hana at her desk. She's now chatting with another faculty member, Sean Clark. I explain my project to Sean and he, like Richard, laughs heartily and agrees to be one of my operatives. Hana doesn't exactly roll her eyes, but she smirks with a kind of patience no doubt born of coordinating the travel arrangements of over a hundred faculty and students in the program, and, more importantly, of being the mother of triplets.

The wallet I have earmarked for Richard I give to Sean instead. I have a good feeling about Sean: he's off to Bratislava in neighboring Slovakia for the weekend. Might as well try a different locale. Sean seems keen on the idea, too, and tries out the wallet in his back pocket. "Usually, I'm Mr. Security," he says. "I'm always the guy looking out for everyone else, telling them to be careful, but I can do this." Sean looks like a well-heeled guy, dressed in a polo shirt and tan slacks, the kind who might attract a pickpocket's attention. But, brawny and compact, he also looks like someone who could hurt you, though he radiates a kind of good humor that Richard doesn't. With Richard, it just looks that, if your hand comes anywhere in the vicinity of his butt, he'll kick yours. Frankly, we all radiate self-confidence and a purposefulness that seems as though it might deter potential pickpockets. I have . . . if not self-confidence, then at least a well-honed sense of street smarts I acquired (eventually) when I lived in

Chicago. It's not easy to unlearn that. I imagine pickpockets have quite specific criteria for the people they mark and one of them has to be befuddlement, a sense of being distracted and lost. I tend to walk with a sense of purpose and self-confidence even when distracted and lost.

After class, I head back in the direction of the Pyramida with a couple of my students, including my teaching assistant Joe, an affable and talkative guy in his thirties who spent years struggling in a band and then as a guitar teacher eking out fifteen bucks an hour, before making the clearheaded and practical decision to return to school to become a writer. Joe is my kind of person, as I have long been a soul of equal practicality and Yankee frugality. I am in fact so impractical that I have never successfully balanced a checkbook in my life, have never once made a sound financial decision, all 185 pounds of me, penny-wise and pound-foolish. The hopelessly artistic type like me, Joe is my perfect accomplice. He's not actually allowed by Richard to participate in my project. No student is. But he can be my sidekick. I have always wanted a sidekick, having instead a sidekick's name: Robin. I grew up as "Robin, the Boy Wonder," which in my case just meant that I wondered about a lot of things. Joe sports an earring in each ear, has a cool bald look going, and likes my jokes, the number one criterion to be hired (at the same hourly rate as dispensers of free advice) as my sidekick while in Prague.

As we walk across the bridge over the Vltava to the 22 tram stop, we talk about the storm the previous night. Evidently, not much happens in the Czech Republic besides "crimes of stealth," not even storms. The TV news that morning is full of The Storm, as though it were a new Russian invasion. There are shots of reporters standing beside fallen trees, looks of utter shock and amazement on their faces as though they were standing in front of the ruins of a tank. Not just one shot, but perhaps fifteen minutes of shots of horizontal trees, reporters speaking frantically into their mikes while stopped trams wait on the other side of the tree. The rest of the news consists of men moving the trees. Perhaps there is a subtext here I'm not getting. The current president of the Czech Republic refuses to acknowledge global warming. Ronald Reagan once famously stated that trees cause pollution. Perhaps the Czech government suspects the trees of a coup attempt.

These and other theories of Czech society I happily espouse to Joe as we head toward the tram. "This looks promising, dude," Joe tells me. Joe is one of the few people I know who can say *dude* and actually not sound ridiculous. He says it with just the right accent and intonation, the result no doubt of his years in the music industry.

"Got my mojo working," I say, and quickly decide I will never utter those words again in this life or the next. The pickings *do* look promising; there must be at least sixty tourists milling about the platform. The 22 tram going to the castle is, after all, one of the prime locales in Prague for being pick-pocketed. There are always only two tram cars, and so it's sure to be crowded. As the red and white tram rounds the corner, I pull my wallet out of my back pocket halfway. It's still too slim, but a good pickpocket won't have any trouble spotting it. The tram pulls in front of us and the doors open. I glance around as surreptitiously as possible to see who's boarding, to see if there are any likely prospects. A couple of policemen board right behind me. Thanks a lot, guys. I push my wallet completely into my back pocket again. The gesture has not gone unnoticed by Joe. "Nice move," he says.

"I've been working on it," I say.

I return full-handed that day to the Pyramida.

When the Pyramida was built in the 1980s it probably seemed the lap of luxury to visiting dignitaries and party bigwigs, but now it has the air of a decrepit cruise ship in dry dock. I like it for this very reason. Among its amenities are the Kafka Bar and the Kopernick restaurant. Somehow I doubt that in its Communist heyday the hotel ever boasted a Kafka Bar. My first visit to Prague was in 1990, not long after the Velvet Revolution, a twenty-four-hour jaunt that involved an eleven-hour train ride from Frankfurt. Kafka isn't a favorite of any totalitarian regime, and his home-town was no exception until the Velvet Revolution. A construction wall plastered with "Up with People" concert posters had blocked me from getting too close to Kafka's house, so I had my photo snapped in front of the wall with a diminutive bust of Kafka poking from the wall of a building behind me. It seemed funny and appropriate to me then that I couldn't actually reach Kafka's residence, which now houses a store brim-ming with Kafka mugs, Kafka posters, and Kafka umbrellas. The whole city is Kafka-crazy, when in his lifetime he was an outsider as a Jew and a German-speaker. He famously wrote of Prague as that "little mother with sharp claws." She still has her claws dug into him, and it's surprising there are no Kafka dinner cruises on the Vltava or a Kafka Karaoke Bar. If pickpocketing is a crime of stealth, so is the tourist industry. In any case, Kafka's house isn't even his house, as it turns out. The building he lived in, on the perimeter of Old Town Square and the Jewish Quarter, didn't exist back then. His house, along with almost all the buildings in the Jewish Quarter, a warren of twisting streets, was demolished, the entire district redone, except for its ancient synagogues, to fit the more orderly notions of Hapsburg urban planning.

At least the Pyramida has one authentic Kafka detail: Elevator C, dubbed (by me) the Kafka Memorial Elevator. Elevators are in fact the safest mode of transportation in the world, but the Kafka Elevator shudders between floors three and zero. Not a shiver, but a full-on shudder, approaching a spasm. And it's a sustained shudder. There's no way to avoid the Kafka Elevator (except by taking the stairs, which is a novel idea) because most often it is the one with the door open, bidding me to enter. And enter I do, mindful of and trusting in my little factoid about elevators being the safest mode of transportation, though I heard a gruesome anecdote about a man getting beheaded by an elevator when the doors closed on him and wouldn't let go even as it descended. Although I have been in the hotel for almost a week, the shuddering elevator has not been repaired, and so I also trust that the shuddering is simply the habit of this particular elevator, that certainly, if it were truly dangerous, they would have done something about it by now.

I wonder if perhaps I should say something about it to the front desk, but then I decide that surely someone already has mentioned something to them. The ambience of the Kafka Bar demands an adjacent Kafka Elevator! Still, I approach the front desk, where a tall young man stands regarding me as though from the top of an elevator shaft.

"Dobriden," he says, and I reply with the same greeting.

"The elevator over there shudders as it moves," I say. "I think it's about to snap its cable and send your guests hurtling to their deaths. Are you aware of the problem?"

"Yes, thank you," he says. "We will look into it."

Sadly, I have said no such thing. I am in fact a Kafka Elevator enabler. I imagine that someone else will say something, a sad but all-too-human reaction known as the Kitty Genovese Effect. Kitty Genovese was a young woman who was stabbed to death in New York in the 1960s with scores of witnesses. Not a crime of stealth. Before she died, she knocked on the doors of all of her neighbors asking for them to help her. None did. Some of them said later that they thought someone else would say something. Bloodcurdling cries for help can be interpreted in hundreds of ways, after all.

Slightly different circumstances, but the impulse is similar. Instead of saying something to the hotel employees, I head for the rack of tourist brochures by the front desk and grab a few to pad my wallet for the pickpocket project:

Welcome to the Casino President
YOU CAN EXPECT AN EXCITING NIGHT
Casino President

PRAGUE WALKS
Daily in English
Licensed Guides . . .
. . . Personal Care

Traditional Thai Massage
MUSEUM OF COMMUNISM
DREAM
REALITY
NIGHTMARE

I stick all the brochures in my wallet, with the Museum of Communism brochure in the front. Stalin is on the brochure's cover, seemingly condemning all pickpockets, his hand raised as if to strike them. Of course, I make sure that it doesn't block the letter with its hundred-koruna note taped to it. The money will still be the first thing a pickpocket sees, an angry Stalin second.

As I'm fooling around with the brochures, someone has placed a red velvet rope in front of the Kafka Elevator. Later that afternoon, the rope has vanished and the next time I ride the elevator, it shudders worse than ever. There seems something wonderfully charming in all this. At any rate, I like the gesture. "We're in control," the rope suggests. "We know there's a problem," it suggests. "Please do not enter," it suggests. And then the rope was taken away. "You might drop dead of a heart attack on the stairs, so why not chance the elevator?" it suggests. "It's already the weekend, and where are we going to find an elevator repairman on a Friday night?" it suggests. "Think positively," it suggests.

ON SATURDAY MORNING, I board a bus along with twenty students in the program for the city of Cesky Krumlov. Our guide is Milosz, a man in his mid-fifties whom I came to know the previous year when I took a trip led by him. Milosz is famous as a guide and has been featured on Samantha Brown's program on the Travel Channel. Bald, round-faced, intense in his fixed gaze, but soft-spoken and a soft chuckler rather than a hearty laugher, he is the type who has piles of books lining his floors, collects death masks and ossuary relics, and visits cemeteries around Europe on his days off, cataloguing information about the movements and lives of vanished peoples.

Sitting behind him on the bus, I wait for an opportune moment to tell him about my project, afraid that he might find it frivolous or vaguely insulting, as has Hana. But when I mention it, he seems intrigued and then delighted as he reads and rereads my letter to the pickpockets.

"You know, Robin," he says, "I like this very much. But this is a dying art. Now they more often than not surround you on the subway, a group of four or more men, and simply go through your pockets. They don't hurt you—it's intimidation, but there's no craft to it. It's simple robbery. I don't want to stereotype, but it might also help to have this put into the language of the Gypsies, the Roma. I have a friend at university who specializes in Romany, and I think he would be willing to translate this. Would you mind if I took a copy of the letter to him?"

This is tricky territory. Milosz is sensitive to the issue, but many Europeans are fiercely racist in their attitudes toward the Gypsies. Along with Jews, the Roma were decimated by the Nazis. To this day, mistrust and persecution dog them quite openly throughout Europe, particularly in the East. As a Jew, I'm terrified of such stereotypes: the Jews became merchants in Europe because they were not allowed to own land, and they lent money because Christians were not allowed to lend money at interest. Hence the reputation that Jews are money-grubbing. American males in nineteenth-century America thought doing laundry was women's work, but Chinese men had no such stigma attached to the activity. So they opened up laundries in the West: hence the Chinese suddenly became known in America as experts at doing laundry, and racist jokes were common in my youth, the punch line being, "No tickee, no washee." The Roma have long been accused of everything from petty theft to child abduction, and if some resort to petty theft as a result of being constantly shunned and run out of town, then it's not hard to see them as the real victims.

Still, I make up a full wallet, complete with a one-hundred-crown note taped to it, for Milosz to give to someone who might stand a chance of having his pocket picked.

I suppose here I should say a few words about fate. I've always been attracted to the concept, though it's much out of fashion among my crowd. There's something decidedly nineteenth-century about it, and perhaps egotistical as well, that each of us has a destiny mapped out by forces unseen, and yet I have to admit that it seems we do. The way to make God laugh, as the saying goes, is to make a plan. Whether the forces guiding us are geopolitical or supernatural, or both, part of living seems to be learning the lesson repeatedly that we are not in control. If you tempt fate, two things generally happen. Let's call one the Law of Oppositional Desire and the other the Law of Fulfilled Desire. Unfortunately, neither is desirable.

When the Nazis marched into Prague, the German "protector" of the city, Reinhart Heinrich, noticed the statues of famous composers atop the Rudolfinum, the imposing state theater catty-corner to Charles University, a structure I pass every day on my way to and from my classes. He decided that the statue of the "Jew composer" Mendelssohn-Bartholdy should be immediately taken down and disposed of. So he ordered this to be done, and a group of soldiers went to the roof to demolish Mendelssohn-Bartholdy's likeness. The problem was that there were no plaques indicating which composer was which and so they decided to determine who was Jewish by other means, namely to find the statue with the biggest nose. After determining which statue that was, they carted it away, only to realize later it was not Mendelssohn-Bartholdy's at all, but Wagner's, Hitler's favorite composer.

This is the Law of Oppositional Desire.

The Law of Fulfilled Desire can be summed up in the famous dictum, "Be careful what you wish for."

I return from Cesky Krumlov with a newly purchased fanny pack, intent on redoubling my efforts in Prague to become someone's victim. Fanny packs are almost irresistible to pickpockets, especially if the packs are turned around on the victim's side. If I were a pickpocket, I would hand out free fanny packs at street corners. Until someone invents a fanny pack with nerve endings, they will remain one of the most pickpocket-friendly items you can buy. It's funny that we keep our money in places where we are least likely to feel it removed. In my case, I want to be fully conscious, even defiant in the face of dispossession. Come on then, world! Here are my pockets. Do I need to turn them inside out for you?

Sadly, I learn that Sean Clark, who went to Bratislava on a pickpocketing mission, has returned with his wallet intact. Sean tells me that his friends in Bratislava took him to an area known as prime pickpocketing territory, a Gypsy area. Again I find myself uncomfortable confronting stereotypes of Roma, but nearly everyone I tell about my project mentions them and tells me I should have my note translated into their language. Sean's friends took him to a Gypsy area and pointed to a square where he was sure to attract attention. By his account, he stood near a group of Gypsy women, who eyed him but kept their distance, though his wallet bulged from his back pocket. "I tried everything," he tells me.

"I know why they won't come near you," one of his friends said after an hour of trying to bait pickpockets. "Because you look like you might arrest them."

Yes, of course. Who but a policeman—and a naïve one at that—would stand "chalantly" (to coin a word), aiming his butt at a group of women he thinks are pickpockets?

But Sean was lucky, because he could have had more than his pocket picked. As Milosz told me, the art form is dying. Not only do men on subways simply surround the victim and go through his pockets, but a woman who in days past might have tried to steal undetected now pretends to proposition the victim. She rubs against him, suggests that they visit a hotel, whispers what she wants to do to him in private, and then reaches down to his groin and starts massaging. If she still has him in thrall at this point, she reaches a little farther down (maybe inside his pants if she can manage it), grabs his balls, and squeezes, digging her fingernails into them.

"Give me your wallet. Now!" And she doesn't wait for him to answer, because he probably can't answer very well. She reaches with her free hand, finds his wallet, and takes it, locking him with her eyes before she lets go, indicating with a little flip of her hair the man standing in the shadows. A stranger? Perhaps part of the ruse, someone she doesn't even know. But the man in the shadows nods to you, raises his eyebrows and smiles, and well, it is best just to cut bait, as they say, and consider yourself lucky.

Not very artful, but effective.

After teaching and lunch, I decide to try out my new fanny pack. I head first to the Charles Bridge. Milosz suggested I might want to go there, listen to jazz played by street performers and thereby have a pleasurable experience while being robbed. Parts of the bridge are cordoned off while repairs are being made, which funnels the tourists into a teeming lane. I check my wallet in my fanny pack to make sure it's unsecured. I have the fanny pack positioned practically on my fanny, zipper open, wallet poking out alluringly. I have even stuck a few dollar bills in the wallet in such a way that they're visible too. I look and feel sluttish. Take me, take me, take me. Does desperation have a scent?

A puppeteer attracts my attention. He works two marionettes, one dressed like a groom with a top hat, dancing with a bear to a tango. How the puppeteer, an elderly man with a silver mustache, is able to manipulate the two as they dance, without entangling them, impresses me, as it impresses the other tourists. The trick is making it look natural. The small group laughs and so do I as the groom puppet bends the bear in a swooning embrace at just the right moment. How much practice that one move must take. I stand with the semicircled crowd, trying to put myself in the way of passersby who will have to pass close by, perhaps brushing me. My senses are on high alert, just the opposite of the ideal of total absorption and distraction. A young man and a woman lounge near the railing of the bridge, below one of the statues of the saints.

This is a problem. They have a clear view of my fanny pack and will certainly notice someone trying to rob me. With my luck, they'll be like disapproving Hana, a concerned citizen who shouts at pickpockets. Why can't people (other than me) mind their own business?

I move on to a group of street musicians playing the Hoagy Carmichael standard "Stardust." Standing in the midst of the circle around them, I scan the crowd for potential pickpockets. As I do so, the woman beside me with a yellow purse on her shoulder shifts her weight away from me and a man in a jeans jacket, one I thought could be a pickpocket, does the same. What's more, neither seems aware of this movement, this subtle protective repositioning of their bodies. Both are completely engrossed as they watch the four musicians play their instruments. But their bodies have alerted them to my presence: the woman cuts her eyes in my direction and touches the strap of her bag. The man separates himself from the crowd and approaches the spot in front of the band where they are selling their CDs. He picks one up and studies it.

I decide to walk home, willing myself to forget who I am, what I carry. I am just some dumb tourist, I tell myself. Lost in the sights. Without a care. I feel something behind me. Turning around, I see blue.

Three nuns stalking me.

The next day, I visit Old Town Square fifteen minutes before the hour and stare up with all the other tourists at the famous clock there with its mechanical figures that dance every hour. This is one of the best locales in which to have your pocket picked. A French tourist taps me on the shoulder and points to my open fanny pack, making a hand motion to zip it up.

Richard told me that in sixteen years of running the program, every year several participants and faculty have been pickpocketed. Every year. Until this one.

On my final day in Prague, as I walk one last time across Charles Bridge, I tug my wallet to make sure that it's poking out of its pouch. A piece of paper, folded many times, pops out of the fanny pack and onto the bridge. I pick it up before it can be trampled and retreat to the side of the bridge, out of the way of the crowd rushing along. "Open me," someone has written on the paper in a printed hand, like a child's. I don't recognize the writing, but it reminds me a bit of *Alice in Wonderland*.

"We have become enormous / just knowing each other / with eyes closed," the note inside reads, identified as a quote from a poem by Octavio Paz. There are no other identifying marks, no signature.

Apparently, someone (one of my students? Joe? Richard? Sean? Even Hana?) has reverse-pickpocketed me, slipped me the unsigned note when I was distracted. An odd but wonderful quote! It unnerves me slightly because it's so intimate, the kind of note one lover would pass to another, not an anonymous note tucked by a friend, colleague, or acquaintance into

ROBIN HEMLEY

a fanny pack. I have been around so many people on this day. It could have been anyone. But that makes it all the more wonderful. The paradox, the beauty of incomprehension. I don't want to find out who has done this, I tell myself.

Passing by the man with the marionettes, who's having a cigarette break, I take out all the accumulated change from my pocket, and pour it into his hat. But I keep the note. Perhaps it's all I need right now. The man raises his eyebrows. Gratitude mixed with perplexity? He isn't doing anything. He's on break. He hasn't given me a thing in return. Why so many coins? What is wrong with them? With me? I nod to him and then I continue on my way across the crowded bridge.

INTERVIEW
Robin Hemley, author of "The Pickpocket Project"

Q: You tend toward the meta-aspects of writing in your work. Why do you think that is?

A: I think that the essay is a particularly interrogatory form. We write in order to see what we think: our own thoughts are revealed to us as we write, kind of like an old ticker tape machine giving us the news as it threads though our fingers. We read the essay to see a mind at work on the page—or at least that's why I read. That's one of the hallmarks of the essay. It's a constantly questioning and recursive form. So it's natural that an essay would concern itself with its own form and ask the question, "Why do I exist?" in much the way its author asks the same question.

Q: From "Pickpocket":

> I love to board trams and buses without knowing where I'm going and let
> them carry me away. I like to pick up real estate books and imagine what
> it would be like to live wherever I go. So this is about curiosity, but it's also
> about imagination. Can I engage imaginatively with a pickpocket? Can I
> turn his or her manipulation of me around and manipulate back?

Being led by a writer through an essay is similar to your penchant for boarding trams and buses for places unknown. What then of this concept of manipulation in the form of the essay? How might you, as a writer, manipulate a reader? Or when do you feel manipulated by a writer?

A: All art manipulates. That's part of the project. You're trying to get the reader or viewer to engage with the world you've created, and in doing so you lead the reader toward certain effects, emotions, questions, concerns. The most obvious example of artistic manipulation is in a film, say, a horror film or a thriller. In Alfred Hitchcock's *Psycho*, there's a highly manipulative moment when a hapless detective sent to investigate Janet Leigh's disappearance climbs the stairs of the scary mansion. The camera angle is a high one, looking down on the detective as he climbs the stairs. The point of view is that of a bird of prey. The music swells and we in the audience are thinking, "No, can't you hear the bloody music! Turn around and flee for your life." That's manipulation, brilliant manipulation, and I'm all for it. I don't want Hitchcock to suddenly appear on screen and say, "Listen, I don't want anyone to be afraid or concerned in the least. This is a film, remember?" No, he wants you to be terrified. Essayists manipulate in various ways: through word choice, pacing, the tone of a piece, the divulging of information, even the degree to which the essayist involves the reader in the dilemma or problem he or she is addressing in the essay. Sometimes the essayist is trying to manipulate the reader simply to withhold judgment, to set aside the usual pieties and confident beliefs the reader holds, to shake these up a bit. In Orwell's famous essay "A Hanging," he takes us through a step-by-step account of a prisoner's last minutes before being hanged in British colonial Burma. At one point, he depicts the prisoner stepping around a puddle on his path to the gallows, a moment that stuns Orwell, who is moved by the fact that the prisoner, knowing he's going to die, retains all the habits of living and self-protection. Frankly, who knows whether this moment ever indeed happened. Personally, I don't care, because I have a high tolerance for manipulation when it's done for some higher artistic purpose. I'm *not* a fan of being manipulated for a writer's self-aggrandizement, as is the case with those sensational memoirs in which you find out after reading a book that the author has made up nearly everything, simply to make the book more saleable. But manipulation in itself is not bad. Famously, Orwell never tells us what the condemned man has been found guilty of. If it's some heinous crime, some of us might feel less sympathy for him, but Orwell doesn't want the nature of the crime to interfere with his opposition to the death penalty.

Artistic manipulation is not a moral issue, but a technical one. I'm much more interested in how an essayist manipulates than whether or not it's done. I always assume I'm being manipulated.

Q: I cannot think of a better example, cinematically, than Hitchcock. Reading your answer, I immediately thought of the technical manipulation in *Rope* (1948), for which the film set had walls on rails that would

be moved so as not to disrupt the scene with a cut. He also had a remarkable sense of play in the placement of the camera (in *Rope*, again, behind
the liquor bottles, or in *Psycho*, through the eyes of Norman Bates into
the motel room next door), to offer the viewer a distinct and unusual
perspective. Technical manipulation indeed, whereas recent filmmakers
(Christopher Nolan, Charlie Kaufman, M. Night Shyamalan) manipulate
at the story level.

In "Pickpocket," you write about how you tried to manipulate reality in
order to write about that created reality (and it didn't work—reality would
not bend to the will of the art). Do you agree with that assessment? And
how do you think writers manipulate reality for or in their work?

A: I think you're right here. Partially right. I tried to manipulate reality,
and it didn't work in that I wasn't pickpocketed. I wasn't going to fabri-
cate an incident for the sake of the narrative. Instead, I changed the way I
thought about reality: that was the solution for this essay. *Not* being pickpocketed was in a sense the best possible outcome. In art, it's the element
of surprise we're after, shock, seeing something new, feeling alive in that
dousing that happens when we're splashed in the face with a new perspective. In a way, I was trying to force the universe to play by my rules and it
wouldn't. I couldn't control it, and I was given something when I wanted
something taken away. Even so, I was of course manipulating the prose.
What I wrote down was not what I experienced. What you write down
is not what you experience. It's always a translation of experience, and in
many ways a crude one. Language approaches experience but never arrives
at it. Reading is of course an experience, but it's not the same experience
as what's being re-created. The goal is not slavishly to set down experience
on a platter, whole and alive and still flopping around, but to present it
artfully, to fillet it, as it were.

Q: "What you write down is not what you experience." Beyond being an
extremely astute observation that I believe all writers should ponder in
relation to their own writing, that should be a creative writing program's
slogan; I can see it in half-page ads in *Poets and Writers*. Your program at
Iowa has a creative nonfiction conference called NonfictioNow, which is
held every other year. What have been some of the most engaging discussions or panels in recent years that you feel encapsulate the genre? Any
involving metawriting?

A: We're a genre full of brewing controversies, which is great. As far
as I'm concerned, all writers should be cultural provocateurs, and that's
what we try to do with NonfictioNow, constantly to reinvent and renew
the genre, without throwing away tradition, of course. So, yes, we had

David Shields and a *Reality Hunger* panel at the last conference, as well as Rebecca Solnit challenging us to write heroically, that is, with an agenda beyond the self, and then an address by Alison Bechdel coming right back at Solnit and claiming that the personal can be heroic at times too. We have or will have all of these talks from the three NonfictioNow conferences on-line, so you can hear for yourself and decide which panels and discussions engage you. I'm sure we've had panels dealing with metawriting and the self-consciousness of the genre, but the specific titles escape me at the moment.

Q: Since you mention the self-versus-other issue, I'd like to point to a review in a January 2011 *New York Times Sunday Book Review*, in which "the age of oversharing" is attributed to the "disgorging" of the memoir by writers who write uninterestingly about the "unexceptional." To be sure, we live in a time of second-by-second status updates and Tweets, yet this reviewer argues, erroneously, I believe, that the ordinary cannot be extraordinary. What do you think has precipitated the rise of the memoir, and what's your take on it?

A: That's a large question. But first of all, what's unexceptional and unoriginal is such a potshot taken at memoirists. It's simply an easy place of comfort where the nonmemoirist may feel superior. Even if such a reviewer can point to a particularly egregious example, what does that prove? That there are bad memoirists? Indeed. As we know, there are no bad novelists or bad poets. None of them are ever self-indulgent. None of them take on the quotidian in a boring fashion. I'm not even sure what the reviewer refers to when she or he writes of the "unexceptional." There are only unexceptional writers, not unexceptional subjects. Nearly anything can be made amazing by an amazing writer. I could list dozens, but how about two, one from fiction and one from nonfiction? In fiction, the winner of the Unexceptional Moments Award is Nicholson Baker for his novel *The Mezzanine*, which takes place in its entirety during a thirty-second escalator ride. After which the protagonist is presumably disgorged into similarly unremarkable moments of his life. In nonfiction, I'd like to nominate Elisabeth Tova Bailey for her memoir *The Sound of a Wild Snail Eating*. This lovely book tracks the progress of a snail as the author lies in bed recovering from a debilitating illness. Both are wonderful books written in different modes about unexceptional moments. It's the writing, of course, that makes the work exceptional.

I also argue (and have done so in print before) that memoir has existed for a long time. In my parents' day, we used to call memoirs "first novels." It was a given that a writer's first novel was likely a thinly veiled roman à clef. I wrote a piece on this for *Creative Nonfiction* recently, and I'd refer the reader to that article if she or he wants to know more on this subject. As for that reviewer for the *New York Times*, please send a copy of your book when it's finished, or at least my answer, with my compliments.

Q: As metawriters, we inherently write about ourselves (as writers). What risks or challenges might we face when implicating ourselves in our own work?

A: I think that the primary danger of self-implication is what I like to sum up as: "A little self-loathing goes a long way." It's possible to be too confessional, too self-conscious. If you don't modulate the tone, if you don't exert some self-control, you might wind up sounding weepy, whiny, self-indulgent, and precious, or some combination of these unwanted attributes. You have to consider the poor reader, after all. There's only so much self-implication the poor dear can stand. You might send him or her running for the nearest vampire book if you're not careful.

"The relationship to truth, especially in memoir, is a little, well, bendy. And that seemed like an apt comparison to what I aim to do when I write a screenplay, or just what I do naturally."

Excerpts from *Creative Nonfiction*

CREATIVE NONFICTION is a tale of a female undergraduate working on a screenplay in hopes of being admitted into a screenwriting program, while struggling with dating and friendship issues in her college dorm. The fictional elements, the italicized portions narrated by Ella's explanatory voice-over (v.o.), are juxtaposed with the nonfictional elements of what is happening in her life. She struggles in her fiction, as her friends question her on elements of plot, setting, and plausibility. The excerpts appearing here highlight the fictional screenplay, Ella's metawriting discussion with her professor, and real-life conversations that address the role that writing plays in her life.

INT. CLASSROOM, DAY

A GIRL sits at a desk in a classroom of girls in school uniforms. A MAN, the teacher, well dressed, about fifty, hands her back a poem with a large A written on it and a note that says, "See me after class."

ELLA (v.o.): *Well, this girl in high school has taken up with her English teacher. He loves her poetry, which is how it starts . . . You know, that whole "see me after class" thing.*

RURAL ROAD, DAY

THE GIRL and THE TEACHER drive in an old-fashioned convertible and pull into the driveway of a country cabin.

ELLA (v.o.): *And he takes her away to this cabin he has in the country . . .*

CHRIS (v.o.): *To buck it?*

ELLA (v.o.): *What does "buck it" mean?*

CHRIS (v.o.): *Y'know . . .*

INT. COUNTRY CABIN, NIGHT

THE GIRL sits at a table. She is tied to a chair with ropes, and she's working at an old-fashioned typewriter. THE MAN, her teacher, leans over her, smiling at her work and pointing out mistakes.

ELLA (v.o.): *He keeps her there for three years. And he just makes her sit there at a typewriter and write. And you'd think she'd be miserable, obviously, but instead she's under a spell of creative happiness.*
[. . .]

INT. ELLA'S DORM ROOM, NIGHT

ELLA, nineteen, played by the same actress as THE GIRL, sits on her bed wearing sweatpants and a t-shirt. Above the bed are a number of old photographs of family members. The room is lit by Christmas lights. CHRIS, about Ella's age, sits in a chair, holding a mug.

CHRIS: I can't follow this, Ella.

ELLA: It's going to be different once it's on the page, you know? I'll tie up all the loose ends . . . And hopefully it'll be funny, you know?

CHRIS: Funny?

ELLA: Well, *I* think the theft and abuse of minors is funny . . . Anyway . . . I'm sure you don't want to hear about this.

CHRIS: No.

ELLA: Well, thank you for your honesty.

CHRIS: I mean, I *do* want to hear about it, but I have to ask you something.

ELLA: Yes, I'll marry you. No, I don't do anal . . .

CHRIS: What?

ELLA: I'm sorry. That wasn't even funny. My brain is decaying.

CHRIS: Well, my *room* is decaying. Seriously, there's a strange mold growing in my room, and it's giving me a headache. I was wondering if I could sleep on your floor.

ELLA: What did you do?

CHRIS: It's not me, I swear! My room is right next to the bathroom, you know, and every time someone flushes, some water leaks through this hole in my wall. Plus the flushing, like, thunders in my ears. I just wanna be like, "Fuckers, don't flush!"

ELLA: That would be selfish of you . . . to make everyone stop flushing.

CHRIS: I'm a selfish guy . . . Anyway, I brought you this mug of jug wine as an offering . . .

ELLA: Well, it's fine. In fact, I don't even want your jug wine. I really don't think that would help me right now.

CHRIS: Okay . . .

CHRIS gulps down the mug of wine.

ELLA: You couldn't sleep at Yvette's?

CHRIS: I don't want to sleep at Yvette's.

ELLA: Because then you'd have to sleep *with* Yvette?

CHRIS: That's not the part I mind. It's the part afterward, you know, when we have to talk.

ELLA: You're mean.

CHRIS: I'm honest.

ELLA: She seems sweet . . . I mean, like, *stupid* sweet, but . . . sweet.

CHRIS: Yeah. I don't know. First, she's a cinema studies major, which is a fucking joke.

ELLA: Hey!

CHRIS: What? You're creative writing.

ELLA: Yeah, but I'm writing this screenplay and I'm feeling feelings.

CHRIS: Feeling feelings?

ELLA: Yeah . . . If I ever had a band, it would be called Feeling Feelings.

CHRIS: If I ever had a band, it would be called the Shadow Band.

ELLA: Oh, that's really good!

CHRIS: Thank you. I know . . .

ELLA: Elucidate for me. Why is cinema studies such a joke?

CHRIS: Cinema studies kids just, like, write papers that overuse the word *hegemony*.

ELLA: Oh, be more creative. *Hegemony* is the token word people use to describe, like, quintessential college pretentiousness.

CHRIS: Whatever . . . And do you know what Yvette's favorite movie is?

ELLA: No.

CHRIS: *Homeward Bound!*

ELLA: The one about the dogs on a massive adventure?

CHRIS: Yeah.

ELLA: Maybe she's just incredibly ironic . . . Like, super-hip in a way we can't even comprehend.

CHRIS: No.

ELLA: Okay . . . Well, you can sleep here, but I'm going to go to bed, like, basically now.

[. . .]

INT. CLASSROOM, DAY

College students at desks form a semicircle. ELLA is one of them. Professor Gibbard stands at the head of the room. A female student named SIRI, dressed in typical semihippie gear, reads a poem aloud.

SIRI: And so
>you left your things to rot around
>the edges of my room
>a fish in a pan
>a sock
>and an old shirt
>of your father's
>I don't
>even know him
>but I know you
>and the way you broke three bones
>in the wrist
>of my heart.

The class is silent.

PROF. GIBBARD: All right . . . Thank you, Siri. Who'd like to start us out with some feedback for Siri? I want you to let Siri know what works in this poem, what's strong in the voice of this poem. I also want you to let her know where it's weaker, where there are gaps.
(beat)
All right, I'll start. Siri, I think you do an excellent job of capturing the way a person's presence can exist even in their absence. I think that is a concept that can easily become trite, you walk that fine line, and you walk it well.

SIRI smiles appreciatively. STEVE raises his hand.

PROF. GIBBARD: Yes . . . (He looks over his attendance list to locate his name) Steve . . .

STEVE: I thought it *was* trite sometimes.

PROF. GIBBARD: All right . . . Well, can you point Siri to some places in the text that you feel could be fleshed out, made fresher . . . ?

STEVE: Um . . . Let's see . . . Okay . . . I felt that the part where you mentioned a motel vacancy sign just felt obvious, like things I've read before. It's, like, a classic Americana image that comes from nowhere.

PROF. GIBBARD: You know, I don't disagree . . .

STEVE: Cool.

ELLA raises her hand.

PROF. GIBBARD: Yes, Ella.

ELLA: Well, to start, I thought that the image of the three bones in the wrist of the heart was wonderful. And it was odd, the idea of the heart as the whole body, but it was poignant, because it can often feel as though the heart, or heartbreak for that matter, *is* the whole body.

PROF. GIBBARD: Yes. That was great.

ELLA: One area I was less enthused about, although this is just really a minor note, was the thing about the fish in the pan. The whole poem had a pretty prosy, like, confessional tone, and then you just threw in this totally surreal detail that really threw me off. Like, everything else felt as though it could have really happened, except this fish in the pan.

PROF. GIBBARD: I agree. I was actually going to make that same note. (SIRI raises her hand.) Yes, Siri . . . I generally like the workshopee to wait until the discussion is done before chiming in.

SIRI: I'll be quick.

PROF. GIBBARD: All right.

SIRI: Um, it's about the fish thing . . . I just don't see how it could be unrealistic, because it actually happened, you know?

PROF. GIBBARD: I'm not sure I do . . .

SIRI: My ex-boyfriend left this fish in this pan in my room. I was just doing what I always do, which is writing what I see.

INT. COLLEGE LIBRARY, DAY

ELLA and HARRY sit at a table. Both are working on laptops, surrounded by books. Harry is Ella's age, with thick-frame glasses.

ELLA: You keep a journal, right?

HARRY: Of course.

ELLA: Okay . . . when you write in your journal, do you, like, think about the quality of what you're writing?

HARRY: I try not to . . . I try to just let it flow. I mean, I'm not writing for an audience, so the whole thing seems unimportant . . . Which is probably why I spend so little time writing in it . . . (He returns to working.) I mean, it's a different story with my blog.

ELLA: You have a blog?

HARRY: Of course I have a blog.

ELLA: What do you mean, "Of course I have a blog"?

HARRY: I feel like I don't know anyone without a blog.

ELLA: Really?

HARRY: Yeah.

ELLA: *I* don't have a blog.

HARRY: Well . . . I'm sorry that you're blogless.

ELLA: Why haven't you ever shown me your blog?

HARRY: I don't know . . . I guess I just show it to my blog friends.

[...]

HARRY: Let's get back to work, come on.

ELLA: I can't do this. I can't write this.

HARRY: Then don't.

ELLA: Easy for you to say. I want to take this screenwriting workshop. In fact, I have to take this screenwriting workshop if I want my degree to say, "Creative Writing" on it . . .

HARRY: See, this is why I'm an English major. I think being an English major is more serious-sounding anyway. Some of those creative writing classes seem so *bogus* . . .

ELLA: (slightly defensive) Which ones?

HARRY: I don't know . . . Exercises in translation.

ELLA: No, that's serious! You have to know a foreign language to do that!

HARRY: Okay, what about creative nonfiction?

ELLA: What about it?

HARRY: Bogus!

ELLA: No! It's like journalistic prose.

HARRY: Then why not just journalism?

ELLA: Because you can be more creative!

HARRY: You mean you can *lie*?

ELLA: No!

(pause)

HARRY: What's the script called?

ELLA: It has been tentatively titled, "50 Ways to Leave Your Lover."

HARRY: Isn't that a Paul Simon song? Don't you need permission from Paul Simon?

ELLA: That's why it's tentative.

HARRY: What have you actually written so far? Has the girl escaped from her teacher's house?

ELLA: (panicked) I already told you about the plot?

HARRY: Vaguely.

ELLA: I'm talking about it too much! I read some article somewhere about authors who talked about things until they were unable to write them, because they'd just talked it all out.

HARRY: And you think you've done that?

ELLA: It's a distinct possibility. (Pause. She looks miserable.) You wanna know where I'm at in the screenplay?

HARRY: I do . . . And then I'll post your progress on my blog.

EXT. UNDERNEATH CABIN PORCH, NIGHT

THE GIRL is on all fours, wearing a white nightgown. She is bleeding from her lip and looks generally battered and manhandled.

ELLA (v.o.): *So she's finally made her escape and she's crouching under the porch. A switch just flipped in her mind and she's done there, she wants out. She told him so, and he beat her. She ran out and is hiding.*

HARRY (v.o.): *What changed her mind?*

ELLA (v.o.): *Just chalk it up to, like, the mysteries of human experience, okay? And you can hear her panting. You hear leaves crinkling under her hands and knees. But I don't know how much detail I'm actually meant to include in the script, about that stuff . . .*

INT. LIBRARY, DAY

ELLA is looking at HARRY questioningly.

HARRY: Don't ask me. I don't know.

ELLA: Well, I have all these details in my head. Like, in her white night-gown, her breasts are just pendulous . . . almost bovine . . .

EXT. UNDERNEATH CABIN PORCH, NIGHT

THE GIRL'S breasts are noticeably larger than they were in the last shot, and her nipples are erect.

HARRY (v.o.): *Why?*

EXT. CABIN PORCH, NIGHT

THE MAN paces on the porch, looking out into the woods for THE GIRL.

ELLA (v.o.): *Because . . . And so the man is up on the porch. She can hear him walking around, and so she makes a run for it. She just takes a chance. It's life or death, she feels. . . .*

THE GIRL emerges from below the porch and goes running through the woods.
[. . .]

EXT. RURAL ROAD, NIGHT

THE GIRL is standing at the edge of the woods and the road, in her white nightgown. She holds her thumb out shakily, waiting for a car. She is cut up and bleeding from her feet and legs.

ELLA (v.o.): *The girl has finally run away. . . . And she's run through the woods. She's all bloody, all shaken up, but she's been through so much she's almost placid. Like, deadened . . . And she's waiting for a car.*

Two cars pass and don't slow down. A third car, a safari jeep, finally slows to a halt.

ELLA (v.o.): *A few pass but don't stop. Finally a safari jeep, the canvas-top kind, stops.*

The passenger side of the car opens. A WOMAN is inside, dressed in military fatigues. She motions for THE GIRL to get in. The girl does.

INT. JEEP, NIGHT

THE WOMAN is talking to THE GIRL, making passionate hand gestures even as she drives.

ELLA (v.o.): *The woman inside the car is, like, a totally militant feminist. The kind who thinks all sex is rape, all men are pigs.*

CHRIS (v.o.): *She sounds like the girls who live in the women's collective off South Quad.*

ELLA (v.o.): *Yeah . . . But more intense. This woman warns the girl not to call the police, that they won't help her escape her teacher because, you know, police are men and don't have the best interests of female-kind at heart. And the girl is so impressionable that she believes her.*

EXT. RURAL ROAD, NIGHT

THE WOMAN and THE GIRL stand in back of the jeep with the trunk open. The girl is holding her arms above her head, allowing the woman to remove her bloody nightshirt and change her into some army fatigues.

ELLA (v.o.): *And she dresses the girl in military fatigues . . .*

EXT. DOWNTOWN CITY STREET, EARLY MORNING

THE WOMAN is letting THE GIRL out of the car. The car drives away, and the girl stands in the street, looking around confusedly. Then she walks forward.

ELLA (v.o.): *And the woman lets the girl loose on the streets of some small city.*

CHRIS (v.o.): *Where is this taking place?*

ELLA (v.o.): *Um . . . Maine? New Hampshire?*
[. . .]

EXT. COLLEGE CAMPUS, NIGHT

All bundled up. ELLA and EDIE walk along a path.

EDIE: So when last I checked in, the girl was being picked up by some radical follower of Andrea Dworkin in a canvas-top jeep.

ELLA: Oh, that lady dropped her off in the city.

EDIE: New York?

ELLA: No. Portland . . . Maine, I think.

EXT. CITY STREET, DAY

THE GIRL stands in front of a store window, dressed in fatigues. A PUNK GIRL with blue hair is begging for change.

ELLA (v.o.): *She meets this girl. This young punk runaway with, like, Technicolor hair.*

THE PUNK GIRL taps THE GIRL. They begin conversing.

ELLA (v.o.): *And she trusts the girl. She explains her predicament to her. And the girl wants to help.*

EDIE (v.o.): *Well, that's nice.*

INT. SQUAT HOUSE, NIGHT

THE GIRL and THE PUNK GIRL are sitting on a bed surrounded by other punks and punk posters.

ELLA (v.o.): *She lets her come stay at her squat with her, listen to lots of punk music, hang with her friends.*

EDIE (v.o.): *What do you know about punk?*

ELLA (v.o.): *Um . . .*

EDIE (v.o.): *Exactly.*

ELLA (v.o.): *Don't be ornery . . .*

EDIE (v.o.): *Sorry.*

EXT. GAS STATION, DAY

THE GIRL and THE PUNK GIRL are opening the door to a bathroom. The sign on the door of the bathroom says, "WOMEN," but the word *women* has been crossed out with a Sharpie and replaced by the word "SLUTS."

ELLA (v.o.): *And the punk girl wants to help the girl stay, you know, incognito. You know, the man is crafty, he could appear at any time. So the punk girl dyes the girl's hair for her. They go to a gas station bathroom where there's running water.*

INT. GAS STATION BATHROOM, DAY

Fluorescent lamps and mirrors abound. The tiles are white but stained. THE PUNK GIRL is washing THE GIRL'S hair out in the sink. The water runs blue. The girl lifts her head and shakes out her newly blue hair in the mirror.

INT. DORM HALLWAY, NIGHT

ELLA stumbles drunkenly along the fluorescent-lit hallway. She reaches her room and breathes deeply before opening the door.
[. . .]

EXT. BEACH

THE GIRL sits on a blanket with a few old women. They are covered in tanning oil and smoke cigarettes.

ELLA (v.o.): *I don't know where this fits in. I don't know how. But she wants so badly to feel like she's a part of things that she joins flocks of old women, groups of old friends, and imitates their physicality.*

[...]

INT. ELLA'S ROOM, NIGHT

The room is lit with Christmas lights. Music is playing. CARLY and CHRIS sit on the rug by the door, talking, and ELLA and DIMITRI sit on the bed.

ELLA: You're glad to be back in school now?

DIMITRI: Yeah. Music, man. It's it for me. I can't imagine myself doing anything else. I have to do it.

ELLA: Well, I hear that's how artists in all disciplines feel . . .

DIMITRI: Chris tells me you're a writer.

ELLA: He does?

DIMITRI: What? Is he lying? Because I'll tell you something. I've known Chris a long time. He was my first friend in the United States, man. I met him at music school. And before I could even speak English, he would play with me on the piano, communicate with me. The greatest guy . . . I could marry that guy. But he lies . . . a lot.

ELLA: Oh . . . Well, he didn't lie about the writing. I write.

DIMITRI: And can you see yourself doing anything else?

ELLA: No. Well, maybe . . . I can maybe see myself being a notary public.

DIMITRI: (laughing) Like someone who stamps documents?

ELLA: Yeah. My grandpa was one. It wasn't his whole career. It was just a side thing. He was heavy into certifications.

DIMITRI: (laughing) You're funny, you know that?

ELLA: Thanks. You too.

DIMITRI: No . . . You're funny.

[…]

INT. SQUAT HOUSE, NIGHT

A party is under way. THE GIRL and THE PUNK GIRL sit on the ground, happily talking with A YOUNG BLACK PUNK GUY.

ELLA (v.o.): *The girl has been adjusting to this punk sort of squatter life, and enjoying it even.* (THE PUNK GIRL gets up and walks away. THE YOUNG BLACK PUNK GUY leans closer to THE GIRL, strokes the inside of her arm, and then kisses her aggressively.) *This black punk guy, this really sort of bad-ass guy, is really into her. He sort of scandalizes her, freaks her out, but she's excited too, you know?*

EDIE (v.o.): *You don't have to bring your perverted* How Stella Got Her Groove Back *fantasies into this.*

EXT. CITY STREET, DAY

THE GIRL and THE PUNK GIRL are crossing traffic.

ELLA (v.o.): *But it all comes to a crashing halt . . . when she sees that the man has found her. Tracked her down.*

THE GIRL sees THE MAN standing across the street, wearing a bowler hat and holding a briefcase. She grabs THE PUNK GIRL'S hand and runs.

EDIE (v.o.): *How'd he do that?*

ELLA (v.o.): *He's powerful.*

EDIE (v.o.): *I'll say.*

INT. WAREHOUSE, NIGHT

THE GIRL and THE PUNK GIRL are in the warehouse, sleeping on an old, bare mattress. Their arms are wrapped around each other. They smile at each other and stroke each other's hair.

ELLA (v.o.): *So they're hiding in a warehouse. The punk girl is using her street smarts to help hide the girl. They're sleeping on a bare mattress.*

INT. PROFESSOR'S OFFICE, DAY

PROFESSOR GIBBARD sits at his desk reading over some papers. ELLA knocks on the door.

PROF. GIBBARD: Yes?

ELLA enters.

ELLA: Hi, Professor Gibbard.

PROF. GIBBARD: (slightly harried) Hello, Ella. Please, sit down. (ELLA sits down at a chair facing her teacher.) I have a department meeting in about fifteen minutes, so we're going to have to keep this brief.

ELLA: Oh, sure. I don't want to take up too much of your time. I just wanted to get a sense of, you know, what kind of edits you want us to make on the final portfolio, you know? Editing poetry always seems like such a ... I don't know ... gray area. I mean, so open to personal preference.

PROF. GIBBARD: Well, sure, yes. I have preferences, certainly. But I also like to think that there are certain ... matters of technique ... that aren't really up for debate.

ELLA: (nodding) Mmm-hmmm. Sure.

PROF. GIBBARD: I looked over your work again and I think ... hmmm ...

(He thumbs through some of Ella's poems.) These are interesting. Vivid imagery, fun language play. However, I feel that there are some poems that, well, in my estimation, they need to go to marriage counseling.

ELLA: Oh ... Okay ... What does that mean?

PROF. GIBBARD: They are having identity crises, in either the voice or the subject. You're trying to cast your net too wide, to make the poems about *everything*, and in the process ... you negate the very real power they might have.

ELLA: Okay ...

PROF. GIBBARD: I'm sure that you'd like an example of this.

ELLA: All right.

PROF. GIBBARD: I can point to "Shellfish." There is this interesting albeit grotesque narrative about the children looking for shellfish in the stream, and then suddenly it takes a very strange turn when the mother appears in the postal worker's uniform.

ELLA: Yes, well . . . I guess I thought there was a place for surrealism.

PROF. GIBBARD: Well, of course there is. But this is more schizo-phrenic than surreal . . . So, I think that's what you need to watch out for. I really do.

ELLA: All right. Thank you.

PROF. GIBBARD: Okay?

ELLA: Yes . . . May I ask you one other question?

PROF. GIBBARD: Sure.

ELLA: Can you give me any sense of what the committee will be looking for when admitting students into the screenwriting workshop?

PROF. GIBBARD: Well, I'm not on that committee, but I do know that they'll want fully realized work, compelling stories . . .

ELLA: Sure. Yeah. Well, I'm working on something. We'll see how it goes.

PROF. GIBBARD: You're writing a script? What's your topic?

ELLA: Well . . .

PROF. GIBBARD: I don't need a play-by-play, but you can give me a basic premise. I mean, there are certain things the committee is less likely to embrace: action films or immature comedies.

ELLA: Um . . . It's about a girl who has previously been kidnapped by her high school English teacher and been kept in a cabin for three years. At the movie's start, she has escaped and is running from this man.

PROF. GIBBARD: She's in the cabin for three years?

ELLA: (nodding) Mmm-hmmm.

PROF. GIBBARD: Well . . . Either the cabin is truly remote, or this young woman is pretty stupid.
[. . .]

INT. ELLA'S ROOM, NIGHT

EDIE puts an arm around ELLA.

EDIE: Hey, you. Let's talk about something else, okay?

ELLA: Mmm-hmmm . . .

EDIE: What's been happening in your screenplay?

ELLA: Oh, that thing . . . Doesn't it bore you?

EDIE: Nuh-uh.

ELLA: Okay . . . Well, I wrote some this afternoon, actually.

INT. WAREHOUSE, NIGHT

THE GIRL and THE PUNK GIRL are asleep on the mattress on the warehouse floor, still cuddled up and wearing their jackets.

ELLA (v.o.): *The punk girl is hiding the girl.*

EDIE (v.o.): *Yeah . . .*

ELLA (v.o.): *And suddenly the man shows up!*

The door to the warehouse opens, and THE MAN enters, carrying his briefcase.

EDIE (v.o.): *He shows up? How does he know where she is?*

ELLA (v.o.): *I told you, he's powerful. So the punk girl tells the girl to run out to the back of the warehouse and hide, and that she'll get her when the man is gone.*

THE PUNK GIRL whispers to the girl. She runs out. THE MAN approaches the mattress. The punk girl stands on the mattress.

ELLA (v.o.): *So the man comes in, he's talking to the punk girl, and he's asking where the girl is. The punk girl just won't give up her whereabouts. She's being loyal. But he knows everyone's weaknesses, you know? He knows the punk girl likes drugs.*

THE MAN pulls out a bag of white powder and dangles it in front of THE PUNK GIRL's face.

EDIE (v.o.): *What drug, Ella?*

ELLA (v.o.): *Um . . . a bad one? Heroin, let's say. Something addictive . . . something tempting.*

EDIE (v.o.): (laughing) *Ok.*

ELLA (v.o.): *And she sees it, takes a moment, and then says she still won't give up the girl's location.*

EDIE (v.o.): *'Atta girl.*

THE MAN walks away.

ELLA (v.o.): *But!*

EDIE (v.o.): *Uh-oh . . .*

ELLA (v.o.): *The punk girl asks if she can have just a little bit, a taste. Like, if you want a small amount of drugs, you call that "a taste," right? So she asks. He gives her a little bit. She snorts some off the back of his hand.*

THE PUNK GIRL snorts drugs off the back of THE MAN's hand.

EDIE (v.o.): *No one would take drugs like that.*

ELLA (v.o.): *What do you mean?*

EDIE (v.o.): *They just wouldn't. Not realistic. They would put it on their gums.*

ELLA (v.o.): *Okay, well, they do that. And the punk girl feels the effect of the drugs, and she just tells him the girl is out in back of the warehouse.*

THE MAN hands THE PUNK GIRL the bag and walks out the back door. The distraught-looking punk girl collapses onto the mattress in a strange and dramatic movement.

EXT. WAREHOUSE, NIGHT

THE GIRL sees THE MAN coming out and runs into the night.

ELLA (v.o.): *So the girl is on the road again, you know?*

INT. GAS STATION BATHROOM, NIGHT

THE GIRL is dyeing her hair brown in the sink.

ELLA (v.o.): *She buys hair dye and changes her hair again, makes it brown.*

EXT. GAS STATION, NIGHT

THE GIRL, who now has brown hair, is climbing into a very high truck.

ELLA (v.o.): *She hitches a ride with a trucker, asks to go wherever he's headed.*

LOADING DOCKS IN MAINE, EARLY MORNING

THE GIRL climbs out of the truck. It drives away. She is standing in the misty morning, near a beach with some docks where fishermen are loading and unloading large boats.

ELLA (v.o.): *So she's at some small-town Maine location. She's just there.*

EDIE (v.o.): *What does she do next?*

INT. DINER, MORNING

THE GIRL sits at a counter, drinking water.

ELLA (v.o.): *She goes to a diner. She has no money, so she just gets water.*

EDIE (v.o.): *Harsh break.*

A HANDSOME YOUNG MAN dressed in flannel sits beside her. They begin to talk. He buys her coffee.

ELLA (v.o.): *But this boy, this guy, buys her coffee. He just finished working on the docks for the morning. And they get to talking, and he offers to let her stay with him.*

EDIE (v.o.): (sarcastic) *That's a good idea. She just got out of an abusive relationship with a fifty-year-old sex offender, so shacking up with a stranger seems like an awesome plan . . .*

ELLA (v.o.): *No, this guy is good. Nice fishermanly stock, you know? She just senses this guy is good.*

INT. CABIN, NIGHT

THE GIRL and THE HANDSOME YOUNG MAN sit at a table eating dinner. She is wearing a flowered dress.

ELLA (v.o.): *He gives her a dress . . . an old one that used to belong to his mom, who's dead.*

EDIE (v.o.): *How sweet.*

EXT. LAKE, NIGHT

THE GIRL and THE HANDSOME YOUNG MAN, all bundled up in winter clothes, troop around the edge of a lake until they reach a small fishing shack.

ELLA (v.o.): *He takes her to his fishing shack, his favorite place.*

EDIE (v.o.): *Sounds sleazy.*

ELLA (v.o.): *It's not.*

INT. FISHING SHACK

The room is lit with a gaslight. THE GIRL and THE HANDSOME YOUNG MAN are petting each other's faces. They begin to kiss, and it becomes more passionate. She is pressed against a wall. He pulls her into his jacket. She lifts her skirt.

ELLA (v.o.): *She has sex with him. It's her first time.*

EDIE (v.o.): *Even though she was the love slave of some sick old man?*

ELLA (v.o.): *Mmm-hmmm.*

EDIE (v.o.): *Does she tell him she's a virgin?*

ELLA (v.o.): *No. But he just, you know, knows to be kind and, like, gentle.*

INT. GROCERY STORE

THE GIRL is wearing the flowered dress and a knit cap, pushing a cart.

ELLA (v.o.): *She loves living with this guy. She totally takes care of him, you know? But then something awful happens.*

EDIE (v.o.): *She gets pregnant!*

ELLA (v.o.): *No. The man shows up.*

THE MAN appears in her aisle. THE GIRL abandons her cart and runs through the store and out the doors.

EXT. HOUSE, NIGHT

THE GIRL is getting into the back of a station wagon. THE HAND-SOME YOUNG MAN watches her being driven away. She presses her hand to the glass of the window.

ELLA (v.o.): *So she has to leave, keep moving. The handsome young man*

understands, and he gets one of his fisherman friends to drive her to a bus station nearby. She's overwhelmingly sad, of course, and so is he. He asks if he'll find her sometime, and she says, "yes," but who knows if that's even true.
[...]

INT. BUS STATION BATHROOM

THE GIRL has dyed her hair black and is cutting it off into a china-doll bob. She is wearing her combat boots and a flowered dress.

ELLA (v.o.): *Well . . . The girl has hacked all her hair off. It's short and black.*

EDIE (v.o.): *All the momentum in the script is hair momentum.*

ELLA (v.o.): *So now she looks like Edith Head . . .*

EDIE (v.o.): *Or like you in the ninth grade.*

INT. BUS

THE GIRL sits, looking out a window.

ELLA (v.o.): *She knows she needs to get far away, so she takes the bus to the desert.*

EDIE (v.o.): *That's completely unrealistic, Ella. One bus? Takes her from Maine to the desert?*

ELLA (v.o.): *So she switches buses.*

EDIE (v.o.): *I thought she didn't have any money.*

ELLA (v.o.): *The handsome young man gave her some.*

EXT. DESERT, DAY

The bus pulls in. Only THE GIRL gets off. The bus drives away and the girl is standing there, holding a black bag.

ELLA (v.o.): *So there she is in the desert, alone.*

EDIE (v.o.): *This is going to be so expensive to film! How will you ever get this made?*

ELLA (v.o.): *It's not that expensive! It's a nature location! No special effects!*

EDIE (v.o.): *Yeah, but the bus. And moving filming from Maine to New Mexico or whatever.*

ELLA (v.o.): *Well, we could use a location that we actually have for the desert . . . like the football field . . .*

INT. WHITE ROOM

There are cardboard cutouts of cacti all over the room. THE GIRL stands on her own.

ELLA (v.o.): *Or we could make it really surreal and just, like, fill a room with fake cacti and film it there.*

EDIE (v.o.): *That's too weird.*

THE MAN enters through the door.

ELLA (v.o.): *The man shows up.*

EDIE (v.o.): *From where?*

ELLA (v.o.): *He just walks up.*

EDIE (v.o.): *And what happens?*

THE MAN and THE GIRL engage for a moment.

ELLA (v.o.): *They talk for a moment. And then . . .* (THE GIRL pulls a small silver gun from her bag.) *The girl pulls a gun from her bag.* (THE GIRL holds the gun up.) *And she holds it up.* (THE GIRL shoots THE MAN, who looks shocked and falls over dead. The girl looks at him for a moment.) *She shoots him. And he looks shocked. And then he falls over dead.*

EDIE (v.o.): *Holy shit.*

ELLA (v.o.): *And she looks at him, and then she walks away.*

THE GIRL walks away.

EXT. DESERT, DAY

THE GIRL is walking away, holding the gun.

ELLA (v.o.): *This part really won't work unless we're in the outdoor location. The effect won't be right.*

EDIE (v.o.): *What effect?*

ELLA (v.o.): *The girl, and how she's just walking away with the gun.*

EDIE (v.o.): *Where's she going?*

ELLA (v.o.): *Who knows. She's just moving, forever into the horizon, walking for miles, becoming a speck.*
[…]

THE END

INTERVIEW

Lena Dunham, author of *Creative Nonfiction*

Q: In June 2010, *Paper* magazine named you one of 140 Characters to follow on Twitter. Did that introduce a level of self-consciousness into your Tweets?

A: I'm always both self-conscious and shameless vis-à-vis my Tweets. As with my relationship to texting, there's always that moment: am I really going to post this? Okay, I am and I just did. In a way, it's analogous to making art and then showing that work. You question yourself but, ultimately, you're compelled. (Not that my Tweets are anything like art; they are usually pathetic reflections on what I am eating or not wearing.)

Q: Reviewers of your films have noted their autobiographical nature. Do you approach your films with self-consciousness and shamelessness as well?

A: I've never been easily embarrassed, and I've always found the line between fiction and reality in my own work very blurry. By the end of the creative process, it's often so hard for me to say what's autobiography and what isn't that I hardly even know what to feel embarrassed about. But insofar as shame is an emotion I experience, my work is what allows me to purge that.

Q: You raise the issue of fiction versus reality, and in *Creative Nonfiction*, you juxtapose a writer working on a story with a writer experiencing reality. The writer is constantly questioned about the verisimilitude of character and plot by her friends, while the more intriguing, "real" story is the one she's currently living. Were you consciously addressing fiction versus nonfiction (or reality)?

A: The truth is that the script began as a straightforward narrative, the narrative that later became the film within a film. The writing wasn't flowing, and it felt stiff, and suddenly my own writerly conundrum seemed like a premise for the film. I'm certainly not the first writer to experience this phenomenon, and I won't be the last. I wasn't making too many consciously "meta" moves in the script, but looking back, I think I was trying to address the way that my unformed life informed my unformed work, and the interplay between reality and fantasy in the stories I (we) tell.

Q: In an early scene from *Creative Nonfiction*, Chris makes a comment about cinema studies majors, and Ella remarks, "Yeah, but I'm writing this screenplay and I'm feeling feelings." Such a metafilmic moment reminds me of Noah Baumbach's *Kicking and Screaming* (1995), when Chet tells Grover, "It's nice, but it's not for everyone. Some people need to have a real career, which is something I've never really understood, you know, why somebody would want to be a vet, or a lawyer, or a filmmaker." Your film *Creative Nonfiction* has been called self-conscious, and the blog *Hammer to Nail* notes, "It *feels* like a real movie." Part of this hyperreality derives from the frequent moments when the actors shoot glances at the camera. Were you striving for cinema verité? Or a parody of it?

A: The goal was to reach an interesting midpoint, or intersection, between the casual reality of what was at the time being called Mumblecore and the hyperstylization of some of the films I loved as a child, such as *Hairspray* or *Bye Bye Birdie*. I've been equally influenced by films that feel almost too intimate, doc-like in their gaze, and by films that paint the world with candy colors and raunchy tunes. There were definitely some wink-wink nods to the audience about what I was making—in hindsight, even the title falls into that category—but it's funny, because the glances at the camera were purely accidental, something nonactors were doing out of inexperience, and also because the camera was so up-close, personal, and hard to ignore in the cramped spaces where we were shooting. When I reached the editing room, I kept and loved those moments.

Q: The title is how I found your film, in fact. I Googled "Creative Nonfiction," and it came up on the Internet Movie Database (IMDb). Thanks to your generosity in sending me a DVD copy, I screened it as the closing text of a nonfiction seminar, and the students were thrilled that your film spoke to them on a personal level, and that it spoke to the issues of creative nonfiction on a theoretical, intellectual level. So you mention the title *Creative Nonfiction*—

A: A creative nonfiction class was one of the first that I took in college. I found the concept incredibly intriguing: you tell the truth, but also bend it to the will of your narrative voice, dilate and contract time, and embellish characters to serve your narrative. The relationship to truth, especially in memoir, is a little, well, bendy. And that seemed like an apt comparison to what I aim to do when I write a screenplay, or just what I do naturally. The title came before almost anything else.

"Yes, I think I write to say what I haven't yet been able to articulate, and to use language to give a name to amorphous emotions and states of mind. Words contain and give a provisional shape to what is otherwise nameless and unexpressed. It seems only logical that the elusive nature of language would be of interest to a writer."

Winner Take Nothing

WHEN I RECEIVED WORD informing me that my first book had been chosen for the PEN/Hemingway Foundation Award, I held the letter in trembling hands while the following thoughts, in precisely this order, shot through my head:

1. I won the Ernest Hemingway award!
2. I don't deserve it.
3. My father's heard of Ernest Hemingway!

I ran a couple of laps around the house, elated, not just because of the letter, but because I remembered seeing a hardback volume of *The Snows of Kilimanjaro* on the shelves in my father's upstairs hall. Perhaps the book had belonged to one of my brothers, or was left behind by Esther. In any case, a novel by the award's namesake was shelved right there in Dad's very own home library, which would, as far as he was concerned, lend credence to the whole affair.

I had to admit that my father had managed perfectly well without literature for his entire life, and I had no illusions that writing, especially mine, could enrich his life. He sometimes read *Consumer Reports*, but largely, I think, to sustain through retirement the image he had of himself as a citizen with buying power. His primary reading material was *TV Guide*, a map by which he and Rosa navigated nights in front of the Sony console, watching *Wheel of Fortune*, followed by the healings of the Reverend Benny Hinn. In the few instances when I told him I'd had something published in a magazine or literary review, the first question he asked was, "How much they pay you?" I suppose he thought of "they" as a faceless jury, twelve arbiters of taste. Imagine telling a man who keeps his cash in a gold money clip shaped like a dollar sign that, after working on a piece of writing for months, you've been compensated with a complimentary copy of the publication. "You're kidding," he'd say, shaking his head as if I'd been duped in a shell game.

Over time, I'd cultivated a certain temperance when sharing literary news with my father. I'd come to consider it unfortunate but not devastating that he was unable to recognize the arc—or was it the bump?—of my career. Still, I ached to have him slap me on the back, wanted to hear his unstinting praise, and in it the honeyed pronouncement: Son.

Toward this end, I'd once given him something of mine to read. I chose a brief reminiscence about my mother, who had once dreamed of writing a book into which she'd pack every anecdote she could recall, starting with her immigration from Russia to the United States. *Immigration* isn't quite the right word; what she told me was that she and her parents swam across the Atlantic Ocean to the shores of North America when she was two. I was young enough at the time to believe such a feat was possible, and my credulity inspired her to add that, if the "authorities" ever discovered she'd entered the country illegally, they'd knock on our door and deport her, and *that's* why she never applied for a driver's license. Needless to say, my gratitude for having a mother grew instantly acute. I thought my father would find the tone of this reminiscence unmistakably fond. And so I handed him the pages one day, neatly stapled. Before I let go of the manuscript (feeling him tug it from the other side was the closest I'd come to his tangible enthusiasm), I told him I hoped he would enjoy reading it and assured him he was under no obligation to offer comments.

Days went by. Weeks. Months. In all the times we saw one another or spoke on the phone, he never mentioned reading it, and pride prevented me from coming right out and asking. If it hadn't been for a chokingly potent vodka tonic I drank when we met for dinner one night at The Brass Pan, I might not have asked him to this day.

"Hey, Dad. You've never mentioned the essay I wrote about Mom."

He peered at me over his bifocals. In the dim light of the restaurant, he looked anything but adversarial. "Well," he sighed. "What can I tell you? You wrote down your opinion."

I stirred the booze with a swizzle stick and took another swig.

MY FATHER WASN'T the first person I called about the award (I reached Brian during his break between clients and then made short work of my address book), but when I dialed Dad's number and told him the news, his "Oh" was as round and buoyant as a bubble.

In my excitement, however, I'd overlooked one crucial hitch: now that it had been deemed worthy by a panel of judges, my father might decide to read the book—specifically the passage where I mentioned his affairs while married to my mother. If only I'd used a pseudonym or the putty nose of fiction, but the man was unmistakable, the ink completely dry.

Sure enough, once my father learned of the award, he phoned several local bookstores and, to my relief, was told that my book, which had been in print for several months, had sold out. Little did he know that the bookstores had ordered only a couple of copies in the first place, one or both of which had been bought by my friends. I wasn't about to disabuse him of the idea that my fame was a wave that swept through the city, washing my work from the shelves. I told him the publisher was planning another print run that would be available *after* the PEN ceremony in New York. By lying, I'd bought myself more time to plan the least upsetting way to let him know he appeared in the book. Should he react badly, at least I wouldn't arrive at the ceremony feeling defeated. No, defeat would have to wait until I received the award.

A few days later, my father and I were talking on the phone about my plan to buy a suit for the big night, and though it usually made me bristle when he gave unsolicited advice, I listened with pleasure to his description of the dress code that prevailed in the courtroom, and to his suggestion that I try a men's store downtown that I was sure had long ago gone out of business. "Listen," he said, "we'll fly to New York together, share a room, and take in some Broadway shows. Rosa will take care of things while I'm gone. To tell you the truth, I could use a break from her, and probably so could she, from me." I was stunned by his offer, and more than a little touched. Since he had no compunction about expressing bemusement at my small successes, it never occurred to me that he might need to take an active part in my large ones.

I didn't know what to say. Without Rosa there to monitor his diet and medications, the responsibility for his well-being would fall to me, and I didn't want to be encumbered. Not on this trip. Besides, Brian had booked our flights and hotel room weeks ago.

"Nothing could make me happier than knowing you're proud of me," I told him, "but I'm only going to be in New York for three days." I explained that I'd made plans to see a couple of old friends and had promised to read for a creative writing class. As terrific as a trip with him sounded, I wouldn't have time to go to Broadway shows or give him the attention he deserved. Although his gout was finally under control, he still walked slowly and tired easily, and I suggested that Manhattan might not be the best city for him to visit, until he had less trouble getting around. "Tell you what," I said. "Let me take you and Rosa to The Brass Pan just as soon as we get back. That way the four of us can relax and celebrate properly."

After I stopped talking, I gave my little speech high marks; it had been a good mixture of respect and autonomy. But the longer he remained silent, the more aware I became of the telephone's static, a sound growing vast, oceanic. "Dad?"

"Fine," he said. "If that's what you want."

BRIAN GAVE ME his window seat as soon as we reached cruising altitude. I thought that looking out the window might make me less claustrophobic, but no matter where I sat, the plane seemed to stay aloft solely because of my death grip on the armrests. When panic finally gave way to the Valium I'd taken twenty minutes before takeoff, my hands and feet grew rubbery, the view of earth abstract.

Once inside the terminal at JFK, the firm ground acted as a conduit, diffusing fear. At the baggage claim, as I watched luggage spill onto the carousel, it finally dawned on me that I'd survived the flight to receive an award. Sunlight burned through a bank of windows and warmed the glaring terrazzo floor. Outside, people swarmed toward a fleet of cabs and were whisked away to meetings and reunions. Possibility charged the air, dense, electric. In my happiness I turned to Brian and faced my father.

At first I thought I might be drugged or dreaming, though by then, only the mildest trace of Valium remained in my system. I looked at him and couldn't speak. The entire busy terminal contracted to a point the size of his face. Was he omnipresent, like Santa Claus or God? Dad looked back and blithely smiled.

"Surprise," he said.

"How . . . ?" I sputtered.

"Your plane. I went first class."

Suddenly I understood that all the questions he'd asked about the details of my trip—time of departure, name of the airline—questions I'd interpreted as paternal concern, were part of a perfectly executed plan.

Brian, who at first had been as stunned as I, rushed in to fill the conspicuous silence. He shook my father's hand. "Are you staying at our hotel?" he asked.

I recalled with a start that Brian had booked rooms at a gay bed-and-breakfast.

"I'm at the Warwick," said my father. "Quite a fancy place, according to the Automobile Club." Two familiar carryalls were making aimless circles in the periphery of my vision, and before I knew what I was doing, I yanked them off the carousel and threw one over each shoulder. "We're going," I announced, a decision I'd regret within minutes. I marched toward the taxi stand.

"Bernard!" shouted Brian, dashing after me.

"Share a ride?" my father shouted.

I didn't look back.

THE CAB RATTLED LIKE AN EARTHQUAKE, the driver barely missing other vehicles as he swerved from lane to lane. "If this Caddy had another coat of paint," my father liked to say after a close call, "we would have been in an accident!" He could be funny, my father, which made me a heel for leaving him at the airport. But he'd gone ahead and followed me to New York. If he and I weren't going to sleep in adjacent beds and take in the town like sailors on shore leave, we were going to arrive on the same flight, split a cab, and share who knew what other adventures. It wasn't that he was "eccentric," as the jacket copy of my book (a book whose publication I was in no mood to celebrate) claimed; he was unpredictable, capable of acts that were unimaginable until they happened. I'd spent much of my life having to appease or second-guess him, and look where a stab at independence had gotten me: grinding my teeth in the back of a cab, vacillating between guilt and fury while Manhattan slipped past the windows, unseen.

Once we settled into our hotel room, with the faux-homeyness of its antique furniture and antimacassars, I took a shower and tried to gather my thoughts. Pelted by hot water, I returned to what was left of my senses and began to worry that I'd acted rashly. Had I been a different person, I might have poked my father in the ribs and teased him for being a stubborn coot. But in order to be a different person, I'd have to have been raised by a different dad. The one I had was an old Jewish genie who materialized wherever he willed and granted any wish, as long as it was his.

After changing into fresh clothes, I called the Warwick. My father answered on the second ring. Allowing himself to sound upset would have presumed he had done something wrong, and so it was to his advantage to act as if nothing unusual had happened. "Hey there," he said.

"We'd better have a talk, Dad."

"It's your dime."

"I thought you understood that I wanted to do this on my own."

"Fine. I'll pack up my goddamn bags and go home."

"No. I *want* you to stay now that you're here. I'm just trying to explain why I reacted the way I did at the airport."

"So now you explained it. Is that what you wanted to talk about?"

There had to be more. In the shower, I'd rehearsed ways to tell him that his surprise was an intrusion disguised as kindness, a success usurped. But now, I couldn't recall what I'd wanted to say, or why we always found it so important to win the other's capitulation. After all was said and done, my father had come here because he was proud of me.

"We'll have lunch tomorrow," he said.

THE DINING ROOM at the Warwick, with its ambient chimes of silverware and ice, offered a quiet retreat from the city. My father looked small and harmless as he sat waiting for us at a table. He peered nearsightedly around the spacious room, hands folded before him in a boyish pose, almost contrite. As Brian and I walked toward the table, it struck me that he was not at all the giant of the nursery I was prone to imagine; when I didn't have the actual man before me, he ballooned into myth.

There arose a somewhat leery conviviality as we seated ourselves at the table. Brian had had experience with couples' counseling, but of course expecting him to mediate the situation between my father and me would have burdened him with a professional responsibility while he was on vacation. It would also mean that the couple to be counseled was you-know-who.

"So, Mr. Cooper," asked Brian, "what have you been doing?"

My father toyed with the silverware. "Nothing much. I watched a little TV."

"What did you watch, Dad?"

My father cocked his head and thought. "They got this channel where they show you all about the hotel, where the lobby is, and the fire exits, and who can remember what other amenities."

Brian and I looked at each other.

"Have you gone anywhere, Mr. Cooper? I hear there are some wonderful restaurants in the area."

"I had breakfast at a deli across the street. Haven't had corned beef hash in so long, I'm telling you I got tears in my eyes! Same with the cream cheese. Don't tell Rosa, though. If it were up to her, I'd be eating air."

"Is there anybody you know in New York who you could go to dinner with tonight?" Please, I prayed.

"We'll find the name of a great place," offered Brian. "And make your reservations."

"I got relatives in Jersey. Or used to twenty years ago. I should look them up next time I'm here." His hearing aid squealed with feedback, and he fiddled with its tiny dial.

"The thing is, Dad, we can't go to dinner with you tonight."

"I know," he said curtly. "You're *very* busy."

The maître d' brought us huge glossy menus, the covers printed to look like marble. I opened mine, expecting an engraving of the Ten Commandments: "Thou shalt honor thy father, who gazeth at the entrées." Without lifting his eyes from the menu, he waved his hand in a gesture of largesse. "Get whatever you want," he said. "Sky's the limit."

THE MORNING OF THE CEREMONY, I added an additional paragraph to my acceptance speech. In it, I thanked my father for reading me stories as a child. His rapt voice had transported me, I wrote, and his enthusiasm for telling tales had introduced me to the power of language. I wasn't certain whether my father had, in fact, read me stories as a child, but he wouldn't contradict the sentimental notion, and our collusion would be a kind of bond.

That evening, when the elevator doors opened on the tenth floor of the Time-Life Building, my nerves lit up like a chandelier. The representative of PEN introduced himself and pointed to a table where the books by the various winners and nominees were on display. My father had stationed himself beside it, staring down at a small stack of my books. I waited to see if he'd pick one up to peek at a page or turn it over to scan the jacket copy, but his hands stayed clasped behind his back.

Half a dozen awards were handed out during the ceremony. Almost every author who received one had written a speech identical to mine, a sort of apologia in which they expressed surprise at having won and either implied or insisted they were undeserving. The motif of modesty had been exhausted by the time I walked up to the podium, but I'd already revised my speech that morning and was far too nervous to change it again. When I came to the part about my father, I looked up from the wrinkled sheet of paper, eager to find him among the crowd and make eye contact, but I had to look back quickly for fear of losing my place. The paragraph I'd added struck me as a little schmaltzy, and I worried that my apparent sentimentality would discourage people in the audience from buying my book. In the end, it didn't really matter; my homage was meant for Dad's ears alone, and reading it aloud righted the night.

Or so I thought. Immediately after the ceremony, I found my father milling in the crowd and raced up to ask him how he'd liked my speech. "Couldn't hear a damn thing," he said, chuckling at his rotten luck. His hearing aid, unable to distinguish between foreground and background noises, had amplified both. From the rear of the auditorium, my father saw me reading in the distance, but he heard ubiquitous coughs and whispers, a battle of creaking leather coats, the rubbery acoustics of someone chewing gum.

THAT TRIP TO NEW YORK completely changed my life. In three days, I'd charged so much money to my credit card that I had to teach two additional classes when I returned. Along with teaching, I began to publish in a few magazines that paid well. My combined income was still meager by any standard except my own, but at last I could speak my father's language, a lexicon of hard, cold cash.

By that time, however, my father reacted to news of my solvency with a foggy acknowledgment. At the mention of money, he'd look at me wistfully, nod his head, then look away. My father was going broke from lawsuits. Although Rosa, true to her word, had paid the phone bill, Dad filed a harassment suit against Mr. Delaney. A judge dismissed the case before he heard it, admonishing my father to pay his phone bill on time and scolding him for clogging an overtaxed judicial system with a frivolous complaint. Next, he took Dr. Corwin to court, and this time a judge not only dismissed his case but ordered him to pay the doctor's attorney's fees. He filed a claim against the neighbor whose sprinklers turned his lawn into "a swamp," and also against the neighbor whose rumbling garagedoor opener purportedly cracked his plaster walls. Most ominous of all, he began to prepare proceedings against Gary's wife Sharleen and Ron's wife Nancy, claiming they had promised to repay him money he'd long ago loaned to my brothers. Had I really ever been naïve enough to ask Rosa if my father had the energy to go through with a lawsuit?

"I'm entitled by law," he'd say when I tried to convince him to drop the suits, "to take action against a party eight times before they can even *think* of claiming malicious prosecution. Believe me, I know what I'm doing. I didn't just fall off the boat, you know." He represented himself in court (such a sadly incriminating phrase) and lost each case. The judges were corrupt, he'd claim, his witnesses inarticulate. Defeat never seemed to give him pause or lessen his zeal for prosecution. He was in the throes of a lawyerly tantrum; if the world refused to yield to his will, he'd force it to yield to the letter of the law.

I protested his plans to sue my sisters-in-law, though to stay in his good graces, my objections were tempered. In the convoluted scheme of things, I found it flattering to be, along with Rosa, one of two people in his life exempt from litigation. My worth as a son was verified daily by the absence of a summons to appear in court. Rosa must have been as backhandedly flattered as I. As a nurse, her bedside manner was stern, but when "off duty," so to speak, she flirtatiously teased my father about his bullheadedness, charmed by the very trait that made him a difficult patient, not to mention a tenacious legal foe.

Every now and then, my father and I met for dinner at The Brass Pan.

Some nights, when the waitress asked for his order, he'd tell her a story based on his choice of entrée, so that filet of sole, for example, segued into a fishing trip with my brothers. At first I thought his brevity—a boat, an ocean, three rambunctious, seasick boys—was in deference to the busy waitress. Then I'd see that he was stranded in the shallows of a thought, unable to remember more. On other nights, he'd stiffen and eye the waitress with suspicion, tense as a man being cross-examined. She'd hover above him, pencil poised, till he blinked and finally lifted his hand, pointing to a dish on the menu.

Eventually, he grew too distracted by his legal battles to return my phone calls. On the rare occasions when we spoke, he said he was too busy to meet me for dinner. More often than not, the answering machine picked up after several rings and played its refrain: "I am not at home at this present time."

AFTER MONTHS OF AN ELUSIVENESS he couldn't be coaxed out of, I drove over to my father's house one afternoon to ask why he'd been unwilling to see me, why he hadn't returned my calls. Such phases of estrangement were nothing new; for as long as I can remember, our relationship had been punctuated by weeks of his withdrawal, followed by fits of generous attention. But there I was, hoping, I suppose, to make the reinforcement schedule a little less variable.

Dad answered the door of his Spanish house, preoccupied but glad to see me. Time had taken a belated toll, as though weariness had waited till now to irrevocably claim his face; his eyes were puzzled, hair unkempt, chin bristling with patches of stubble the razor had missed. His polyester jumpsuit, after years of looking supernaturally pressed, was finally the worse for wear.

Rosa rushed in soundlessly from the kitchen. She'd recently left the home-care agency, taking short-term jobs that didn't require her to drive too far from Hollywood, and she was dressed in her uniform and silent white shoes. "I'm going to say hello and good-bye," she announced, slinging her purse over her shoulder. As she had on the day of her interview, Rosa stood squarely, the very picture of dependability with her bulging shoulder bag, and yet she had about her a breathlessness, an air of agitation I hadn't noticed before. Even this slight change in her seemingly limitless composure—it had to be limitless, I thought, if she maintained a peaceful relationship with my father—forced me to recognize just how much I depended on her to take care of him. "Your dinner's in the refrigerator," she shouted at my father. "Give it five minutes in the micro."

She looked at me and whispered, "Remind him. Five."

"What?" said my father.

"I left Mrs. Travisi's number near the phone," she shouted. And then she was gone.

My father and I sat down at the dining room table. Yellow legal tablets and manila folders were scattered across it, scraps of paper saving his place in law books that rose in precarious stacks. He lowered himself into a chair with a troubled gust of breath. Age had robbed my father of the prowess he believed a triumph in court could restore.

"Are you sure you're not angry at me about something?" I asked. "Because, if you are . . ."

My father fiddled with his hearing aid. "What makes you think I'm angry?"

"You're so . . . unavailable these days."

"How many times do I have to tell you? I'm busy. Swamped. Do you need me to spell it out for you?" He rose to his feet, and I thought he might begin to sound out the letters. "You have no idea. No goddamn concept."

I stood, too, trying to rise above the childlike vantage point that came with being seated. "All I'm saying is that you have to eat dinner anyway, and we might as well . . ."

"Who says?"

"What?"

"Who says I have to eat dinner? Where is it written? Is it written here?" He hefted a law book and let it slam back onto the table. Stray papers jumped and fluttered. I made a move to calm him down, but he began to prowl around the table, stirring up motes of sunlit dust. "Don't you ever tell me what to do!"

"Having dinner is not something to do! I mean, it *is* something to do, but I'm not *telling* you to do it." At a loss for logic, I was barking back.

"Don't you raise your voice at me!" He rushed up and grabbed the back of my shirt, a hank of fabric twisted in his grip. "I'm seventy-six years old," he shouted. "I can do whatever the hell I want whenever the hell I want to do it." He pushed me toward the door, breathing hard, his face red and alien with effort.

"Dad?"

"That's right," he said. When he opened the door, the daylight was blinding. "Don't ever forget that I'm your father. Now get the hell out and don't come back."

Since high school, I've been both taller and stronger than my father, but just as we reached the threshold of the door it occurred to me that I might flatter him into relenting if, instead of resisting or fighting back,

I let my body be heaved outside as though from an admirable, manly force.

Acquiescence didn't help. Before the door slammed shut behind me, I turned and glimpsed his indignant figure sinking inside my childhood house. The door hit the jamb with a deafening bang, the birds falling silent for half a second before they went back to their usual racket.

ON A DAILY BASIS I relived the particulars: the shirt taut across my chest, the heat of his breath on the back of my neck, the flood of light as the door swung wide. As with so much that's transpired between us, the sheer abruptness and implausibility of what had happened made me wonder if I'd perhaps misperceived it. Had I said something thoughtless or cruel to set him off?

In lieu of an explanation, I started making changes to the story. Suppose I hadn't mentioned dinner? Suppose I hadn't raised my voice? Suppose we'd stood instead of sitting? Say the day had been cooler, the hour later, the dust motes churning in another direction? Would the outcome of my visit have been any different? Who knew what crucial shifts of fate had hinged on the tiny details?

Several nights a week, I had to drive past his house on the way home from teaching, and the closer I came, the greater its magnetic pull. More than once, I turned the steering wheel at the last minute, aiming my car through a tunnel of trees and parking across the street from his house. So this is what it was like, I thought, for my brother Bob: parked and watchful for hours on end. My behavior pained me, yet the urge to spy on my father was nameless, as deep and murky as the darkness it required.

There was little to learn from my nights of surveillance. Light would suddenly burn in a window, but I couldn't see anyone move through the rooms. Even if I had, what would a glimpse of his silhouette tell me? A walkway led toward the large front door, the stepping stones flat and blank in the moonlight. Rosa's yellow station wagon was parked in the driveway on the nights she wasn't working, but my father's Cadillac always sat there, gleaming, impassive, white as an iceberg. Despite my vigilance, nothing happened, except that every now and then I'd glance at my phosphorescent watch, its ghostly hands advancing.

During the first year of our estrangement, my entreaties and apologies and furious demands for contact were recited into his answering machine. On a few occasions, he picked up the phone and then slammed it down at the sound of my voice.

By the second year, resignation took hold. I'd lost the desire to drive by his house or reach him by phone. I recalled that afternoon less often, and when I did, I refused to probe the memory for meaning.

By the third year, his absence settled inside me like a stone.

"I REALIZE MY PHONE CALL must come as an unpleasant surprise," the social worker told me. "But I believe your father's deterioration is significant enough to make legal guardianship a necessary step. We routinely ask the nearest relative before resorting to a court-appointed guardian, since it's in the client's best interest to place their finances in the hands of someone they know."

Mr. Gomez assured me that I didn't have to make up my mind right away; it would be several months before the case came before a judge. An anonymous caller had phoned Adult Protective Services to say my father needed help. If I assumed legal responsibility, my father's Social Security checks would be placed in a trust, and he'd need my permission for every expenditure: medicine, groceries, clothes.

"Careful monetary management is especially crucial in your father's case," said Mr. Gomez. "As you may know, the bank has begun foreclosure on the house."

I couldn't bring myself to tell Mr. Gomez that I hadn't known a thing about it, afraid the admission would portray me as a callous son. I certainly couldn't explain that even if Dad and I *had* been on speaking terms, he might not have bothered to mention foreclosure till a moving van pulled up to the curb.

"Hello?" said Mr. Gomez.

If the city was a compass, my childhood house was magnetic north, and always would be no matter where I moved.

I promised Mr. Gomez that I'd give our discussion serious thought, and said good-bye. I'd become so guarded against any emotion having to do with my father that the prospect of seeing him again aroused only a dull ambivalence. After three years, I'd finally decided it was *I* who didn't want contact with him, a decision that redefined circumstance and made my banishment bearable. And now, out of the blue, a social worker urged a reunion.

If I did take responsibility for my father's finances, wouldn't receiving an allowance from his son—an *allowance!*—cause him to resent my authority, just as I once resented his? How well would he be able to understand that I hadn't wanted or asked for this role?

Had I been in my father's position, I'm the last person to whom I'd give fiscal responsibility. I can barely balance my checkbook, let alone manage someone else's finances. Ask me about money, and instead of thinking of stocks and bonds and dividends, I remember a trick my father showed me when I was six. He rolled up his sleeves and waved his empty hands in the air. "See," he said. "There's nothing there." With a little flourish, he reached out and plucked a quarter from my ear—were there more coins, I wondered, hidden in my head?—leaving me, as only he could, slack-jawed with astonishment.

I'D BEEN WRITING when the telephone rang. Though I don't usually answer the phone when I'm working, I was expecting a call from Mr. Gomez.

"Bernard?"

"Dad?" Saying the word made my mouth go dry.

"I sold the house and the people who bought it want to move in pretty soon, so I've been cleaning out closets and I came across all sorts of drawings and photos of yours. You wanna come get them? Is four thirty good?"

"Four thirty's good." I wasn't sure I was ready to see him, but assent was automatic.

"Okay. See you later."

"Wait," I blurted. "How have you been?"

"Fine. And you?"

Three years. "I'm fine, too."

"Good," he said, "as long as you're fine." His harried voice softened. "Well," he said, "I'm really swamped."

Only after I hung up the phone did I realize he hadn't said hello.

I APPROACHED THE HOUSE with apprehension; who knew in what condition I'd find him. Since I'd last spied on the house, the first-floor windows had been covered with bars. The front door stood behind a wrought iron grate, and no matter how decorative its design, it made the house look so aloof it might as well have been surrounded by a moat.

No sooner had I rung the doorbell than my father appeared behind the bars, pale and unshaven, jangling keys like a castle keep. All the while he burbled greetings. My hands were jammed in my pockets; I simply couldn't act as if things had been normal without damaging a sense of reality that, especially in my father's presence, could founder like a little boy's. "Come on in," he said, unlocking the grate. I found his hospitality suspicious, and as much as I wanted to make amends, I also wanted to run the other way. I'd come to think of my boyhood house as a place I'd never visit again, and now that I stood on the verge of return, I practically had to perform astral projection and give myself a push from behind.

The house was even more crammed with memorabilia than I remembered. He must have strewn souvenirs about the rooms as he cleaned out the closets, a last-minute effort to make his mark on the home he had to forfeit. The breakfront doors yawned open, his scrapbook packed in a cardboard box. The portrait of JFK leaned against the wall, as did still-lifes and landscapes by my brother Ron. Spread across the coffee table, in the careful, printed letters of childhood, were compositions I'd written about the sun's brightness and my love of dogs; they called back the distant, mesmerizing triumph of being able to describe the world and contain it on a piece of paper. Pictures from a photo booth showed a mugging ten-year-old who bore as much resemblance to me now as I to my father; I wanted to warn that oblivious boy of what was to come. I couldn't look at the stuff for long, and I gathered it up, ready to go.

"Sit," said my father.

I did as he asked.

"What's new?"

"Lots."

"Written any more books of yours?"

"Trying to. Yes."

"I see," he said. "Tell me, what else has been going on?" He leaned forward in the chair, cocked his good ear in my direction.

"Look, I appreciate your willingness to get together, but I'd think you'd be glad that you raised a son who has enough integrity to feel he deserves to know why his father hasn't spoken to him in three years."

His brows furrowed.

"Why haven't you talked to me?" I shouted.

"Look. You live, things happen, you go on. That's the way it works."

"That's not the way it works for me."

"Well, the truth of the matter is that you were getting irritated with me about my hearing aid. You were always screaming, 'What? What? I can't hear you! Turn up your damn ear!'"

"First of all, Dad, you're the one who shouts 'What? I can't hear you.' Second, I'd never scold you because you're hard of hearing."

"I'm telling you, that's what happened."

"It didn't."

"Did."

"Okay," I said. "Suppose you're right. Is that any reason not to speak to me for three years?"

My father sat back, stared into space. He gave the question due consideration. "Yes," he said, lurching forward. "Yes, it is."

"You see, this is why I can't just 'go on.' Unless we can talk to each other like two mature adults, I worry that some misunderstanding might set you off again."

"All right," he said. "All right already." He looked at his feet, then back at me. "I've lived in this house for fifty years. Do you remember when we moved in?"

"I wasn't born yet."

"Do you remember what day it was?"

"I wasn't . . ." It seemed pointless to repeat myself. "Tuesday?" I guessed.

"No," he said. "It was your mother's birthday. Did you know that she never knew her real birthdate?"

"Her birthday was the Fourth of July."

"Ach," sputtered my father, waving his hand. "That's the birthday they gave to lots of greenhorns at Ellis Island, people who didn't know or couldn't say in English the year they were born."

"Dad," I asked, "what's our original family name?"

"I sold the place to two very nice guys. By the way, how's that friend of yours, what's his name?"

"Brian's fine, he . . ."

"What do I need all these rooms for, anyway? It was either sell the house or get kicked out on the street."

I shook my head in commiseration, pretending to know nothing about the foreclosure.

"Some meshugga social worker wanted to have someone else do the real estate negotiations. Said I couldn't handle the sale myself. I showed him. Closed escrow on my own, then told Hernandez to take a hike."

I stopped myself from blurting "Gomez."

"The kicker," he continued, picking lint from his jumpsuit, "is that I got Rosa to report me to the guy in the first place."

"What!"

"See," said my father. "You *do* shout 'What.'" He bristled a moment, shifted in his seat. "It was the only way to save myself. If she said I was, you know, soft in the head, the bank couldn't foreclose."

Rosa walked into the living room and sat beside my father, her hair dyed a metallic shade of blonde. She'd gained weight since I last saw her and it took her a couple of labored adjustments to settle into the valley of the couch. "Non compos mentis," she said, shaking her head at the whole mess. "That's what the social worker called it."

I must have been wide-eyed, because my father added, "Don't look like that! She didn't tell them I was crazy out of the kindness of her heart. She gets something out of it too."

Rosa glanced at him sharply. "I was protecting us both."

My father nodded, but I don't think he heard her.

"Did you know that Gomez called me?" I asked.

My father sighed. "I figured he might. I got a pretty penny for the place, but I owe a lot too. There are liens and things. A second mortgage. I'm looking at a mobile home in Oxnard. Not the best place in the world, but it looks just like a regular house, and it's what I can afford."

"We," said Rosa. "What *we* can afford."

"Rosa's from Oxnard. She knows some people up there, so it's not exactly like starting from scratch. You'll come up and visit." He cleared his throat. "You sure have grown since the last time I saw you."

"Dad, I've been this tall since high school."

"Taller than me?"

"For years," I said.

My father shrugged. "Then I guess I'm shrinking."

AFTER LOADING MEMENTOS into my car, I came back inside the house to say good-bye. Rosa nudged my father and this reanimated his grave face. He slapped his palm against his forehead. "Almost forgot your present," he said. I followed them into the kitchen. Dad stationed himself in front of the counter, then beamed at me and stepped aside.

A pink bakery box yawned open to reveal a cake, its circumference studded with strawberries of an uncanny size and ripeness. The fruit was glazed, and beneath the kitchen's fluorescent lights it looked succulent, moist, aggressively tempting. Slivered almonds, toasted gold, had been evenly pressed into a mortar of thick white frosting, every spare surface dotted with florets.

What I noticed next made me catch my breath. Written in the center, in gooey blue script, was "Papa Loves Bernard." For a second I thought there'd been some mistake. I'd never called my father "Papa." "Dad," yes. "Pop," perhaps. The nickname belonged to another parent, didn't mesh with the life I knew.

I looked at Rosa. For the moment her attention was elsewhere. Probably in Oxnard.

My father began yanking open drawers and kitchen cabinets, offering me anything that might not fit into his new trailer, which was just about most of what he owned. A punch bowl set, napkin rings, two-pronged forks for spearing hors d'oeuvres: artifacts from his life with my mother, a life of friends and fancy repasts. His barrage of offers was frenzied, desperate. All the while I politely declined; "this is more than enough," I said, gazing at the cake. As hungry as the sight of it made me, I knew a slice would be sickening, dense with sugar, rich with shortening, every bite a spongy glut. Yet it looked so delectable sitting in his kitchen, Betty Crocker's Sunday bonnet. If years of my father's silence had an inverse, that clamorous cake was it. Within it lay every grain of sweetness I'd ever declined or been denied. While my father jettisoned old possessions, I swiped my finger across the frosting and debated whether to taste it.

It didn't hurt that Hemingway's reputation was surrounded by an aura of manliness and adventure. My idea of manly adventure was getting my car past the McDonald's drive-through window without scraping the wall. If my father harbored the apprehension that I'd chosen an insular, effete career, what better antidote than a dose of Papa Hemingway?

My father and I didn't discuss his lawsuits on the rare occasions we met for dinner at The Brass Pan. To do so only prompted me to try to talk him out of pursuing one or the other. To disagree, even mildly, was an act of betrayal. At the least hint that I didn't share his litigious point of view, he'd angrily recite the facts, as if they were so persuasive, so incontrovertible, that merely to list them would win me to his side. But the details were vague, the court dates ever-changing, the numerous parties hard to keep straight. Any question about the motives behind his legal spree made him glower and huff and shift in his seat—to ask "why" was to deem him wrong—and so I learned to sidestep the topic. The more entangled his strategies, the more enraged my father became. He was in the throes of a lawyerly tantrum; if the world refused to yield to his will, he'd force it to yield to the letter of the law.

The decline was apparent in visit after visit. Age had robbed my father of the prowess that he believed a triumph in court could restore.

His disinterest in reading my work had allowed me to write about him without fretting over the consequences. I'd tried to capture the moodiness with which he presided over my childhood: a C on my report card, say, might be met with indifference, detonating rage, or a fatherly pep talk. One never knew what familial infraction or offhand remark might cause him suddenly to leave a room and brood for hours. Lavish generosity, bursts of goofy humor: these traits were also abundant in the book, but if he hadn't recognized the affection in the essay I'd written about my mother, how would he respond to what I'd written about him?

Not that my father had continued to disapprove of my being a writer; he'd come to understand it to the extent that he could understand a person gambling with his or her life in order to pursue a profession he found frivolous and fiscally unsound.

(Over the years, I'd cultivated a certain temperance when sharing literary news with my father.)

Q: Bernard, for writers, whether in fiction or nonfiction, our characters or personas are not always writers, yet in your memoir *The Bill from My Father*, a significant aspect of your persona is that you are a writer. Why was that important to emphasize in this work?

A: I'm both a teacher and a writer, and since these aren't necessarily lucrative lines of work, it allowed me to show what I'd consider a class difference between my father and myself. He tended not to understand why someone would choose the gamble of writing as one's life's work, and this choice on my part wasn't something he approved of. So much of the book is about my striving to win his approval, one of the story's driving forces.

Also, his way of speaking often revealed his identity as a first-generation Jew, though he tried hard to assimilate the English spoken by his lawyer colleagues. In court, language is power, it can color the case and persuade the jurors. For me, even as a boy, language was power because it allowed me to articulate complex feelings and ideas. My use of English marked me as an American Jew. My father was sometimes defensive about my grasp of language. Conversely, he could keep me out of conversations by speaking Yiddish to my mother. Each of us wanted to use words to be superior to the other: this was a kind of father-son competition. In this too, being a writer was important to emphasize.

Q: In the memoir, you allude to writers such as Elizabeth Bishop, Sylvia Plath, James Merrill, Ernest Hemingway, James Baldwin, and John Cheever, who many times built a chapter around a story or a poem. The literary allusions work to reinforce this theme of language, but as I read it, I couldn't help but think that writers view the world through the lens of writing, their own, for sure, but many times, the work of others.

A: All the writers I've mentioned in *The Bill from My Father* not only have written books that have been life-changing for me but have written single lines that have served as touchstones as I try to make sense of life's often nameless sensations and states of mind. In the case of Bishop, the line "then try losing harder, losing faster" has often come into my head like an incantation, assuring me not that loss is easy but that it is inevitable and, as we live into old age, that the loss of all we hold dear accelerates. What a chilling thought that is, so difficult to reckon with, and yet this line, with its repetition of "losing," offers a driving, rhythmic counterpoint of defiance. Certain lines, like Bishop's, are unforgettable for being distilled and epigrammatic. They speak worlds.

Q: "Almost Like Language," from your work *Truth Serum: Memoirs*, is not metawriting, but it is about language and how it often eludes us. References to words on refrigerators, "no vocabulary was large enough to describe," "a word sat inside him," "distant chatter," an allusion to a Dylan Thomas poem and one to Benjamin Whorf's *Language, Thought, and Reality* (I could go on, and when I teach it, I ask students to exhaust the memoir for all allusions to language) create a linguistic foundation for a series of moments that defy articulation. It fascinates me, as the writing self-consciously emphasizes language to convey what you were not able to at the time. Do you think this is why you write?

A: Yes, I think I write to say what I haven't yet been able to articulate, and to use language to give a name to amorphous emotions and states of mind. Words contain and give a provisional shape to what is otherwise nameless and unexpressed. It seems only logical that the elusive nature of language would be of interest to a writer. In the visual arts, painting and sculpture tend to take the materials into account, their texture and color and effect on the viewer. Abstract expressionism, for example, was in large part about how the artist manipulated the paint, or allowed the paint to have a physical life of its own, the medium both in and beyond the artist's control.

Also, one of the pleasures to be had in writing from memory is the chance to go back in time and give voice to what was vague and overwhelming.

BRIAN OLIU

"There is something amazing to me about immersing yourself in a world while the world around you continues without you. Part of my understanding of worlds, narrative, and even literacy was formed through playing video games as a child."

Adventure Island

DARLING, LET ME TELL YOU about the time I created an island. The island was a volcano once, a place where there was nothing to say but nothing—I continued forward with my face looking up toward the spiders, but my eyes always on my feet. On the island I created, I can see through the sand to the layers of earth: a blanket on top of a blanket on top of a creature, sleeping. Please do not touch me—I will be poisoned. I will fall through the trees and into nothing, perhaps, into water I cannot swim in. I could not swim in the water, so I created this island to walk across, to move from left to right, eyes to the ground. I do not know why I placed this rock here. I do not know who started this fire. During the fall, there is a bridge that will turn to dust as I walk across it—my feet destroying what my eyes created—please do not touch me. Do not feed me apples. Do not feed me bananas. I am very hungry, creating, but please don't let me eat the fruit I am creating in the trees. When you peel the orange, a spider will come out of the pulp. One leg will follow another. It will crawl up your hand like it is dancing, like you are interrupting a process. Drop the orange. Let it roll across the ground. Follow it until it hits something: a snake, a snail. Do this until I stop existing. Watch me fall from the sky like a helicopter, like a cannon, like a head cut clean from its body. You must understand this: when I walk, I am not the one that is moving. I will create this all by standing still, by marching in place. You are fooled. You should have eaten the orange. There is no spider hiding, waiting for your hands. There is no wonder here: all of it has been replaced except for the snails. The sky, darling, is moving opposite the ground. As I move in place, I move the world—I adjust the grass to my footing. In a room with no floor I die again, I roll backward. In front of me I can touch you—I have thrown out everything I have. These things I throw move against the world; they cut in front of dead leaves and clouds; they mean nothing, I promise. When I am done with all of this, we can go outside. We can have a picnic. I will peel the orange for you. I will slice the apple. I will pull the body out of the lake, I will tell you about the time I created an island. I will tell you about other islands I have created, smaller ones. I will tell you about the people whom I know who have drowned, whose bodies were found months later. I will tell you about falling backward into the water, about the red shorts I was wearing, about taking showers, about pressing my forehead against the white tile, about my feet bleeding from where my feet could touch something. You shouldn't have listened. You are faster than me, but I cannot be brought down, darling, I promise. Darling, it is cold and I am wearing a hat. It was a gift from my grandmother. I will try to pull the earth closer. I am not moving fast enough, please help me pull the earth closer. If we can pull the earth closer, we can punch the wasp's nest, we can kick over the traps. The insects will eat the garden. They will bite at my legs. Don't listen to them. They will put holes in the fruit, and then there is nothing that we can do: I cannot make more. Darling, in my heart, there are people. In my heart there are people with torches, with axes. I will stuff them with seeds from the garden. Let me tell you about the time I created an island that was a volcano once. I will fill their mouths with it until they cannot breathe. I know that this island is a line, but it is not a worm, it is not a night moth, a snail without a shell. It is not the leg of a spider bent like an elbow, like your hair on your shoulders. The shape of the island I created has nothing to do with this. It has nothing to do with an egg or the desire to go faster: if I go faster, I will fall into the fire, through the trees, through the earth. The next shell I crack open, the next rind I peel, could be you. We will run through the island inventing it. We will turn fire into smoke, rock into smoke, spiders into smoke. Darling, run with me until the feeling is gone.

INTERVIEW

Brian Oliu, author of "Adventure Island"

Q: In an August 2010 issue of the *New Yorker*, Nicholson Baker confesses, "I'd never held a video-game controller until last fall. Which is a pretty sad admission, as if I'd said in 1966 that I'd never watched 'Bonanza' or heard a song by the Rolling Stones." The piece, titled "Painkiller Deathstreak: Adventures in Video Games," catalogs Baker's excursions in three games. As a person whose last video-game controller was an Atari joystick for repeated rounds of *Frogger* and *Asteroids*, I'd like to ask you how you came to be interested in video games and their relationship to writing.

A: I've always been interested in the relationship between storytelling and video games, specifically those of my youth, which were relatively basic and rudimentary games without much of a story behind them. The player was given a world, a set of simple instructions and rules, and was forced to abide by those rules. "Adventure Island" is one in a series of lyric essays based on eight-bit Nintendo games, all of which take on the characters and settings of the games and juxtapose experiences that have occurred in my life with them. There is something amazing to me about immersing yourself in a world while the world around you continues without you. Part of my understanding of worlds, narrative, and even literacy was formed through playing video games as a child. Back then, the games were so basic that I found myself creating entire narratives as I played through them. I constantly wrote in to *Nintendo Power*, a Nintendo-run magazine, with video-game ideas and what I recognize now as fan fiction about my favorite games and characters.

Furthermore, video games constituted my introduction to and my first experiences with death: the idea of losing lives is a strange concept that I didn't understand the weight of until I was much older. These themes of the loss of life, worlding, and storytelling are very much at the forefront of the piece. Playing these games now has allowed me to observe a lot of the absurdities of these worlds and the parameters set for the gamer, and to overlay them with things that have occurred in my life, to synthesize the game and the gamer. I've come to realize that, for me, video games took the place of fairy tales: strange worlds with bizarre creatures, places where I was given a template to fill with whatever stories I could imagine. In an on-line discussion, Matt Bell has stated that he sees video games "somewhat as containers, with their spare stories ready to hold certain kinds of fictions and essays if we fill them right. It's really the same thing you do when you retell a myth, or use the structure of a fairy tale or other archetypal story to structure your own work." I wholeheartedly agree: to many, Link in *Legend of Zelda* was our first champion, Bowser our first evil. By juxtaposing these known stories with more personal accounts, I believe the effect achieves something familiar yet startling.

Q: For me, it was films, and as an only child, I was introduced to serious ones, as my parents took me along to *Reds*, *The Big Chill*, *Out of Africa*, *On Golden Pond*, *Tess*, and, I admit, *Flashdance*. I would come home and write down lines that I loved, and I kept them in a notebook, loving the way the words evoked the scenes I remembered. But also, like you, when I tucked the words into my own notebook, they became mine, and I transformed (in the mirror in my bedroom) into the character (again, even the welder/stripper). And I confess, I even wrote a letter or two to actors, though I never sent them. Most of us have a desire, I believe, to become another, and stories and storytelling allow us to do that. Yet to this idea of meta-storytelling, when storytellers—whether in fiction or essays or the films of Woody Allen—refuse to abide by the rules and become a self-conscious part of their stories, is there an equivalent in video games?

A: The most famous example of metastorytelling is in the game *Metal Gear Solid*, in which a boss named Psycho Mantis is presented as having psychic powers. During the battle, your controller will start to rumble, and the player's controls will be backward. Furthermore, the boss will claim to read the player's mind, and it will talk about how you are a fan of other video games. (In actuality, it is reading the memory card of the system and seeing what other saved games you have on the card.) In addition, the screen will suddenly turn black, as if someone has turned off the game system—I for one thought I had sat on the television controller. The solution to defeating the boss and advancing in the game is to unplug your controller and plug it into the secondary slot: Psycho Mantis could only read the "Player One" controller port.

While this is the most dramatic version of metastorytelling in video games—the act of doing something outside of the game in order to impact what is actually occurring in the game—I find that metaelements are everywhere in video games. One could argue that, anytime there is a minigame (for instance, a game within a game), it is in fact a metagame. In *Super Mario Bros. 2*, after each level, the player plays a slot machine in order to gain more lives. In the context of the game, it makes no sense: the rules that were established are now entirely different. Games such as *Grand Theft Auto IV* have these minigames as well, but they are what are referred to as "sandbox" games, meaning that there is a world that has been established, but there is no linear narrative. So, if you don't want to follow the (excellent) story line of the main character, you can opt to walk your character to a pub and play darts all day. These minigames operate within the world of the actual game and therefore feel more realistic.

I will say this: one of my most vivid memories of playing video games, which I now realize was a result of metastorytelling, came from the game *Dragon Warrior*, which is considered to be one of the first role-playing games to have success in the U.S. market. (This was the case mostly because you received the game for free if you renewed your subscription to the aforementioned *Nintendo Power*—a brilliant marketing strategy for a game that was hugely successful in Japan but considered too cerebral for an American ten-year-old.) After fighting your way past various evil creatures, you arrive at the final boss, the Dragonlord. Instead of immediately fighting the final boss, he offers you the opportunity not to fight but instead to join him and rule the world. I'm not sure what compelled me to join him, but immediately after choosing not to fight, the entire screen turns red and your character is killed. The game is then frozen—any buttons you press aren't going to do anything. Instead, you have to get up from the couch and manually press the reset button. This small moment gave me nightmares: video games as I knew them did not ask you to make moral decisions with consequences. You kill the bad guys because they are bad; anything you can kill is your enemy. Furthermore, when you die in *Dragon Warrior* or in any other game, there is an opportunity to start over, whether it's at a save point earlier in the game or from the beginning. The fact that there was no option to do this when choosing to join the Dragonlord was horrifying, because there was some element of finality in your decision. Instead of accidentally jumping in the pit and restarting, you had to acknowledge the facts that you had made the wrong decision and that your character was dead. So to me, any game that takes you out of the gamelike element is not only metatextual but also extremely powerful and jarring. The breaking of the fourth wall is so much more startling in video games than in, say, films or writing, because you have felt as if you were in control the entire time. When you lose that control, the effect is shocking.

Q: In his introduction to a study of video games called *Half-Real: Video Games between Real Rules and Fictional Worlds*, Jesper Jaul notes, "To play a video game is therefore to interact with real rules while imagining a fictional world." You and others (I'll add Tom Bissell's *Extra Lives: Why Video Games Matter*) who write about video games use the pronoun *you*, and I'm thinking of the use of *you* in writing, a choice that implicates the reader, though not with the dynamic of moral decisions or consequences that you attribute to video games. Sure, Holden Caulfield warns us, "Don't ever tell anybody anything," but if we do, we will not lose our lives (at least not in a tangible way).

I wonder, why not the *I* of the game? Also, to this notion of half-reality: is this a term apropos of writing, in your opinion?

A: To me, video games are a series of directions. Some of the most entertaining things to read are video-game instruction manuals, small booklets that teach you how to play the game. A lot of times, they provide the back story that is absent from the game. Video-game sequels are most guilty of this; they often reveal something like, "Guess what? The princess got captured again!" These manuals usually go one of two ways: they insist that *you* are the hero in the story or that you are *helping* the hero in the story. As a result, in these essays I tend to default to the other—it's always *you* and *we*. All video games make you interact with the other, whether it is an enemy visible on the screen or someone you are trying to save.

My favorite thing to read when I was younger was the Choose Your Own Adventure series, which was pretty much reading for the video-game set. The majority of those stories were told in the second person. I find something very beautiful about using the word *you*; it sounds so immediate and automatically makes things personal. The idea of being forced to take responsibility for someone else's story is a very intriguing concept to me, and that is what I hope to do with these essays: to make the reader a part of my experience, whether he or she would like to be or not.

That said, utilizing the *I* is important. In a conversation about the game *Super Mario Bros.*, friends and I shared similar experiences of pausing the game right before we knew Mario was about to fall into a pit. The player, the *I*, is always present, always interacting, and in most cases always manipulating.

As to half-reality, I think that is an excellent term with which to describe writing. The majority of the essays in my eight-bit Nintendo game collection, where "Adventure Island" comes from, allude to dreams and making wishes. The object of my affection is not a kidnapped princess in the literal sense of the term, nor am I a knight, a superhero plumber, an elfin swordsman. Yet these games have become such a part of my memories and my consciousness that I can't help but see parallels between the world of the video games that I played and the world that I live in. To me, good fiction and good nonfiction are able to layer worlds on top of ideas and concepts: Joan Didion uses historical contexts and the events of the time in order to delve into her psychological exhaustion, in the same way that *As I Lay Dying* uses Addie's death as a vehicle. The world where the lesson is neatly packaged within the action does not exist in reality; it exists in some sort of alternate dimension. It's both half-real and hyperreal at the same time. But to me, all writing is re-creating some reality, whether it's the most abstract poem or a historical memoir attempting to get every single fact right.

Q: You have published your first book, *So You Know It's Me* (Tiny Hardcore Press 2011). Like "Adventure Island," the pieces employ the second person, though it's a different usage of the second person, yes? And in the pieces, you "re-create some reality." Tell me about this collection.

A: The book is a collection of Craigslist Missed Connections—they were originally posted on the Tuscaloosa Missed Connections board during the summer of 2010. I've always been fascinated by Missed Connections;

they're direct addresses to someone but they're also complete shots in the dark—they are for one specific person, and yet they are read by everyone. There's always some sort of sad desperation to them as well—they are all re-creations of reality: "you were wearing this/you were making eyes at me/I think I sensed a connection." In a way they are artifacts of inaction: a lack of reaction while in the moment and then instant regret.

For those unfamiliar with Craigslist policy, posts start automatically deleting themselves after 45 days, and so this brings up another concept of the "missed" Missed Connection; something that is even more tragic. The voice of the collection is aware of this policy: that the pieces are slowly disappearing, and by a certain date everything will be gone. As a result, the collection becomes about loss: both in the fact that the person being addressed has already been "lost" as well as the fact that even these attempts at connection are fleeting.

Q: I cannot help but connect your last statement with regard to writing to an absent reader with the desire for connection to what writers do. Perhaps metawriting does, as other contributors have noted, "press on I" (Ander Monson), to emphasize his or her presence to the reader or to the writer's "self" (Sarah Blackman).

In metawriting, writers incorporate that struggle to "get every single fact right," or present another struggle in the writing of the writing. For example, one of my favorite metafictive moments is Tim O'Brien's "How to Tell a True War Story," when he writes, "It's difficult to separate what happened from what seemed to happen." What are some of yours?

A: A favorite metafictive moment of mine has to be in Salvador Plascencia's *The People of Paper* where the book "reboots" in the middle of the novel because a character was based on a real-life acquaintance of "the author" and they took offense. Seeing a brand new title page in the middle of the book was one of my first genuinely "wow" meta-moments. One of my favorite lines is from Carolyn Forche's *The Colonel*: "What you have heard is true." I often introduce my students to metawriting with that poem and have them use it as a first line of their own work. To me, it's always exciting to be aware that things are occurring outside of the story—that what is being told is all that can be told right now: these characters and this world exists beyond the page and beyond the stories that you're hearing. In the same way that in between *Legend of Zelda* and its sequel, Link isn't running around killing monsters, in stories we are zoomed in on a particular moment in a particular world—this is the world that interests me: what happens when evil is plotting its revenge, and what happens when the story has already been written.

"Many writers of meta-nonfiction, as well as those who write metafiction, take ironic pleasure in pointing to the status of the narrative as dramatic construction, as artifact, as illusion."

How to Be Tough in Creative Nonfiction

WHEN I WAS A CHILD, we went on long Sunday drives in the mountains, which we hated with a passion. The four of us—my two sisters, my impish little brother, and I—rode morosely in the backseat of a lizard-green station wagon with faux-wood paneling on the sides. My parents were from Scandinavian farm families in Iowa and Minnesota. Colorado was a mystery, a luxury, a tourist trifecta of high peaks, winding roads, and picture-perfect family togetherness enforced by no bathroom breaks.

My mother was a master of logistics and orchestration. We gave up going to church as a family by the time I was eight, and Sunday mornings were meant for sleeping. She had to work to get everyone out of bed and more or less committed to the project. "Let's go, kids!" she'd call, standing at the bottom of the stairs in her pedal-pushers and Keds, hair and makeup perfect. One by one we shuffled into the bathroom and tugged combs through our snarled tresses. My mother tried to fix our long, straight hair with frizzy perms we endured once a month at the Arvada Beauty School, but they never took very well. Once we were dressed, she'd pack us into the backseat of the station wagon, side by side, and then go rouse my father, who insisted on driving but wouldn't emerge from the house until everyone else was ready to go. He liked to sleep.

Sunday mornings were the only time I saw my father. I knew the back of his head like the palm of my hand.

This trip, though, was different. My brother had broken his leg, the result of a fall from a horse. The horse was a payment from a client of my father's. My father had little business sense, and when someone couldn't pay for their divorce or their DUI, he'd take something in trade. Sometimes it was a couch or a grandfather clock. Sometimes it was a horse. This horse hadn't been broken yet.

My mother put down blankets and pillows in the back of the station wagon for Kurt, still in his body cast, so he could lie flat. "I guess you'll have to look at the ceiling, honey," she joked.

"I can see fine," he said. He propped his pillow against the backseat and braced his foot against the rear window.

My mother slid behind the wheel and started the engine. "Where's your father?" she muttered. She tapped the horn. A minute or two passed, and she honked three short barks. She rolled down the window and lit a cigarette. "I get so sick of this," she said. She blew a thin stream of smoke and honked again.

"The neighbors probably don't like honking on Sunday morning," my sister Karin said. Karin was never afraid to speak up. Sometimes she refused to go on Sunday drives at all.

"He's coming," Mom said. She glanced at her watch, counted under her breath, and then laid on the horn for a good long one.

Dad burst from the house. "I'm coming, Marilyn. Christ." She smiled and slid over so he could get behind the wheel. He hadn't showered, but his shirt was clean and he smelled minty, like mouthwash.

"Hey, guys!" he said, grinning into the rearview mirror. He was his best on Sunday mornings. He put the car in reverse and backed down the driveway.

"You're going too fast," my mother said. "You'll hit one of the dogs."

He ignored her. "Where are we going today, guys? Where do you want to drive? Golden Gate Canyon? Rocky Mountain National Park?"

We didn't want to drive anywhere. It was hard to see from the backseat, even with my mother pointing out the scenery, and the winding roads made us all carsick.

"Let's drive up to Rocky Mountain National Park," Mom said. "We haven't been there in ages."

"That's a long drive," Karin piped up. "I have homework."

"This is a family day," Mom admonished. "Maybe we'll see some elk. Don't you kids want to see the elk?"

The silence was taken as agreement. "There's that nice little restaurant in Estes Park," Mom said. "We can have lunch."

"All these kids deserve is a hot dog stand!" Dad joked.

"I like hot dogs," Kurt called from the back.

"We'll have a very nice lunch," Mom said, and gave my father a look. "It's the least you can do for your family."

It would be years before I'd learn to share my parents' appreciation for mountains, and it would take a backpack and a pair of cross-country skis for me really to understand what wilderness meant. In those days we never got out of the car. "Look, kids!" Mom exclaimed. "There's snow on top of that peak—in July!"

"If we're lucky we'll see a mountain lion," Dad warned, though we never did. Maybe it was the flat cornfields of Iowa that made them so ecstatic about Colorado mountains, but they never tired of driving and looking, the car mostly quiet except for the hum of the tires. It was a sin to doze off. Sometimes we saw deer standing alone or in groups at the edge of the road, or a hawk floating on air.

We stopped for a late lunch at a restaurant in Estes Park, and as soon as we cleaned our plates, our parents dismissed us while they finished their manhattans and had a cigarette. We stood outside and felt the cool wind on our faces. If we were lucky, we'd get to stop at the fudge shop—a tourist trap—but the fudge was good nonetheless. Already the sun was beginning to slip behind the mountain.

"Let's go," Mom called, emerging with Dad, smiling, and we took our seats. Kurt braced himself in the back of the station wagon. It would take a couple of hours to get home; the road was narrow and winding. No one saw the deer until it was too late.

"Damn!" Dad yelled, and slammed the brakes. For a moment I glimpsed the deer in the windshield and then it vanished. The car stopped, shuddering, the hood hissing, and the deer appeared again, dazed, and staggered into a ditch by the side of the road.

Karin, Dad, and I jumped out of the car. The front of the car was pushed in like the nose of a bulldog, and the deer lay bleeding, one eye calmly looking up. "We need a veterinarian," I said.

"No," Dad said. "There's nothing a vet can do." His voice was tense.

The road was dark, the car steaming, and what happened next seems unreal. My father walked back into the forest and came back with a large rock. "I'm sorry about this, kids," he said, and in one swift motion he crushed the deer's skull. He dropped the rock to the ground and spoke in a low tone. "He was suffering," he said. I felt the sadness in his voice, the compassion. "I'm sorry you had to see that," he added.

But it wasn't my father who killed the deer. Years later I learned that no one in the family remembered the incident the way I did. The truth was that another man killed the deer, a stranger who drove up behind us in a pickup truck with big headlights, a man in a flannel shirt and heavy boots—a real mountain man, my sister Karma said later—who looked things over, found a rock, pulled the deer's carcass further off the road, and then left to call the cops so we would be sure to get home safely.

This was years before the law practice collapsed, the house was lost, and my father had collected enough of his own DUIs and DWIs to keep him in a place locked away from us, where it was hard to see him at all, even on Sunday mornings.

That Sunday, I wanted to believe it was my father who killed the deer.

The sheriff arrived, and he and Dad examined the car. "It's fine!" Dad barked. "The car is fine!" It looked bad, but it was drivable. We climbed back in to begin the slow journey home. But all was not fine. The cast on Kurt's leg had been crushed in the jolt, and when we got home my mother took him back to the emergency room. He returned with a fresh cast—the leg had been broken again—and he had a new doctor's order of six more weeks of no soccer.

"He'll be all right," Mom said. "He's tough."

We were all tough. Or so we thought.

THIS STORY, like many of my family stories, is remembered differently by the people involved. Some facts remain the same: it was a Sunday, we had lunch, we hit a deer. The differences lie mostly in the details; one of my sisters, for example, swears it was raining. But we all agree on one thing. None of us ever forgot the experience. It was a tough day, in retrospect the beginning of many tough days.

The details of the day dim with time. The emotional intensity of it does not.

Memory is clouded by desire and disappointment. Facts depend on who's doing the telling. Research is limited by what's available at the moment. Story hinges on what you leave in and what you leave out.

Verisimilitude is not art.

Creative nonfiction attempts to do the impossible: to represent reality and to create literary art. All the tools we use to create literary art—characterization, dramatic tension, scene development, sensory image, metaphorical language—can and will be used against us by those who put their faith in reality.

All the tools we use to represent reality—real characters, events anchored in time and place, information and facts and statistics—can and will be used against us by those who put their faith in art.

The writer of fiction moves without hesitation from one scene to the next, from one sentence to the next, confident in the fact that the veil that exists between writer and reader—the mask of the fiction writer that explicitly declares this is *not* real, this is only a story, this is maybe me and maybe not me—is present, in place, and fully understood.

The writer of creative nonfiction has no such mask. She represents herself as herself on the page. Or rather, herself as a version of herself.

It's real. Yet all is artifice.

The writer of creative nonfiction must stop to examine each step along the way. Did this really happen? Did it happen like this? What part of the story should I develop? What am I leaving out? (The reader will never know!) Have I represented the story, the character, the event, accurately on the page?

And is this dramatic *art*?

Prose writers of all stripes aim for that same magic moment, that thrilling little leap of faith when the reader suspends his or her disbelief and falls into the story hook, line, and sinker. That moment—you remember, right?—when you were a kid sitting on the back porch, book in lap, hiding from your mother who wanted you to come in and do your chores. You were hiding because you were reading. It was a good story. It was a drug. It was the moment that made you think you might want to grow up and be a writer.

And the drug was even better if the story was also *true*.

Fiction and creative nonfiction are two sides of the same coin.

Many writers of meta-nonfiction, as well as those who write metafiction, take ironic pleasure in pointing to the status of the narrative as dramatic construction, as artifact, as illusion.

Yet all creative nonfiction, memoir in particular, questions the relationship between narrative and reality.

Creative nonfiction is inevitably, unavoidably, uncomfortably meta-narrative.

SOME OF MY STUDENTS tell me they feel cheated if they know that a creative nonfiction author has decided in advance that he or she is going to write about a particular experience, as if the decision to write about the experience before actually having it somehow taints the intention and meaning of the work. Anything less than a raw and unbidden reflection upon a random and spontaneous experience begins to look like a dramatic construction, somehow false or manufactured. Which means, of course, it's not *real*.

It's even worse if a writer has accepted a contract or an advance from a publisher to work on a book of creative nonfiction. She knew going into it that she was going to write about it! As if the author marched forth with plot and epiphany in hand and returned just to pick up a royalty check.

If only life were that tidy. If only art were that easy. If only book contracts were that effortless.

And as many writers will be happy to tell you, if you're getting paid for it, it's not art.

Call me guilty. I will confess right here that I have sought certain experiences in order to write about them. I have a couple of friends who belong in the same jail cell.

I once bungee-jumped by my ankles from a hot-air balloon suspended three hundred feet in the air on a windy day. It did not result in art, or a royalty check. My mother nearly disowned me, and I had a headache for a week.

Was it worth it? Yes.

ONE OF THE GREAT IRONIES of my life is that I spent a great deal of time—years, in fact—trotting around the globe, looking for things to write about. I grew up in the suburbs. Nothing had ever really happened to me, or so I thought.

The biggest story, as it turns out, was in my own backyard.

I grew up in a suburban neighborhood in Arvada, Colorado. Unbeknownst to us, we were directly downwind from Rocky Flats, a secret nuclear weapons facility that produced plutonium triggers for nuclear bombs for decades. We never knew what they did out there. The plant was operated by Dow Chemical Company. We thought they were making household cleaning products.

We were on the front line of the Cold War, but no one bothered to tell us.

I had always wanted to be a writer. As a kid I kept secret notepads and spiral-bound journals with curled-up edges. I wrote in the margins of my Big Chief wide-ruled pads. I collected pens, and only the right kind would do: very fine-tipped ones, with black ink that didn't smear. Things were happening all around me, and I had to write them down, fast. In the third grade, I read *Harriet the Spy*. Harriet was like me. She sneaked around with a secret notebook and took notes on everyone. I stuck ragged little notebooks in the back pockets of my jeans, carried them in my book bag, stashed them under my mattress, stacked them under my bed. I wrote about everyone: my friends, my enemies, my family, my teachers, my horse, the lake. As I grew older, I was always running out of space, so I wrote on anything that was handy: receipts, napkins, bookmarks, the backs of movie tickets. I couldn't keep track of it all.

Profoundly contaminated after decades of weapons production, Rocky Flats had countless fires, leaks, and accidents. Tainted barrels leaked plutonium into the soil. Wind and water carried radioactive and toxic elements into surrounding neighborhoods, including mine. It turned out that we were in one of the primary contamination zones. We didn't know. Plutonium is invisible: you can't see it, taste it, or smell it. One millionth of a gram of plutonium, if inhaled or ingested, can cause cancer.

Like many other kids in my neighborhood, I eventually worked at Rocky Flats. When I worked there in 1994 and 1995, fourteen tons of plutonium sat on the premises in various stages of disarray. They told us it was safe.

I knew the day I took the job that someday I was going to write about it.

There was a sense of bravado among the employees at Rocky Flats. Like everyone else, we were instructed not to talk about Rocky Flats to anyone outside of the plant. I didn't mention it to my family or friends. I spent my days working next to fourteen tons of plutonium. I joked about it with the other secretaries and administrative assistants. We're tough. Not dead yet!

Yet part of me was petrified of the place and always had been. I wanted to see. I wanted to understand. I wanted to get on the inside and figure it all out. So I did what I always do: I took notes. At first it was on envelopes and napkins, notes and Post-it notes that I crammed in my purse at the end of the day. Guards could search a purse or briefcase at any time without warning, but rarely was my purse searched. I kept my cool. Gradually I got a little bolder. I bought a small notebook and started keeping a daily journal. I was the post–Cold War Harriet the Spy, reporting from the front line. The rest of the world thought the Cold War was over. Not at Rocky Flats.

And I wanted to tell the story.

YOU HAVE TO BE TOUGH to write creative nonfiction. That doesn't mean you have to leap from hot-air balloons or work at bomb factories. Sometimes just riding in a car is enough.

People love to tell you what you're doing wrong. They'll tell you it's not real enough, it's not literary enough, it's a lion with zebra stripes, and maybe it's best not to bother at all.

As writers of creative nonfiction, we bear a responsibility to witness the world in ways that are a little different from those of writers of fiction and poetry.

Creative nonfiction carries a sense of consequence in the real world. Something happened. It matters. It matters that it really happened.

Memoir is about fact and memory, dream and desire, reflection and regret. It's an intimate journey of self-examination and self-reflection undertaken with a reader on your shoulder. But it's more than that. It seeks to reveal the self in relation to the world; to broader social, cultural, or political themes or issues; to an event or series of events; to a person, a government, a culture.

Memoir, along with creative nonfiction in general, often reveals atrocities or injustices large and small. Yet it cannot fall into the realm of propaganda or proselytism, sentimentality or melodrama. It must inform and illuminate, but it must not be satisfied with those goals alone. Creative nonfiction seeks a higher literary aesthetic even as it tries to maintain a hold, however tenuous, on what we call, or think we call, reality.

INTERVIEW

Kristen Iversen, author of "How to Be Tough in Creative Nonfiction"

Q: In your essay, you point out that the writer of nonfiction "represents herself as herself on the page. Or rather, herself as a version of herself." In your work, do you feel that you present a consistent persona, or does it vary with each essay?

A: It's a little bit of both, honestly. There are an abiding voice and a presence that are relatively consistent, yet that presence changes given my age at the time, my experience, and my perspective at that particular moment. When I write an essay, I'm trying to re-create a significant moment of my life, a moment that turned out to be meaningful in some way, and I try to refigure myself on the page as accurately as I can. Sometimes I'll use triggers to help me get back to that point in time. I'll look at photographs, or call one of my sisters, or look back on my journal. I've kept a fairly detailed journal since I was about thirteen. But of course my perception and understanding change with time as well. There is the girl or woman—the character on the page—who experienced the event, and then there is the older woman writer—the narrator, visible or invisible—who is looking back on the event and giving it dramatic shape.

A few years ago, I visited my mother just after she'd had a small stroke. She was in the early stages of Alzheimer's disease. Her bouts of confusion were punctuated by moments of remarkable clarity. She was a vibrant woman, a proud woman, and always paid attention to her appearance. The stroke had caused the left side of her face to dip. I was unprepared for how she had changed, and she must have seen me react. "Oh Kris," she said, "I've changed, haven't I?" She turned to the mirror that hung on the wall behind her dining room table. "I'm old. Yes, I'm old now!" She said it with complete and utter disbelief. "The funny thing," she added ironically, "is that I'm the same inside. I'm the same girl I was when I was seventeen and living on the farm, or when I married your dad, or when I had you." Life, she felt, had been a kind of cruel trick.

The beautiful moment in an essay or memoir happens when the writer can capture that utterly impossible yet inevitable, paradoxical moment: I am the same, yet I am changed.

When I write an essay, I try to re-create a precise moment in time, a precise emotional moment. I might be a young girl, or a parent, or a daughter, or a friend. Sometimes my narrative voice and presence are almost invisible. Essays, even those that are lyrical or speculative, tend to be framed by time, feeling, and—thankfully—a certain page length. Writing *Full Body Burden* has been a challenge because I move through so much time and I experience so many dramatic changes, emotional and physical changes. I'm a very young child at the book's outset. By the close of the book, I'm a parent with half-grown children of my own.

The circumstances, the feelings, my understanding and perspective, all that changes. But I'm always, as my mother said, the same girl inside.

Q: Your allusion to interior versus exterior self reminds me of an e-mail from Ryan Van Meter during the earliest phases of this project, in which he discussed "the difference between the writer assembling the essay and the character of that writer living the experience of the essay." He went on to explain that perhaps he writes in order to "figure out why one memory hovers above [his] present life more than most others." I'm thinking of the Joan Didion line from "On Keeping a Notebook" in which she claims to write in order to remember "how it felt to me." Why we write—it's different and specific for each of us. Why must you write?

A: The world is a random, confusing place. I've kept a detailed journal ever since I was a kid. My notebooks fill several large plastic crates. Every few years I sit down and browse through them all. It's astonishing what the mind forgets or overlooks. On a very basic level, I write to remember what happened, to remind myself that it all matters (to me, at any rate), and to figure out what matters most. And why.

I write to seek some sense of understanding and—perhaps—peace. I look for patterns, repetitions, coincidence. Coincidences that would be impossible to pull off in fiction happen in real life. Actions or events that were inexplicable or obscure or emotionally laden in the moment become more clear, not just with time and reflection but with the actual, physical process of writing. It's hard to realize and understand an emotion in the present moment, and we rarely if ever experience one single, pure emotion at any distinct point in time anyway. Usually we feel several emotions in the same moment, and those emotions can be quite dissimilar. Love and hate can be close bedfellows, for example. Clear writing takes courage and a steady gaze. Writing about an experience expands it and allows me to unpack and unravel the thorny knot of emotion that has kept a particular memory close over the years.

I'm always trying to peek behind the veil, to look beyond the obvious.

Virginia Woolf wrote, "It is a constant idea of mine, that behind the cotton wool [of daily experience] is hidden a pattern; that we—I mean all human beings—are connected with this; that the whole world is a work of art; that we are parts of the work of art."

The writing brings me closer to understanding who I am. If I'm lucky, I'll have a reader who connects or resonates with that in some way.

Q: Let's talk about that connection between writer and reader. Couldn't metawriting be seen as a distancing mechanism? Or a technique that dissolves the distance between writer and reader? I'm thinking in particular of your piece, in which you write an essay, and then you write about that essay. Beyond the scope of metawriting in an anthology of metawriting, to what end does this device work (for you)?

A: I like the conversation that happens in metawriting. Metawriting makes its own rules. I love its playfulness, its insistence on conversation, dialogue, dialectic, debate. In creative nonfiction, it's a particularly charged dialectic or debate, because we've placed so much emphasis on distinctions between truth and untruth, and along the way questioned not only the truthfulness of the story but the authenticity and intention of the author herself. Is the story real? Is the author real? That is, is the author truly believable, of good intention, with impeccable credentials? Metanarrative in creative nonfiction turns this kind of questioning on its head. No one asks these kinds of questions about fiction or poetry, or writers of fiction or poetry, because the mask between reader and writer, and art and reality, is firmly in place. In fiction, metawriting lays bare the mask; in creative nonfiction, it demonstrates that the mask is never entirely nonexistent. Sometimes metawriting can ask bigger questions because it's so unfettered.

At some point, all writing is about the act of writing. To write creative nonfiction, to focus on the aesthetic qualities of language and form and style as much as the topic or subject being explored, is to make art. Art that is tethered to reality. Metawriting in creative nonfiction investigates those tethers. It shakes them a bit to see what holds. It reminds us that the tethers are there. The story points to itself as artifice, however "real" that artifice may be, or may appear to be, and at the same time it points to something beyond itself.

Metawriting moves the conversation forward. We can stop arguing about whether or not something is really "true"; we can stop—for a moment, anyway—trying to fix firmly that line between reality and imagination, fact and memory, in a way that's really going to stick. We can start talking about more interesting things. I'm not saying that truth doesn't matter, or facts don't matter. They do. But other things matter, too.

In the journal I edit, *The Pinch*, we published an essay by Ander Monson entitled "Solipsism." It was one of the most innovative works of creative nonfiction I've ever seen. It was visually delightful; it was playful and soulful, and it made you think. In my own writing, I've been experimenting with things such as footnotes, asides, and even graphics. How far can I push the limits of language and still tell a story that's "true"?

Metawriting questions how language represents reality and why that question matters. This goes to the very heart of why we write creative nonfiction rather than fiction. The danger of metanarrative is that it can become too intellectual or too busy with its own pyrotechnics or—worst-case scenario—trivial or dull. You can always find a good chess game. I want a good chess game with heart.

Q: "Metawriting makes its own rules" is one of the central concepts of this anthology, and "metawriting moves the conversation forward" is one of its goals. You mention Ander Monson's piece and the ways in which he employs metawriting to cause the reader to think. This aspect of metawriting is one of the reasons I am drawn to it. It demands that I, as a reader, think about writing, thereby offering not just a good essay or story, but an epistemological, theoretical exercise. In that way, I hope that this anthology encourages readers and writers to contemplate its existence, purpose, and effects.

To another point, you write, "In fiction, metawriting lays bare the mask," but I also think it adds complexity to the mask and the story, the reader's response to it and the writer's relationship with it. I'm thinking of Tim O'Brien's *In the Lake of the Woods*, a novel that infuses chapters with footnotes from factual documents, thereby throwing a shadow across the story. O'Brien seems to be nudging us: *This story has a foundation in fact, and because I am writing a mystery, I am also writing about questions that may never be answered or about how the answers are sometimes not factual. So how can we ever get to the truth?* I also have in mind the way in which Bret Easton Ellis in *Lunar Park* creates a character named Bret Easton Ellis, who mirrors his fictional characters as a means, I assume, of challenging readers' naïve assumptions about character as a mere stand-in for an author. I like your metaphor of the chess game, but might I offer the idea of metawriting as a fun house? Oh wait, John Barth beat me to that one.

You also address the concept of truth, which is what I as a nonfiction writer write toward, yet the truth in nonfiction has in recent years been held hostage via a mandate for accuracy.

I find this dangerous in that the concept of *creating* becomes the sole property of those who live on the fiction side of the block, leaving those of us on the nonfiction side in dark, empty houses. But any nonfiction writer will confess that, in every essay, we turn on all the lights in the house and run from room to room, playing with the memories of the spaces we left long ago, or we light candles and sneak through those hallways we currently inhabit. In other words, no genre has property rights on truth. Or art.

I wonder if you play with notions of truth (the concrete and the abstract versions) in your writing.

A: I read *Lost in the Funhouse* when I was fourteen, around the same time I read *In Cold Blood*, and both those books influenced my becoming a writer and how I think about writing. I fell in love with writing when I read those two books.

Aiming for truth in writing—any kind of writing, or any kind of art, for that matter—is like trying to shoot at a moving target. I'm not a hunter, so that's an awkward metaphor. I'll talk about a camera instead, which is what we're trying to do in creative nonfiction anyway. We want to shoot an accurate picture. So you try to hold the camera steady, and you hope your eyesight is clear. But the target keeps slipping out of your viewfinder. That doesn't mean the target doesn't exist. It just means that it's not fixed or static. Similarly, the connection between truth and art is not a clear or simple one. Fiction, which historically is more clearly considered an art form, explores the possibility of events, of things that happened, or might happen, or might happen in various ways. Fiction asks, what if? Creative nonfiction explores the actuality of events: what happened, why it happened, how we interpret it, how we feel about it, why it's meaningful. Creative nonfiction asks, why this? And, by extension, what now? Creative nonfiction insists on the connection between truth and art, on the real consequences of storytelling and narrative in the real world.

But to insist on literal truth in creative nonfiction simplifies or overlooks the complex connection between reality and art and the role of the author or artist. There is a type of nonfiction that is transactional; that is, its primary purpose is to convey information. Alternatively, in creative nonfiction, the writer brings a filter, a sharpness of perspective and talent, to the shaping of the text. To write an essay, a memoir, or any sustained form of creative nonfiction is to create a plausible narrative that is both true and not true. The author chooses parts of life or experience and shapes them into a pattern, a pattern that by necessity hints at a larger order of things. Stories, real or imagined, have no natural beginning or end. The author chooses from what moment to begin the story, and at what moment to end. Where one chooses to end the story, for example, profoundly influences the meaning of the story. In between these two points, the author creates scenes, passages of description, moments of reflection, and so on, and links these things together in subtle and not-so-subtle ways. These links give significance to what would otherwise be random chaos; that is, no story.

Writers talk about emotional truth in creative nonfiction; I think that term is inadequate. We're really striving toward a truth of life or living, an attempt to express what it means, emotionally and intellectually, to be human. Our experiences are no longer random and inexplicable if we can relate them as story, as a grouping of cohesive events or ideas. Even the most experimental writing in creative nonfiction suggests, as Virginia Woolf wrote, a peek behind the veil. Creative nonfiction is rooted in reality, but it seeks the symbolic character of art; that is, it seeks to discover the universal in the particular, and asks us to consider what it is that makes us human and connects us to one another. Metawriting reminds us that even when we stick to the facts, we are nonetheless creating a plausible mirage on the page, a story real and believable and yet also contained, created, contrived.

We are creating an illusion with a promise of the real.

We can look all the way back to Aeschylus to see how our wounds, our deeply felt experiences and tragedies on a scale both grand and small, define us. Our wounds give us our myths and our mythologies. Creative nonfiction, and perhaps memoir in particular, helps us to see the apocryphal in the actual, the mythic in the real. There are no new stories, really, only new and different ways of seeing. Creative nonfiction is a new frontier of seeing and storytelling. Metawriting in creative nonfiction moves us along the road of finding ways, in the words of Ezra Pound, to make it new.

Contributors

SARAH BLACKMAN earned an MFA in fiction from the University of Alabama and is the coeditor for fiction of *DIAGRAM*. She is currently the director of creative writing at the Fine Arts Center, a public high school focusing on the arts, in Greenville, South Carolina. Her most recent prose is published or forthcoming in the *Alaska Quarterly Review*, the *Gettysburg Review*, the *Fairy Tale Review*, and *American Fiction*. Her chapbook is *Such a Thing as America*.

BERNARD COOPER's most recent book is *The Bill from My Father*. He is the author of four other books, including *Maps to Anywhere* and *Guess Again*. Cooper is the recipient of the 1991 PEN/Hemingway Foundation Award, a 1995 O. Henry Prize, a 1999 Guggenheim Fellowship, and a 2004 National Endowment for the Arts fellowship in literature. His work has appeared in several anthologies, including *The Best American Essays* of 1988, 1995, 1997, 2002, and 2008. His work has also appeared in magazines and literary reviews, including *Harper's Magazine*, the *Paris Review*, and *Los Angeles*. He teaches creative nonfiction at Bennington College and USC.

CATHY DAY has been teaching creative writing for almost twenty years, most recently at Ball State University. She is the author of *The Circus in Winter* (2004), a linked story collection that was a finalist for the Story Prize, and *Comeback Season* (2008), an immersion memoir. Her stories and essays have appeared most recently in the *Millions*, *Ninth Letter*, the *North American Review*, and *Sports Illustrated*. She is the recipient of a Bush Artist Fellowship, a Tennessee Williams Scholarship from the Sewanee Writers' Conference, and a Beatrice, Benjamin, and Richard Bader Fellowship in the Visual Arts of the Theatre from Harvard University's Houghton Library.

LENA DUNHAM is a New York–based writer, director, and actress. Her film *Tiny Furniture* was released in 2011, and her HBO show *Girls* will air in 2012.

ROBIN HEMLEY is the author of eight books of nonfiction and fiction and has won many awards for his work, including a Guggenheim Fellowship for nonfiction. He has two books forthcoming in 2012, *Reply All*, a collection of short stories, and a book on immersion writing. He is the founder of the conference NonfictioNow and the director of the Nonfiction Writing Program at the University of Iowa.

PAM HOUSTON is the author of two collections of linked short stories, *Cowboys Are My Weakness* and *Waltzing the Cat*, the collection of essays *A Little More About Me*, and the novel *Sight Hound*. Her stories have been selected for volumes of *The Best American Short Stories*, *The PEN/O. Henry Prize Stories*, *The Pushcart Prize*, and *The Best American Short Stories of the Century*. She is the director of creative writing at UC Davis and teaches in the Pacific University low-residency MFA program. Her newest book is *Contents May Have Shifted*.

KRISTEN IVERSEN is the author of *Full Body Burden: Growing Up in the Nuclear Shadow of Rocky Flats*, forthcoming in 2012; *Molly Brown: Unraveling the Myth*, winner of the Colorado Book Award and the Sudler Award for Nonfiction, and *Shadow Boxing: Art and Craft in Creative Nonfiction*. She directs the MFA program at the University of Memphis and is editor-in-chief of *The Pinch*, an award-winning journal of prose, poetry, art, and photography. She is also on the faculty of the low-residency MFA program at the University of New Orleans, held in Edinburgh, Scotland, and is cofounder of Orphan Press.

DAVID LAZAR's books include *The Body of Brooklyn* and *Truth in Nonfiction* (Iowa), *Michael Powell: Interviews* and *Conversations with M. F. K. Fisher*, and *Powder Town*. The anthology *Essaying the Essay* is forthcoming. His essays and prose poetry have appeared widely. Several of his essays have been named "Notable Essays of the Year" by *The Best American Essays*. He has lectured widely on nonfiction and editing and founded the PhD program in nonfiction writing at Ohio University, as well as the undergraduate and MFA programs in nonfiction at Columbia College in Chicago. He is the founding editor of *Hotel Amerika*.

E. J. LEVY's anthology *Tasting Life Twice: Literary Lesbian Fiction by New American Writers* won a Lambda Literary Award. Her essays have appeared in *The Best American Essays*, the *New York Times*, the *Nation*, the *Kenyon Review*, *Orion*, and *Salmagundi*; her fiction has been published in the *Paris Review*, the *Gettysburg Review*, and the *Missouri Review*, among other journals. She has received national awards for fiction and nonfiction, including a Pushcart Prize, a Michener Fellowship, a Nelson Algren Prize, and the Margaret Bridgman Scholarship to Bread Loaf. Her collection of short stories *Life in Theory* is forthcoming.

BRENDA MILLER is the author of *Listening against the Stone* (2011), *Blessing of the Animals* (2009), *Season of the Body* (2002), and coauthor of *Tell It Slant: Writing and Shaping Creative Nonfiction* (2003). Her work has received six Pushcart Prizes and has been published in numerous journals. She is a professor of English at Western Washington University and serves as editor-in-chief of the *Bellingham Review*. Her book *The Pen and the Bell: Making Room to Write in a Crowded World*, coauthored with Holly Hughes, is forthcoming in 2012.

ANDER MONSON is the author of a host of paraphernalia, including a decoder wheel, several chapbooks and limited-edition letterpress collaborations, a Web site <http://otherelectricities.com>, and five books, most recently the poetry collection *The Available World* and the nonfiction *Vanishing Point: Not a Memoir*. He lives and teaches in Tucson, Arizona, where he is an editor for the magazine *DIAGRAM* <http://www.thediagram.com> and the New Michigan Press.

BRIAN OLIU is originally from New Jersey and currently lives in Tuscaloosa, Alabama. His work has been published in *Brevity*, *DIAGRAM*, *Ninth Letter*, *Sonora Review*, *Hotel Amerika*, and elsewhere. His collection of Tuscaloosa Craigslist Missed Connections, *So You Know It's Me*, was published in June 2011.

RYAN VAN METER is the author of the essay collection *If You Knew Then What I Know Now*. His work has also appeared in journals, most recently *Ninth Letter*, the *Normal School Magazine*, the *Iowa Review*, and *Fourth Genre*, as well as in anthologies including *The Best American Essays* and *Touchstone Anthology of Contemporary Creative Nonfiction*. He lives in California, where he teaches creative nonfiction writing at the University of San Francisco.

Permissions

Bernard Cooper's "Winner Take Nothing" appeared in *GQ*, *The Best American Essays 2002*, edited by Stephen Jay Gould, and *The Man I Might Become: Gay Men Write About Their Fathers*, edited by Bruce Shenitz.

Cathy Day's "Genesis; or the Day Adam Killed the Snakes" appeared in *Freight Stories* 3:3 (September 2008).

A version of Ander Monson's "Facing the Monolith" appeared in *Ecotone* 7:1 (Fall 2011).

Index

Addison, Joseph, 57
Agee, James, 33
Alice in Wonderland, 132
Allen, Woody, xxv, 48, 190
Anderson, Sherwood, 20
Arbus, Diane, 33
Arthur, Chris, xxv
As I Lay Dying, 192
Atwan, Robert, 23, 27
Auden, W. H., 57

Bacon, Francis, 52
Bailey, Elisabeth Tova, 136
Baker, Nicholson, xxiii, 136, 188
Baldwin, James, 33, 184
Barth, John, 205, 206
Barthes, Roland, xxiv
Baumbach, Noah, 164
Bausch, Richard, x
Bechdel, Alison, 33, 136
Bell, Matt, 189
Berger, John, 44
Bernheimer, Kate, 44
Bishop, Elizabeth, 184
Biss, Eula, 33
Bissell, Tom, 191
Blackman, Sarah, xxvii, 27, 193

Bourke, Joanna, 24
Byatt, A. S., 44

Capote, Truman, xxi, 113, 206
Carson, Anne, 33
Carver, Raymond, 19
The Catcher in the Rye, 191
Chabon, Michael, xxv
Cheever, John, 184

D'Agata, John, 73
Danticat, Edwidge, xxv
Davis, Kathryn, 44
Day, Cathy, xxviii, 66
DeLillo, Don, 73
Detweiler, Susan, 29
Didion, Joan, 33, 73, 192, 203
Dinesen, Isak, xxi
Dunham, Lena, xxiv

Easy A, xxvi
Ellis, Bret Easton, 205
Erdrich, Louise, xxiv, xxvii

Facebook, xxii, xxv, xxvi, 10, 85
Fakundiny, Lydia, 55
Ferris Bueller's Day Off, 18

Fielding, Henry, 57
Fisher, M. F. K., 33
Flynn, Nick, 33
Forché, Carolyn, 193
Fremont, Helen, 29
Frey, James, xiv, xv, xix, xxiii, xxviii

Gardner, John, xxiv, 18
Gordon, Fox, 33
Gornick, Vivian, 31
Gulliver's Travels, 26
Gutkind, Lee, xxviii, 65

Hampl, Patricia, xxv
Harriet the Spy, 200
Harrison, Kathryn, 33
Hazlitt, William, 33
Hemingway, Ernest, xxi, xxiii, 167, 183, 184
Hemley, Robin, xxviii, 112
Hemon, Aleksander, 20
Hitchcock, Alfred, 116, 134, 135
Houston, Pam, xxvi
Hurd, Barbara, 22
Hutcheon, Linda, xxii, xxiv

Isherwood, Christopher, xxiv
Iversen, Kristen, xxvi

Jaul, Jesper, 191
Johnson, Joyce, xxi

Kafka, Franz, 126-7
Karr, Mary, 29, 33
Kaurismäki, Aki, 48
Keene, Carolyn, 112
Kerouac, Jack, xxi
Kincaid, Jamaica, 73
Kingston, Maxine Hong, 20, 29, 30, 33

Krakauer, Jon, 29
Krauss, Nicole, xxii, xxiii

Lamb, Charles, 48
Lawrence, D. H., 44
Lazar, David, xxvii
Lish, Gordon, 24
Lopate, Phillip, xxviii, 67
Lorde, Audre, 33
Lukács, Georg, 55

Maclean, Norman, 20
Mandelstam, Nadezhda, 33
Martin, Lee, 30
Maugham, Somerset, 23
McCarthy, Mary, 29
McCullers, Carson, 115
McPhee, John, 31
Merrill, James, 184
Merton, Thomas, 33
Miller, Brenda, xxvii
Mitchell, Joseph, 33
Monson, Ander, 33, 193, 205
The Monster at the End of This Book, 18
Montaigne, Michel de, 52, 53, 55, 56
Moody, Rick, 20
Moore, Lorrie, 20, 24, 65
Munro, Alice, 20

Nabokov, Vladimir, 23, 29

O'Brien, Tim, 193, 205
O'Connor, Flannery, 54
Oliver, Mary, xxv
Ondaatje, Michael, 33
Orr, Gregory, xxviii
Orwell, George, 134

Paola, Susan, 64
Plascenia, Salvador, 193
Plath, Sylvia, 184
Pound, Ezra, 207
Purpura, Lia, 33

Ross, Lillian, 33
Rousseau, Jean-Jacques, 53

Sebald, W. G., 57
Shields, David, 23, 27, 28
Slater, Lauren, 33
Solnit, Rebecca, 136
Soucy, Gaetan, 44
Spiegalman, Art, 33
Statemeyer, Edward, 112
Steele, Richard, 57
Sterne, Laurence, 57

Strayed, Cheryl, 11
Swift, Jonathan, 57

The Things They Carried, xv, 18, 20
Thomas, Dylan, 185
Trilling, Calvin, 53
Twitter/Tweets, xxii, xxvi, 10, 81, 163

Van Meter, Ryan, vi, xx, 203

Wallace, David Foster, 33, 73
White, E. B., 23, 33
Whorf, Benjamin, 185
Williams, Joy, 33
Wood, James, 19
Woolf, Virginia, 32, 33, 204